THE CHAMPION
BUFFALO HUNTER

THE FRONTIER MEMOIRS OF
YELLOWSTONE VIC SMITH

Other books by Jeanette Prodgers:

The Only Good Bear Is a Dead Bear:
A Collection of the West's Best Bear Stories

Butte-Anaconda Almanac: A Day by Day History of Montana's
Two Greatest Mining and Smelting Towns

THE CHAMPION BUFFALO HUNTER

THE FRONTIER MEMOIRS OF YELLOWSTONE VIC SMITH

by Victor Grant Smith

Edited by Jeanette Prodgers

T W O D O T

HELENA, MONTANA

A · TWODOT · BOOK

10 9 8 7 6 5 4 3 2 1

TwoDot is an imprint of Falcon® Publishing Co., Inc.

Published by Falcon® Publishing Co., Inc.
Helena and Billings, Montana

Printed in the United States of America.

Library of Congress Cataloging-in-Publication Data:

Smith, Victor Grant, 1850-1925.
    The champion buffalo hunter : the frontier memoirs of Yellowstone
Vic Smith / by Victor Grant Smith ; edited by Jeanette Prodgers.
        p.   cm.
    Includes bibliographical references and index.
    ISBN 1-56044-586-6
    1. Smith, Victor Grant, 1850-1925. 2. Pioneers—West (U.S.)—
Biography. 3. Hunters—West (U.S.)—Biography. 4. Frontier and
pioneer life—West (U.S.) 5. American bison hunting—West (U.S.)—
History—19th century. 6. Montana—Biography. 7. North Dakota—
Biography. I. Prodgers, Jeanette, 1958- . II. Title.
F594.S66   1997
978' .02'092—dc21
[B]   97-31004
                                                                            CIP

For extra copies of this book and information about other TwoDot books, write Falcon, P.O. Box 1718, Helena, Montana 59624; or call 1-800-582-2665. To contact us by e-mail, visit our homepage at http://www.falconguide.com.

Cover photo credits:
Front cover, upper left: Vic Smith, ca. 1912-1925, detail. Richard Anderson, photographer. Courtesy Montana Historical Society, Helena. Front cover, upper right: Vic Smith, age fifty, detail. From the *Anaconda Standard*, December 16, 1900. Courtesy Montana Historical Society, Helena. Front cover, bottom, and back cover, top (detail): *Theodore Roosevelt and His Hunting Guide, Vic G. Smith*, oil painting, ca. 1890. Artist unknown. Courtesy Theodore Roosevelt National Memorial Park, Medora, North Dakota.

In memory of my beloved brother Dave,
whose life and death affected me deeply.
As Vic would have said,
"He died with his boots on."

—J. P.

CONTENTS

Preface   *ix*
Introduction   *xiii*
Chronology   *xxxii*

PART I—*BOYHOOD*
    Early Days, Wayward Ways   *1*
    Whitewater Adventures   *7*
    Indian Tales   *10*

PART II—*INTRODUCTION TO THE FRONTIER*
    Carrying the Mail   *14*
    Smith Averts Hanging   *19*
    Early Buffalo Adventures   *24*
    Conversion Through Immersion   *29*
    Smith Takes His First Scalp   *32*
    An Indian Love Story   *36*
    Dodging Danger in the Black Hills   *41*
    A Horse Raid with "Red" Mike   *45*
    Buck Marsh's Puppy Love   *48*
    Rollicking with Joe Taylor   *51*

PART III—*SCOUTING*
    Ambushed in the Black Hills   *55*
    Smith Just Misses the Little Bighorn Battle   *58*
    "Yank" Brockmeyer Is Killed   *63*
    Delivering Dispatches—A Dangerous Duty   *68*
    McCormick's Hair Turns White   *71*
    Wolfers Versus Sioux   *75*
    End of the Indian Wars   *78*
    Delivering Mail   *82*
    Catching Brockmeyer's Horse   *83*
    "Slippery Dick"   *84*
    Chief Joseph   *85*
    "Liver-Eating Johnson"   *86*
    The Scalping of Jennie Smith   *87*
    The Bewitching Rosa   *90*
    Humiliated by the Sioux   *92*

PART IV—*BUFFALO DAYS*

  Buffalo Exploits   *96*
  On the Trail of "Limber Jim"   *100*
  "Dutch Jake" on the Make   *104*
  Smuggling Whiskey   *106*
  Hard Luck at Hardscrabble   *110*
  The Demise of George Grinnell · *115*
  Resurrection of the Virgin   *122*

PART V—*BIDING TIME IN THE BADLANDS*

  Hunting with Theodore Roosevelt   *128*
  Old Chief Sitting Bull   *131*
  A Trip Underground   *134*
  "Flopping Bill" and the Stranglers   *137*
  Medora Days   *139*
  Bear Hunting with Madam de Morès   *144*

PART VI—*ADVENTURES OF AN AGING
        FRONTIERSMAN*

  Odd Neighbors   *149*
  Elk Ranching   *156*
  Predator Control in the Big Hole   *162*
  More Bear Tales   *168*

Appendix: Other Stories   *175*
Endnotes   *211*
Bibliography: Archives and Reference   *240*
Index   *249*

PREFACE

In 1984, while perusing many frontier newspapers, my interest in Victor "Yellowstone Vic" Grant Smith was piqued. I was collecting pre-World War II bear stories for my book *The Only Good Bear Is a Dead Bear: A Collection of the West's Best Bear Stories,* and Smith's bear hunting experiences were featured in more than a few publications.

Articles about Smith frequently referred to him as "the famous hunter." The reason became obvious. He first gained notoriety as a professional buffalo hunter on the ranges of eastern Montana and western North Dakota in the late 1870s. Then, in the mid-1880s, he attained a reputation as a trick shooter, giving exhibitions in some of the larger eastern cities. Later he was a renowned bear hunter and successful big-game guide. He was distinguished among his peers, so naturally I wanted to learn more about him.

My search turned up a possible great-great-nephew, Jim Metcalfe, who had discovered some old news clippings and photographs of Vic Smith in his family papers. Several articles in the *Bad Lands Cow Boy* (1884-1886) mentioned the Smith brothers, Vic and Frank, but neither Jim nor I could find any documents that showed a direct relationship between Victor Grant Smith and Frank M. Smith, Jim's great-great-grandfather. U.S. census records for 1860 indicate that Vic Smith had three brothers: Ottram, Ray, and DeMorny. Census records for 1870 only listed two brothers, Rae and Morny—it was possible that Frank was a nickname for Morny. At any rate, Jim Metcalfe had family information about Vic Smith and shared his findings with me. From this material and other information, I published an article for *Old West* magazine in 1986.

In 1990, I renewed my research on Smith because his story—real or fabricated—deserved to be told. I found a reference noting that Smith had recorded some of his frontier experiences, and I hoped to locate these writings. During my search, I dug up many new pieces on his life, including articles by or about him. Then, to my surprise and delight, I discovered his manuscript, written in the third person, cached in the Theodore Roosevelt Collection at Harvard's Houghton Library, which granted permission for its publication.

Originally titled "Vic G. Smith of Montana," Smith's manuscript is reproduced here with minimal but much needed editing. It was not my intent as editor to rewrite the manuscript. Rather, I wanted to retain Smith's vernacular and fondness for clichés—as well as his prejudices, for reasons of historical accuracy—and maintain his voice as storyteller. I did not change the text's character or vocabulary, and readers should note that Vic Smith's viewpoints, common among frontiersmen at the turn of the century, will offend many modern readers.

Smith used the third person when writing his memoirs. Numerous accounts by reporters state that Smith was reticent regarding his exploits, and he may have used the third person as a means to write freely about himself without feeling self-conscious. His grammar and spelling were impressive considering he had at most an eighth-grade education, but his manuscript was sparingly punctuated and was composed of a single paragraph. Without changing too much of the original layout, I created paragraphs and sections to facilitate reading, and silently corrected a few misspellings. Generally, the manuscript flowed along smoothly, but at times Smith blended the years of some adventures; when necessary I reordered them chronologically, based on other contemporary accounts. In addition, I supplemented the text with an introduction, chronology, and endnotes to enhance or clarify the material.

Although Smith would reside in a particular location for several years at a time, wanderlust would eventually strike. Keeping track of him during some periods was difficult, but with the help of his manuscript, some personal letters, and other documents, I was able to trace most of his seventy-five years. Sometimes information in his manuscript did not match official records, and Smith exaggerated on occasion—perhaps when his memory failed.

Based on a few dated excerpts, such as the death of Calamity Jane, I estimate that Smith wrote his memoirs between 1906 and 1912, long after most of the events he describes occurred. He added a few notes by hand after 1912. However, most of the manuscript centers on a twenty-year period between 1870 and 1890, when Smith was actively engaged on the frontier.

In July 1925, one month before he died, Smith wrote to Theodore Roosevelt biographer Hermann Hagedorn asking whether he would be interested in buying his manuscript. It is unknown whether Hagedorn responded, but the Theodore Roosevelt Association obtained the manuscript in October 1925 as a gift from the author. The Houghton Library at Harvard acquired the manuscript in 1943 as a part of the Association's entire research collection, according to Wallace Finley Dailey, library curator.

Although I attempted to verify or clarify many of Smith's accounts, this task proved onerous. Research or corrections by others would be welcome.

I would like to thank these individuals and institutions that have helped me complete this project: Billings County Historical Society, Medora, North Dakota; Butte-Silver Bow Archives, Butte, Montana; Diane, John, and Mike at Butte-Silver Bow Public Library, who ordered numerous items through interlibrary loan; Carnegie Library, Deadwood, South Dakota; Cass County Historical Society, Walker, Minnesota; Chicago Public Library; the staff at the Chateau de Morès, Medora, for an interesting and informative tour; Wallace Finley Dailey at Houghton Library at Harvard, who made my day by informing me of the Smith manuscript and other materials, and who granted permission to use the original manuscript; Dickinson Public Library, Dickinson, North Dakota; Duluth Public Library; Sam Eagle, who offered information on the Henrys Lake area; the Glendive Public Library staff, Glendive, Montana; Aubrey Haines; the staff at Hearst Free Library, Anaconda, Montana; Bonnie Hortick, who traveled all the way to Bismarck and assisted with research on that trip; Itasca County Historical Society, Grand Rapids, Minnesota; Kansas State Historical Society, Topeka; the Library of Congress staff, who provided copies of magazine articles when I couldn't get them elsewhere; the staff at the Mansfield Library at the University of Montana, Missoula; Jim Metcalfe, who provided photographs and miscellaneous documents; Miles City Public Library, Miles City, Montana; Minneapolis Public Library; Minnesota Historical Society, St. Paul; the staff at the Mon-Dak Heritage Center, Sidney, Montana, who were especially helpful when I visited; the Montana Historical Society staff in Helena, who are always helpful in all my research endeavors; the *Montana Standard*, Butte; the Museum of the Badlands staff in Medora, who allowed me to tour before it officially opened for the tourist season in May 1992; North Dakota State Historical Society, Bismarck; Northeast Minnesota Historical Center, Duluth; the Oenota Cemetery staff, Duluth; Minnie Paugh; Richard Prodgers, my best critic and support; Renne Library at Montana State University, Bozeman; Jack Stewart for interesting information from North Dakota; the Theodore Roosevelt National Park and Museum staff, Medora, who showed me the Smith and Roosevelt oil painting and provided the photograph; Topeka Genealogical Society; Tri-County Historical Society, Anaconda; the Universal Genealogical Center, Salt Lake City, for invaluable help in closing gaps in Smith's life; Washburn University, Topeka; Doris and Edwin Watkins, who generously did research for me in Minneapolis; Pascal Wick; Wisconsin Historical Society, Madison; Wyoming Historical Society, Cheyenne, and numerous unnamed librarians in Idaho, Minnesota, Montana, North Dakota, Oregon, South Dakota, Wisconsin, and Wyoming, who assisted in tracking down documents.

INTRODUCTION

Sometimes called "Yellowstone Vic," Victor Grant Smith had many exciting adventures as an Indian fighter and scout for Colonel Nelson A. Miles and General Alfred Terry, and as a professional hide hunter and guide. During his day, Vic Smith was widely known and respected as an expert marksman and a prolific hunter.

According to his contemporaries, Smith was one of the West's most famous frontiersmen, but his renowned reticence created a path to obscurity. Other notable frontiersmen such as "Yellowstone Kelly," "Liver-Eating Johnson," and "Buffalo Bill" Cody are all remembered today, in part because their biographies were published. Writing in the third person, Smith also recorded his experiences; however, due to his modesty, most of his escapades remained unknown, except to his closest companions. Unknown, that is, until now.

Reporters often commented that Smith was loath to talk about himself, and, for the most part, his manuscript reflects this trait. Much of his narrative discusses other people rather than himself. When he does talk about himself, however, he seems a trifle boastful. Looking longingly back to the past, Smith's autobiography generally focuses on a twenty-year period (1870-1890), when his life was full of adventure. Experiences occurring after 1890 until his death in 1925 are generally ignored. Smith does briefly include his wife of twenty-five years, Eugenia, in his manuscript, but he omits their divorce and never mentions their only child, Rae, who died while a boy.

According to U.S. census records, Victor Grant Smith was born in January 1850, near Buffalo, New York. As far as it can be discerned from documents, he was the second son and child of Thomas and Elizabeth (Margaret) Robinson Smith. His father, a blacksmith by trade, was born in England, while his mother hailed from Canada. Vic had at least three brothers: Ottram, Rae, and DeMorny.[1]

Ottram, two years older than Vic, also was born in New York. Around 1851, the Smith family moved to Omro, Wisconsin. While there, at least two more sons were born: Rae (Ray), a.k.a. Bill,[2] two and a half years younger than Vic, and DeMorny (Morny), five years younger. It is unlikely that any other Smith children were born after DeMorny, because the 1870 census records for Thomas and Elizabeth Smith do not list any more children, and because Elizabeth was almost fifty years old at that time.[3]

When Smith was about thirteen years old, he ran away from home, which was then in Alexandria, Minnesota, and spent a few years with a family in Missouri. He eventually returned to Alexandria and lived with his family for several more years. Then he came west at about age twenty-one. One of his first frontier jobs was delivering mail by dog team in what today is North Dakota, between Fort Totten on Devils Lake and Fort Abercrombie on the Red River of the North. This route traversed land occupied by the Sioux, who were increasingly hostile to the continual horde of white invaders pushing westward. Smith quit this position in 1872 after Indians murdered the only white inhabitant between these two forts.[4]

Seeking other forms of adventure, Smith took up hunting and trapping for the next few years. In 1875, as he and two other men headed for the Black Hills, Indians ambushed them at the Cannonball River. One of the men was killed, and their horses were stolen. Smith managed to escape and landed in Bismarck.[5] A year later he became a government scout and dispatch rider for Colonel Miles and General Terry.

As a scout, Smith gained the respect and friendship of many men, including Luther S. Kelly, better known as "Yellowstone Kelly"; Jack Johnson, a.k.a. "Liver-Eating Johnson"; Billy and Bob Jackson; and John "X" Beidler. Once when Miles asked "Yellowstone Kelly," his chief of scouts, to locate a camp of hostile Sioux, Kelly chose Smith to accompany him, because he knew him to be an invaluable and experienced scout.[6]

Smith had some close calls as a dispatch rider. Although he does not relate this story in his manuscript, a buffalo hunter named Smith and William Harrison Cheney narrowly escaped from Indians near Sidney, Montana. Traveling through the Lower Yellowstone Valley in the fall of 1877, they were seeking dispatch carriers to relay a message. Near Savage, Montana, they found two freshly scalped and emasculated bodies, stripped of guns and belongings. As they examined the dead, Cheney's horse "Nig" spooked, and the men realized they were not alone. Some Indians hidden in nearby cottonwoods whooped and began a chase that continued until they were almost at Sidney. Cheney promised "Nig" if he got him out of this trouble, he would care for him the rest of his life. When they reached the river, the horses plunged in. "Nig" struggled up a small bluff, but Smith's horse staggered and fell dead. Smith climbed onto "Nig's" back, and "Nig" carried the men fifteen miles to Fort Buford. When Smith and Cheney arrived at Fort Buford, they reported the deaths of the two dispatch riders, and from that day Cheney faithfully tended Nig, who lived forty-two years.[7]

Smith remained a scout and game provider for the U.S. Army during the peak of the Indian wars in Montana. Then he devoted his attention to slaughtering buffalo for profit, a job he did most effectively. Often described as "the famous hunter," Smith gained notoriety on the range in western North Dakota and eastern Montana during the height of the northern buffalo era in the late 1870s and early 1880s.

In the winter of 1881-1882, Smith tied the record of another buffalo hunter, Charles Rath, by killing 107 buffalo at one stand within an hour in the Redwater area, about 100 miles northeast of Miles City, Montana. A stand refers to a single time and location. That same winter, Smith reportedly killed 5,000 buffalo in the Little Missouri and Yellowstone River areas.[8]

Between 1880 and 1882, Smith settled at a little community on the Yellowstone River, twenty-five miles above Fort Buford, called Hardscrabble, Montana. While there, he occasionally wrote for a nearby newspaper, and articles were written about him. In 1882, Hardscrabble had a population of more than fifty, consisting mostly of emigrants and a few old frontiersmen. Two years earlier, Seymour's Ranch had been the only habitation there. At age thirty-two, Smith was said to be the oldest frontiersman in the settlement.[9]

During his time in Hardscrabble, Smith lived with a woman, whom he doesn't discuss in his autobiography. Although this two-year liaison is absent from his manuscript, several contemporary sources refer to a "Mrs. Smith,"[10] and the 1880 census for Dawson County, Montana, lists twenty-eight-year-old Fannie Smith as Vic's wife.[11]

Referring to Smith as "Sunda," Joseph Taylor, Smith's former trapline partner, poignantly recounts Vic and Fannie's tragic love story in his book *Kaleidoscopic Lives*. According to Taylor, Smith hired a lad and picked up a woman "from across the track" in Bismarck for a campkeeper as he prepared to slaughter buffalo on the northern range. Taylor said the woman came upriver on a Kansas City steamer. As a girl, she had seen desperados kill her father and brother, and later she had been betrayed by a man and had fallen by the wayside. From Bismarck, the trio took the train to Glendive. The boy, most likely Jim Aglew, whom Smith does mention in his manuscript as a runaway and would-be Jesse James, died after accidentally shooting himself on a buffalo hunt. The woman stayed with Smith for two years. However, when most of the buffalo were gone, Smith became restless and irritable and ended the relationship. He gave the woman a thousand dollars for her troubles, but she said she would be gone when the money was gone and left in tears.[12]

With the Indian wars over and most of the buffalo slaughtered, Smith left the Redwater in eastern Montana and drifted back to North Dakota, spending time between Dickinson and Medora, hunting, guiding, roping buffalo calves, and collecting fossils. Contradictory accounts in local newspapers reported that Smith was either capturing buffalo calves to preserve the species or killing any stray buffalo that he encountered. In the summer of 1882, the *Glendive Times* noted that Vic Smith was outdoing himself as a rustler. Another article reported that Smith was in town waiting for his fast horses to come from Newlon, because he had a big order for buffalo calves to fill.[13] In June 1883, one press account reported that Vic Smith, "the champion shot of Dakota," brought in eight buffalo calves from the range, stating that he believed he was the only person interested in saving buffalo from extinction.[14] Later that summer another news account noted that Vic Smith, "the champion buffalo hunter of the northern ranges," came in with his partner J. W. Anderson. They had several thousand buffalo to their credit since the previous fall. Early in August "the famous hunter" was again in town but left for the range within a few days after obtaining supplies.[15] Still one year later an article noted that Smith had killed sixty-five buffalo on his way to the range to hunt.[16]

Months after leaving his girlfriend and the Redwater area, Smith received a letter from one of his friends in Deadwood, telling of a richly dressed woman who killed herself with a pistol in a dance hall. From a newspaper article describing some mementos found with her, Smith knew this was his former sweetheart. When he related the incident to Joseph Taylor, tears streamed down Smith's cheek.[17]

At the beginning of the hunting season in 1883, about ten thousand remaining buffalo roamed between the Moreau and Grand rivers in western North Dakota. Smith and numerous other hide hunters quickly reduced this herd to about twelve hundred. When Sitting Bull learned of the herd's location, he and a thousand Sioux Indians came up from the Standing Rock

Agency to kill the remainder. Within two days, the last of the northern herd was slaughtered by both whites and Indians.[18]

In those days, when the western prairies teemed with wildlife, many thousands of other game animals fell to Smith's rifle, and he lived to regret his role in the extermination of the buffalo. In 1900, he told *Anaconda Standard* reporters that he wished his aim hadn't been so good;[19] but, as he later remarked, few men considered the consequences of their actions until it was too late. Game was so abundant that many hunters could not fathom the extinction of species.

In 1884, seemingly at a loss for what to do now that his livelihood had disappeared with the buffalo, Smith contemplated going north. As the *Bad Lands Cow Boy* reported, "Vick Smith, one of the best of the hunters, trappers, and scouts of the west," said settlers were getting too thick for him, and he planned to go to Alaska after visiting Coeur d'Alene.[20] However, Smith remained in the vicinity of Medora for a few more years, after the Marquis de Morès hired him that fall as a hunting guide and pathfinder for a suitable railroad route through the badlands. De Morès had a grand scheme to ship beef in refrigerated cars to customers in the East. He built a packinghouse and needed a railroad route to complete his plans.[21] Smith discovered a route along a natural gravel roadbed from the first stage station on Davis Creek all the way to the second station on Rocky Ridge.[22]

While living in Medora, Smith and a man named Frank Smith, frequently referred to as his brother,[23] collected interesting artifacts for a local museum. The *Bad Lands Cow Boy* noted that Frank Smith, not to be outdone by his brother, brought in a curious piece of petrified cottonwood.[24] Another article said Frank Smith brought in the best gypsum specimens for the badlands collection. "The Smith Brothers alone, if they keep on, will give us a splendid collection by fall," the editor wrote.[25] A third article lauding Frank Smith's contributions to the badlands exhibit noted: "If we don't have a collection to be proud of it won't be the fault of the Smith brothers."[26] After Frank Smith brought in a specimen with the plain print of water flags found on top of a high butte, the editor said: "Again has Frank Smith placed our Bad Lands museum under obligation to him."[27] Another week the *Cow Boy* reported that Vic Smith brought in a petrified knee joint from a mastodon.[28]

Smith had other duties besides gathering items for the local museum.

Bob Roberts, deputy commissioner of Dakota for the New Orleans Exposition, hired him to kill various animal species to be stuffed and sent to the exhibit.[29] Smith's reputation for bringing down game was well known, as *Bad Lands Cow Boy* excerpts indicate. The paper wrote, "Vic Smith brought in another lot of antelope, coyotes, and mountain deer. Vic never comes home empty-handed."[30] Another article reported Vic Smith and J. L. White had recently returned from a two-week hunting expedition, in which they killed 16 deer.[31] A third article noted Vic Smith killed 89 deer and antelope, taking 69 of them in five days. "Vic is not given to drawing the long bow on his hunting exploits, and as he has the saddles to show for it, we acknowledge that our record has been beaten," the editor remarked.[32] Other accounts told of Smith guiding Count Rembielinski of Russia just 15 miles out of Medora, where they killed 225 deer and antelope.[33]

In November 1884, Smith was hired to take some Russian noblemen for an extended hunting trip.[34] But according to North Dakota pioneer A. C. Huidekoper, the outing was not as successful as Smith was accustomed to. Smith located a band of antelope for the hunters, but they could not hit any. Then Smith found another herd. The Russian dukes shot again with no better results. Spotting a third group lying down against a sunny bank, Smith thought the men had an easy opportunity. Yet they shot again and missed. Frustrated by their lack of skill, Smith killed two antelope as they ran away, which infuriated the Russians. They told him if he had dared to shoot game in their presence in Russia, they would have sent him to Siberia. By this time Smith was disgusted and said, "Well, this is not your country. You are no good, and you can go to hell. I'm going home."[35]

These dukes must have rubbed Smith the wrong way, since he was not usually that impatient with the dudes he guided. Noted North Dakota historian Lewis Crawford related a different incident where Smith guided another unsuccessful antelope hunter. When Smith located an antelope over a hill, he motioned for the fellow to come up with another box of cartridges. After the dude had shot these he said, "For God's sake, keep still. The joke is on me." He couldn't knock the antelope down either.[36]

When Smith wasn't guiding, wolfing, or hunting big game, he was shooting or trapping beaver and otter. One of his trapping partners, Joseph Taylor, said Vic Smith was one of the best shots in the Upper Missouri country. Taylor recalled one year during the spring breakup when Smith went down the Knife River and brought down around sixty beaver, securing about one in every ten that he killed. Taylor remarked that if the best shot could do no better than that, imagine how much useless destruction there was from the multitude of poor shots lining the banks of every beaver stream during the ice breakups in early spring.[37]

Before embarking on one of his beaver outings, Smith stopped at the *Bad Lands Cow Boy* office. Editor A. T. Packard reported that Smith had again gone off on one of his "neck or nothing" expeditions, heading several hundred miles above Fort Buford. After buying a skiff, Smith planned to float down the Big Missouri to shoot beaver when the spring breakup commenced. If successful, Smith would probably net a large amount, Packard said, but then gave the odds of ten to one that his skiff would be ground to pieces by the ice before he fairly started. With this prediction, Packard concluded by wishing Smith the best.[38]

When he had been gone about a week, the *Bad Lands Cow Boy* reported receiving money for a subscription and a letter from Smith saying that Medora was booming compared to other places he visited.[39] Surviving this perilous adventure, Vic Smith and his brother Frank returned to Medora, where they planned to settle.[40] Back in Medora, Smith gave the *Bad Lands Cow Boy* his diary. He left Medora March 4, 1885 and reached Glendive in time to see a "Democratic twenty-years' drunk." Traveling from Glendive to Poplar Creek in a buckboard stage, Smith had a series of drunken drivers. At Wolf Point, he found Indians eating two hundred government cattle that had frozen to death. At Fort Galpin, Smith got a team to take him to Milk River, where he camped until the spring breakup in the deserted shack of Tom Campbell, a man who reputedly kept forty-seven different Indian women.

Before the ice breakup, Smith survived on sage hens and prairie dogs. However, one day he shot a goose, which fell in a gorge. Just as Smith secured the bird with a long pole, the gorge broke,[41] and he had great difficulty getting back on shore. When he returned to his camp, Smith discovered Indians had stolen all of his "grub." Here in his diary he wrote that he observed the fourth commandment. (Since the day was Sunday, it was uncertain whether he meant the fourth or fifth commandment, the editor commented.) Smith killed several beaver, and when the river broke on March 26, he started downstream. After still more dangerous experiences, Smith landed in Bismarck with $300 worth of beaver pelts.[42]

In January 1885, Bob Roberts and Vic Smith headed for Louisiana for the New Orleans Exposition, but Smith never got that far.[43] Upon hearing bad reports about the exposition from friends and learning that his father and brother were very sick, Smith went to Chicago instead and planned to return to Medora at the end of February.[44] Heading north to Milwaukee, he demonstrated his marksmanship at a shooting gallery and was offered forty dollars a week to stay. Smith declined, saying Medora was good enough for him. Wearing Bob Roberts's buckskin suit, Smith won first prize at a masquerade. While in Milwaukee, Smith was fined five dollars and court costs after a policeman caught him showing some tenderfeet how to shoot in a backyard. "Vic can make lots more money shooting here than in Milwaukee. He is already pining for the Bad Lands, and will return soon," reported the *Bad Lands Cow Boy*.[45]

In 1886, Smith again toured eastern cities showing off his shooting skills and earning a great reputation as a trick shooter. A news article, alluding to Vic Smith and his brother Bill (possibly Rae), under the names of "Yellowstone Vic" and "Montana Bill," reported that they were having a jolly time at a big salary. "The fancy rifle shooting of the two scouts, now at the Dime museum, is an exhibition of wonderful skill. Last evening 'Yellowstone Vic' snuffed a two-inch-long candle at seven or eight paces, held between the teeth of his companion, 'Montana Bill.'"[46] When Smith returned to Medora on his way to Billings, where he planned to reside, the *Bad Lands Cow Boy* reported that he carefully held his plug hat under his arm, because the cowboys in Medora disliked plug hats.[47]

North Dakota author Zena Trinka also wrote about Smith's renowned marksmanship and referred to his fondness for gambling in several of her books. Trinka said that, like most of the old-time crack shots, Smith never drank but was an inveterate gambler. Trinka's contention is plausible, at least in part, since luck is a consistent theme throughout Smith's autobiography, and he is frequently broke despite an ability to earn a good living with his rifle.

Once after making a cleanup from Bismarck to Glendive, Smith boasted he was going to Chicago to "bust them tinhorns wide open!" A few weeks later when some badlands cowboys delivered a load of beef in Chicago, they saw a man in front of a Clark Street museum who was advertising the latest attraction: Vic Smith. Smith was on stage wearing buckskins, shooting plaster of Paris earrings, and snuffing lighted candle stubs held by an anxious-looking assistant, never missing by a hair. When Smith saw his friends, he motioned them to come backstage. He said he had been cleaned out and was trying to make enough money to get back home. Within a week he was back in North Dakota on the range.[48]

Eda Benson, who interviewed some pioneers in the Gallatin Valley who knew Vic Smith, noted that Smith was a good shot with both pistol and rifle and was called a snapshot, indicating that he could shoot very quickly. According to Benson, Smith traveled with the Cole Circus for a while but quit the show to come west.[49] Although Smith's standing as a marksman followed him throughout his life, he seemed to devote more attention to earning an income as a showman between 1884-1886, immediately following the demise of the buffalo.

In his book *The Cowboy*, Philip Ashton Rollins tells an amusing anecdote confirming Smith's reputation. Once a drunken drifter came into Charley Scott's saloon in Gardiner, Montana, and began to harass the patrons, but he quickly changed his mind when Vic Smith walked in and was greeted by some friends. When the troublemaker heard Smith's name, he said, "Vic Smith, my God! Vic Smith!" and jumped out through the window.[50]

While employed by the Marquis de Morès, Smith occasionally guided the de Morès family and their friends on hunting trips. In the summer of 1885, the Marquis de Morès, his wife Medora, J. N. Simpson, and several friends planned a month-long pleasure trip into the Big Horn Mountains in Wyoming.[51] Last-minute business prevented the Marquis from going, and on July 16 a party consisting of the Marquise, William Van Driesche, Vic and Frank Smith, Tom Skinner, a man named Sweet, and several others left for Huntley, Montana, where their horses had already been shipped.[52]

William Van Driesche, the Marquis's valet, was the first to return to the town of Medora. The Marquise delayed her return to hunt mountain sheep; she and most of the other hunting party returned several days later. When Van Driesche arrived in town, he told the *Bad Lands Cow Boy* the trip was extremely pleasurable, but said hunting would have been better if they had gone into the mountains. He said they had hunted on the Meeteetse River on the west side of the Big Horns. Numerous bears were killed, with Madam de Morès getting an old bear and two cubs, and Van Driesche a silvertip. Contrary to the Marquise's and Smith's accounts, he said neither elk nor mountain sheep were abundant, but antelope and small game were plentiful. Trout averaging between one and three pounds abounded in every stream.[53]

While Van Driesche told his story in Medora, the Marquise gave her version to the *Billings Gazette,* saying she had been bear hunting in northern Wyoming under the guidance of "the famous hunter and shot" Vic Smith, a former scout for Terry and Miles. They saw seventeen bears in four days. On Meeteetse Mountain, she shot four bears, while Smith shot two that came "unpleasantly near the intrepid huntress." Although elk, antelope, deer, and other game were abundant, the Marquise wanted bear and would not allow other game to be shot except as necessary for food. The news article described Medora de Morès as an excellent shot who shined as "brilliantly in the field as in the cultivated society." On the way home, the Marquise rode to Billings in the mess wagon, because her carriage broke down and temporarily was abandoned.[54]

Meanwhile, Vic and Frank Smith stayed behind for another engagement, and several weeks later Vic Smith wrote to the *Bad Lands Cow Boy,* giving more details of the hunting trip. On the third day of the trip, he said he was down with mountain fever, but that same morning Mrs. de Morès killed three bears, and he killed one near the campfire. Smith said he was sick for five days. On the sixth day, he and the Marquise went higher into the mountains, where they each killed a bear, making six in all, in addition to the silvertip Van Driesche killed. Brook trout was the staple food, but elk, antelope, and sheep were also numerous. The nights were so cold large fires were kept constantly burning. Smith described the Marquise as "an excellent shot and as fearless as a cowboy," while Miss Sophia, who accompanied the Marquise, was praised for being always pleasant under difficulties. He ended by noting that he and Frank would be gone about a month.[55]

Later that fall, Vic Smith again wrote from his camp on the Meeteetse to the *Bad Lands Cow Boy,* saying the Smith family was flourishing. Wild berries abounded and elk ran in herds about their camp, keeping them awake nights by bugling. Mountain sheep were as plentiful as antelope were near Medora. The Smith brothers had two tons of smoked elk meat, which they sold on contract at fifteen cents a pound. They also planned to bring down about thirty-five elk heads and as many sheep heads. Bears were abundant, and Smith said he would send a bear head to Medora. They planned to leave for Medora in about a week.[56]

In addition to the Marquis de Morès and his wife, Smith's circle of acquaintances ranged from an outlaw to a U.S. President. Some of his more illustrious companions included Cole Younger, "Liver-Eating Johnson," "Yellowstone Kelly," and Theodore Roosevelt. The history of the friendship between Younger and Smith is unknown, but Smith reportedly visited the outlaw at the Stillwater penitentiary after Younger was captured during a botched bank robbery. Cole Younger was wounded and arrested when he and seven other members of the Jesse James gang tried to rob the Northfield, Minnesota, bank on September 7, 1876. Of the eight bandits, only Jesse and Frank James escaped. Two others were captured with Younger, and three were killed. One news account said Younger gave Smith a gold charm bridle bit, which he wore suspended from the clasp of an elaborate hair-woven watch chain.[57]

Smith met "Liver-Eating Johnson" and "Yellowstone Kelly" when they scouted for the army during Indian campaigns in Montana in the mid-1870s. Theodore Roosevelt and Smith became friends in the fall of 1883 when Roosevelt came to Medora. One day Roosevelt rode over to Smith's buffalo camp on the Cannonball River, where they discovered their mutual love for hunting. While talking to Smith, Roosevelt spotted a herd of buffalo. The two men decided to pursue them, and from that day they became fast friends. Roosevelt was impressed with Smith's reputation as an excellent shot, and Smith was awed by Roosevelt's conservation beliefs.

Although some historians question whether Smith and Roosevelt actually hunted buffalo together because the animals were nearly extinct when Roosevelt arrived in North Dakota, other evidence suggests that they did. Housed in the Theodore Roosevelt Museum in Medora is a 25.5-inch by 34-inch monochrome oil painting (circa 1890) titled *Theodore Roosevelt and His Hunting Guide, Vic G. Smith*, depicting the two men hunting buffalo together in the badlands.

In a letter to Roosevelt, Smith said he was sending him a moose antler that he picked up in Glacier National Park as a token of their friendship.[58] Roosevelt replied that he looked forward to receiving the antler. On the bottom of this letter from Roosevelt, Smith wrote: "I sent Roosevelt a large moose horn with a painting on it of a huge bull moose battling with dogs. In return he sent me a fine oil painting of our first buffalo hunt."[59]

This painting was later given to Dr. F. C. Grover, the physician who attended Smith at his death in 1925 in Duluth, Minnesota, as payment for services. Dr. Grover's son Eugene F. Grover donated the painting to the Theodore Roosevelt Museum in Medora in 1959. It had been rolled up and stored under a bed. The canvas edges had been trimmed, and the artist's signature or colophon was not visible. According to Eugene Grover, his mother took the painting to framers who tried unsuccessfully to locate the name of the artist.[60]

Smith related the buffalo hunting story to *Anaconda Standard* reporters, and the account was later reprinted in other Montana newspapers and in newspapers along the coast.[61] The press misinterpreted (or perhaps Smith intimated) this adventure as Roosevelt's first buffalo hunt rather than his first trip with Smith. In 1905, Smith received a letter from Roosevelt's secretary William Loeb remarking that Roosevelt would not object to Smith writing about this trip as long as he was "careful to state only the facts."[62]

It is evident that Roosevelt and Smith did hunt together occasionally and remained friends long after Roosevelt became President. In his book *Hunting Trips of a Ranchman,* Roosevelt wrote that "old Vic" was "concededly the best hunter on the Little Missouri" and that probably there were not a dozen men in the West who were better shots or hunters than Smith. Roosevelt then described some of Smith's shooting feats, indicating that he had firsthand knowledge of his abilities. He said Smith's secret to success was constant practice, averaging from fifty to a hundred cartridges a day, and nearly twenty thousand in a year.[63] Smith did go through ammunition; Yellowstone Valley pioneer John O'Brien recalled once selling Smith a ton of lead.[64]

In the fall of 1886, Smith guided the Marquis de Morès on a bear hunt near Big Timber, Montana. During that trip, Smith encountered one of his former buffalo skinners, Richard "Rocky Mountain Dick" Rock. Smith and Rock renewed their friendship and decided to start a game and dude ranch, which they called Smithrocksian. Locating their ranch in eastern Idaho, near Yellowstone National Park, they remained partners for about five years. Besides capturing and raising wild animals for eastern menageries, they guided wealthy clients on hunting and fishing trips.

Although neither Smith nor Rock specifically mentions him as a partner, Charles Marble, a.k.a. "Buckskin Charley," claimed he was their partner. Marble lived near Henrys Lake and may have been one of Smith and Rock's hired men, but parts of Marble's manuscript and an interview with Marble conducted by Elva Howard contain erroneous information about both Smith and Rock. It is likely that Marble exaggerated.

Marble remarked that Smith and Rock were buffalo hunters from eastern Montana. He said Smith had been a fancy trick and snapshooter who toured the East with the Cole Circus before returning to the Rockies, while Rock was a pistol expert, who hunted big game with two .45 Colt six-shooters. In his memoirs, Marble described how the men fulfilled their first contract to secure live elk for Walter (Austin) Corbin, a millionaire with a game preserve in the Adirondacks. After building a cabin along the west fork of the Madison River near Red Rock Lakes and the Continental Divide, they hauled a mowing machine and rake through the mountains nine miles from the nearest wagon road with a team and two-wheeled cart. There they cut and stacked hay, built a ten-foot-high fence around the hay and a ten-foot-high corral, and put up much wood.

Later that fall they brought in grub, snowshoes, and other necessary provisions. At the end of February the snow was four feet deep, which drove elk from the timber onto the windbeaten ridges. A chinook came and crusted the snow, then another foot of snow fell the first of March, followed by a three-day chinook and rain. Within thirty-six hours, it was forty degrees below zero, and a stiff crust had formed on the snow.

After seeing several bands of elk on the ridges, each man donned a pack with belt, axe, knife, and several twelve-foot ropes with loops on the ends. Mounted on skis, they went through the timber to keep hidden and to get above the elk to get a downhill run on them. The elk scattered when they saw them, but the men chased the fleeing animals until the elk became exhausted and were easily overtaken, roped, clogged, and brought back to the corral. According to Marble, they tried several different tactics before perfecting a technique. Tying one end of a fifty-foot rope to the rope on the elk, one man walked ahead holding the rope, while the other two pushed the animal along until they reached the corral. Depending on the distance or terrain, it could take all day or just a few hours to bring one in.

By the end of March temperatures had warmed, and the snow had settled. Once the snow became soft, they could not outrun the animals. By then twenty-seven elk, including two old bulls, had been corralled. The men had cut enough hay to last until the end of May, when they could transport the elk by wagon. They built crates onto several wagons, each wagon holding two elk. While waiting for the spring thaw, the men constructed a road to connect with the nearest wagon road. They took the elk seventy-five miles over rough roads to the railroad station at Monida, Montana, where they got a hundred dollars a head.[65]

Smith sold out to Rock in 1890 or 1891 and moved to the Big Hole area, where he earned a living mainly by killing predators, especially bears, for local ranchers. In 1892, at age forty-two, Smith tackled what he termed "the horrors of matrimony," when he wed fifteen-year-old Eugenia Amelia Dengler (sometimes spelled Dingler or Dingley) in Silver Bow County. It is unknown where or how Vic and Eugenia met, but both lied about their ages on their marriage license. Smith said he was thirty-seven, while Eugenia said she was eighteen.[66]

As he had done on the prairies of eastern Montana and western North Dakota, Smith gained notoriety for his deadly aim with the rifle in south-western Montana. Replacing earlier tales of buffalo slaughter, the press focused on Smith's skill as a bear and big game hunter. Reporters often nabbed him when he brought pelts to town and asked him to tell his adventures. (Some of these accounts are included in full in the Appendix.) One chronicle related how Smith hunted elk before game laws were enacted. Once, when there was heavy snow on the ground, Smith pursued a herd of elk that was resting on a hillside below him. Taking a white sheet from his coat, he wrapped up in it and rolled down the hill, hugging his rifle until within shooting range. Then he fired and killed five elk before the herd fled in panic.[67]

During their early married life, Eugenia often accompanied Smith on hunting and fishing trips. After eight years of marriage, they had a son on November 15, 1900.[68] They named him Rae Victor. Two days after the boy's birth, the *Anaconda Standard* reported that Vic Smith now had an assistant hunter.[69]

Smith resided in southwestern Montana for almost twenty years between 1891 and 1909. The first ten years, he lived variously between the Centennial and Big Hole valleys and Silver Bow County,[70] but by 1902 he was considered an Anaconda resident. While he generally made money killing predators and guiding wealthy hunters, he occasionally worked for the Anaconda Company as a laborer or watchman.[71]

One of the best physical descriptions of Smith appeared in the *Anaconda*

Standard, when he was fifty years old. At that time, the reporter noted that a few wrinkles were beginning to crease his tanned and weatherbeaten face, and a touch of gray hair showed among the black. Despite a life of dangerous adventures and exposure to the elements, Smith maintained an arrow-straight form, a firm tread, a steady grip, and a keen eye. Slightly above medium in stature, he was described as well-knit but not bulky. His muscles were as hard as steel and as flexible as rubber.[72]

Smith's motto was "Don't worry about the river until you get there and then the chances are that you can wade it." Generally described as genial, generous, and good-natured, his modesty was deep-rooted, and he rarely spoke about himself in public. When he did talk about his adventures, reporters noted that Smith tended to draw attention away from himself. He often wore black, donned a light-colored hat, and tied a handkerchief around his neck. According to a news account, Smith seldom drank, didn't use tobacco, and had clear ideas of right and wrong. He became a Methodist about 1896 and was respected by his peers for his morality.[73]

Time and fatherhood had changed Vic Smith. Although he began to forego the rugged life, he enjoyed taking his son into the mountains. Once when Rae was about six years old, Smith tried to teach him to shoot a .22. As they practiced shooting stumps and other inanimate targets, a gopher appeared in the distance. Smith called Rae's attention to the rodent before shooting it. When the gopher fell in death throes, the lad ran to pick up the quivering form and began to cry, asking his father why he had killed it.

When Vic replied, "To show you how to shoot," Rae asked him many more questions: Was it going to hurt you? Was it doing any harm? Is it good to eat? Will it go to heaven? Touched by his son's concerns, Smith swore from that day on he would never again take the life of a creature for sport, or to show off his skill. He would confine his deadly rifle to game that did somebody harm, was liable to do so, or that which was good to eat.[74]

It is interesting to note that Smith does not mention his son in his own manuscript, although he has entries that occurred years after Rae's birth. One article written after Smith's death mentioned that he had two sons,[75] while another noted that his only son died as a youngster.[76] According to U.S. census records, Vic and Eugenia had only one child,[77] and he died when he was twelve years old.[78]

While living in Anaconda, Smith maintained a house in town and a ranch outside of town. The location of his ranch has been given variously as French Gulch, Dry Gulch, Sheep Gulch, and Seymour Creek. His town address was listed as 620 Spruce from 1902 until 1908.[79] Then in 1909, Smith was listed at two other local addresses.[80] Eugenia's thirteen-year-old sister, Olive (Ollie) Dengler, was with the Smiths during the June 1900 census,[81] but it is likely that she was just visiting rather than living with them. At that time, the Smiths resided in the German Township of Silver Bow County, near Anaconda, while Eugenia's parents Minerva J. and William J. Dengler and some of her siblings lived in Anaconda.[82]

Vic and Eugenia stayed in Anaconda until 1909. In September 1909, a news brief in the *Anaconda Standard* noted they were headed for Seattle and Puget Sound, where they were scheduled to remain until mid-October.[83] One news article said Smith loaded the family into a prairie schooner and headed for the coast, where he had a small farm at Heppner, Oregon, for several years.[84] It is unknown whether the Smiths actually had a farm at Heppner, but they did share a residence in Grants Pass with Eugenia's parents. Another reference noted that Smith resided in Oregon circa 1912, where he lived "a consistent Christian life."[85]

In 1910 Vic, Eugenia, Rae, and Eugenia's parents were all listed as living at 511 Rogue River Avenue in Grants Pass. Eugenia's younger brother Fred, his wife Maud, and their four children also lived on the same street.[86] In March 1910, John Bradley wrote to Smith at his Rogue River address thanking him for inviting him to hunt in Oregon.[87] However, in a letter to Hermann Hagedorn, Smith said he was in Canada on a coal survey in 1910.[88]

Smith was truly a man of wanderlust. As he wrote in his manuscript: "Vic still flits from bush to bush, a veritable bird of passage, as it were." After leaving Anaconda, and until his death in 1925, Smith's whereabouts are somewhat sketchy. For example, in July 1912, George Roosevelt, writing for Theodore Roosevelt, sent a letter to Smith in Portland,[89] but that fall Philip Roosevelt wrote to Smith at Glacier National Park, Columbia Falls, Montana.[90]

Smith remained in Oregon for a few years but left around 1912 or 1913 to lecture on his frontier life around the country. He eventually landed in Minnesota, where he spent at least the last fifteen years of his life. From U.S. Census records, it appears that Eugenia remained in Oregon while Vic traveled. When his and Eugenia's only child Rae Victor died of diabetes at the Dengler home in Grants Pass in March 1913, Smith was in Chicago.[91] Rae was buried in Grants Pass, and Smith was charged with the burial expenses at his Grants Pass address.[92]

After leaving Oregon, it is likely that Smith traveled often. In April 1913, he wrote to Theodore Roosevelt from the Jefferson Hotel in Chicago, saying he came to Chicago "to lecture in the movies" on his frontier life.[93] A month later, Smith again wrote to Roosevelt from Chicago to say he was starting his stereoptical lecture tour in a few days with C. Dempsey, a full-blooded Cherokee.[94] Smith planned to travel throughout the West and down the coast. With the letter, he also sent Roosevelt a photograph of himself. This photograph was with Smith's manuscript in the Houghton Library. Neither letter from Chicago mentioned any family members.

Four years after Rae's death, Eugenia filed for divorce in Josephine County, Oregon. At the time, Vic was living in Minneapolis, while Eugenia remained at the family home in Grants Pass with her parents. According to the divorce record, they did not have any children or any joint property to settle.[95] A year later, Eugenia married Alvin Albert Mathes at the home of her parents, who signed as witnesses.[96] Eugenia and Alvin were still living with the Denglers at 511 Rogue River in Grants Pass during the 1920 U.S. Census.[97]

Sometime around Rae's death, it appears that Smith relocated to Minneapolis. In 1912, the Minneapolis City Directory lists a Victor G. Smith living at 3337 Minnehaha Avenue; his occupation was a packer. In 1913, he was listed as a helper, then in 1914 a clerk, at Selby Lake Grocery, and in 1915 he shows up as a display writer. According to the 1916 Minneapolis City Directory, Victor G. Smith was a janitor at City Hospital and had a room at 515 Seventh Avenue South. In 1917, Smith is listed in the Minneapolis directory at the same address, this time as a porter.[98] That fall, in a letter to Theodore Roosevelt, Smith gave his address as 613 Sixth Street South, Minneapolis. In the letter, Smith offered to accompany Roosevelt as an independent sharpshooter if Roosevelt went to fight the war in Europe.[99] Smith is also listed in the 1918 Minneapolis City Directory at that same address as a porter.[100] Two Victor Smiths are listed in the 1919 Minneapolis City Directory, but not Victor G. Smith; both of these Victor Smiths had different middle initials.[101] Victor Grant Smith may have been traveling when information for the 1919 directory was collected, because he was listed as a lodger in Minneapolis during the 1920 U.S. Census.[102]

In 1920, Smith received an interesting letter addressed to him at 917 Fifth Avenue South in Minneapolis, from Medora de Morès. Her letter suggests that Smith recently wrote to her about some personal problems. Mrs. de Morès expressed sympathy for Smith's losses (perhaps his divorce, the death of Rae, and his own failing health). The tone of her letter implied she had not heard from Smith in years. The Marquise noted that she, too, was ill and planned to go to the Swiss Alps. She said she longed for the days when they were on the Meeteetse in Wyoming, and asked Smith to send photographs of himself during the different stages of his life to her in Paris, and she would return them. It is unknown whether they corresponded again, and in less than a year, Medora de Morès died in France.[103]

After 1920, Smith was no longer listed as living in Minneapolis. About this time, he probably relocated to Federal Dam, Minnesota, where he reportedly lived the last few years of his life.[104] Shortly before his death, poverty possibly compelled Smith to seek publication of his manuscript. In July 1925, he wrote to Theodore Roosevelt biographer Hermann Hagedorn asking him about buying his manuscript, but Smith died virtually penniless a month later in Duluth, and it is unknown whether Hagedorn ever responded to Smith's inquiry.

In a lengthy letter to Hagedorn, Smith lamented getting old and being sick. Smith wrote in part:

> I had never been sick abed a day in my life until last March and then I fell heir to "broken arches." I dropped all hold and went to the hospital. It seemed to scatter all over my youthful frame and I suffered anguish galore. Hospital treatment done me no good—I returned home and had all the ills that flesh is heir to came flocking down on me. I developed lumbago in its most acute form—and my legs at the present writing is big as lamp posts. I have to hire a man to cut and carry in my stove wood—I carry the water for the cabin in a 5 lb. lard pail. That is all I can lift. I am reciting my little tale of woe that you may know why I delayed in writing you a long letter also for using a lead pencil which I find more convenient than a pen while lying on my back trying to write this letter.

In another part of the letter, Smith panned Hagedorn's book *Roosevelt in the Bad Lands*. Smith especially disliked the depiction of Medora as a home to ruffians. He also criticized Hagedorn for interviewing the Marquis de Morès's enemies rather than his friends and discounted the rumor that Theodore Roosevelt and de Morès were enemies. After thanking Hagedorn for the book, he said, "It is really interesting—but more so to a person that was not on the ground at the time."[105]

Shortly after writing this letter, Smith contacted his friend Cecil R. Hughes,[106] telling him he thought his end was near and instructing him on what to do with his belongings. Hughes went to Federal Dam and brought Smith to his home in Duluth, where he and C. C. Marston cared for him until he died, August 9, 1925. Dr. F. C. Grover was called, but he could do little because Bright's disease[107] had already advanced.[108]

Smith's death certificate indicated he was divorced and did not list any heirs or next of kin. Cause of death was attributed to myocarditis and nephritis.[109] One obituary noted that "little was known of the family of the old frontiersman, who was always reticent about his own affairs to the small circle of friends here in the city," except that he had been married and that his only child, a boy, had died as a youth. Little would be known of the old scout's life from his own telling, but Hughes said he had documents (probably Smith's manuscript) that gave a history of stirring deeds in a wild country. According to this obituary, Hughes had known Smith more than thirty years. If so, it is surprising that he didn't know more about Smith's personal life.[110]

Another obituary noted funeral arrangements were pending until word from relatives, trace of whom was being sought by Hughes.[111] After the Bell Brothers Mortuary prepared his body for burial, Smith was interred August 12 in Oneota Cemetery in Duluth, with the Reverend H. W. Clough, a Baptist pastor, conducting the services.[112] His few belongings were given to friends, except for the painting of Smith and Roosevelt, which was given to Dr. F. C. Grover as payment for services. According to a curator at the Houghton Library, the Theodore Roosevelt Association obtained Smith's manuscript in 1925, the same year Smith died, and the Houghton Library at Harvard acquired it in 1943.[113]

CHRONOLOGY

1850	Vic Smith born in January near Buffalo, New York.
1851	Thomas Smith built John J. Ryan Building in Omro, Wisconsin.
1851-55+	Smith family lived in Omro, Wisconsin.
1853	Rae Smith born in Omro, Wisconsin.
1855	Thomas Smith family in Omro, Wisconsin, census. DeMorny Smith born in Omro, Wisconsin.
1860-63	Smith family lived in Oshkosh, Wisconsin.
1863-70	Smith family resided in Alexandria, Minnesota.
1863-65	VS ran away from Alexandria and lived in Missouri with Jeff Gumm for two years.
1865-66	VS returned to Alexandria.
1867	VS and brother Rae (Bill) went to Minneapolis.
1867-69	VS at White Earth Indian Reservation, Minnesota.
1870	VS listed as a machinist in Douglas County, Minnesota, census with parents and brothers Rae and Morny. VS hunting and trapping in winter at Aldrich, Minnesota.
1870-71	Smith family moved to Chicago about this time. VS and Billy Preston at Fort Ransom, North Dakota, supplying meat for the post.
1871-73	VS went to Fort Abercrombie, North Dakota, and secured government mail contract to Fort Totten.
1873-74	VS drifted about hunting and trapping with Santee Sioux. VS visited family in Chicago.
1874-75	Capt. Anderson hired VS to take cattle to Fort Buford. VS supplied post with meat, carried dispatches, hunted, trapped, and captured buffalo calves.
1876	Eugenia Amelia Dengler born October 9 in Cawker City, Kansas.
1876-77	VS was government scout.
1877-78	VS wolfed and carried mail for Major Pease.
1878	Frank M. Smith and Mary J. Watson married in New Lisbon, Wisconsin, September 26.
1878-79	VS contracted to eastern firm to collect 50 buffalo calves. VS killed more than 4,000 buffalo and many wolves in the Yellowstone triangle.
1880-82	VS lived near Glendive, Montana, with girlfriend.
1881	VS became a fugitive after smuggling whiskey onto Sioux Indian Reservation.
1882	VS moved buffalo camp to Cannonball River in North Dakota in the fall.
1883	VS met Theodore Roosevelt and slaughtered last of buffalo with Sitting Bull.
1883-86	VS in Medora, North Dakota, employed by the Marquis de Morès, gathered specimens for New Orleans Exposition, performed at eastern shooting galleries, and visited family in Chicago.

1886-91	VS ran game ranch with Dick Rock near Henrys Lake, Idaho.
1887	Olive Dengler was born in Montana or Wyoming.
1890-91	VS sold out to Rock and went to the Big Hole area of Montana.
1892	VS and Eugenia Dengler married in Silver Bow County, Montana, July 28.
1892-95	VS resided in southwestern Montana.
1896-1909	VS resided around Anaconda, Montana.
1900	Son Rae Victor born November 15 in Anaconda.
1900-02	Eugenia's family (Denglers) lived in Anaconda.
1902-09	VS listed in Anaconda city directories as a watchman or laborer for Anaconda Company.
1906-07	VS son Rae in school this year.
1909	VS and family move to Oregon in fall.
1909-10	Fred and William Dingley (Dengler) are listed in Dillon, Montana, City Directory.
1910	VS, Eugenia, Rae, and Eugenia's parents lived together in Grants Pass, Oregon. Eugenia's brother Fred and family lived on same street.
1911	VS probably still in Oregon.
1912	VS in Oregon until fall. VS in northwestern Montana in fall; VS listed as a packer at 3337 Minnehaha Avenue, Minneapolis.
1913	Son Rae Victor died March 23 in Oregon. VS listed at Grants Pass address, but obituary said he had been in Chicago since last fall. VS at Jefferson Hotel in Chicago. VS also listed as a helper at 3337 Minnehaha Avenue, Minneapolis.
1914	VS listed as a clerk at Selby Lake Grocery at 3337 Minnehaha Avenue, Minneapolis.
1915	VS listed as a display writer at 3337 Minnehaha Avenue, Minneapolis.
1916	VS listed as a janitor at City Hospital Rooms, 515 Seventh Avenue South, Minneapolis.
1917	VS listed at 515 Seventh Avenue South, Minneapolis, as a porter and at 613 Sixth Street South, Minneapolis. VS and Eugenia divorced April 9 in Josephine County, Oregon.
1918	VS listed as a porter at 613 Sixth Street South, Minneapolis. Eugenia married Alvin Albert Mathes April 3 in Grants Pass.
1919	VS probably in Minneapolis.
1920	VS listed as a lodger at 917 Fifth Avenue South, Minneapolis. Eugenia and Alvin Mathes still at Grants Pass with Eugenia's parents.
1921	Medora de Morès died March 1 at Cannes, France.
1921-25	VS probably at Federal Dam, Minnesota.
1925	VS went to Duluth to Cecil R. Hughes's home in July and died August 9. Dr. F. C. Grover acquired painting of VS and Theodore Roosevelt. VS manuscript given to the Theodore Roosevelt Association.
1943	Houghton Library at Harvard obtained VS manuscript.
1945	Eugenia died April 23 in Grants Pass.
1959	Theodore Roosevelt Museum in Medora received VS/Roosevelt painting.
1990	Editor located VS manuscript.

THE CHAMPION BUFFALO HUNTER

THE FRONTIER MEMOIRS OF YELLOWSTONE VIC SMITH
[VIC G. SMITH OF MONTANA]

by Victor Grant Smith

From Theodore Roosevelt Collection,
Harvard College Library
(Shelfmark: Roosevelt R332.Sm6)

Publication is by permission of the
Houghton Library, Harvard University

PART I

BOYHOOD

Early Days, Wayward Ways

Vic Smith, or "Yellowstone Vic" as he was known in later years, first saw the light of day at Buffalo, New York.[1] When a cherub of about six hands high,[2] his parents moved to Oshkosh, Wisconsin, where undesirables go to when they die. Nothing occurred to mar the enjoyment of his youth except the lambasting that his sturdy Scotch mother administered almost daily, and which he richly deserved.

Among his choice collection of bad habits was that of sucking the eggs that his mother would put under the setting hens. He would suck the contents of the egg through a small opening in the shell and then put back the shell and thus delude the poor hens until his mother found him out. Then she would entangle her fingers in the bosom of his panties, and with the other hand on his neck, she would souse him in a barrel of water head first until he was nearly strangled.

He attended school until he had thirteen rings on his horns. Then his parents moved to Alexandria, Minnesota.[3] Vic thought a better knowledge of geography could be obtained through traveling and experience than at school or from behind the plow while gazing at the oxen's tails all day. One clear night, when all hands were in the embrace of old Morpheus, Vic separated fifty dollars from the family vault that was under the carpet. Not even bidding his kind mother goodbye, he hiked about twenty miles to the high road and boarded the stage for St. Cloud, where he took the train for St. Paul.

After wandering around for three days, he hopped on board a steamer that was bound for St. Louis. At Dubuque, Iowa, the boat loaded corn all night; the mate rushed the coons[4] unmercifully and swore most horribly to prove he was an artist in profanity. On a boat adjoining the steamer was a crowd of deckhands and coons playing craps. In a dispute about midnight, two large coons got cut across their tummies with razors. Fearing trouble, the players took them outside and laid them on the wharf in a dying condition.

At daybreak the noise and bustle of the steamer in getting ready to start awoke Vic. Rolling out of his berth, he went to look at the descendents of Ham who had been carved up. In the frosty dawn of the morning, side by side, lay the two men with their intestines protruding from the gaping razor slashes. At the edges of the wounds a thick fringe of frost had formed. One was dead and the other at the expiring point.[5]

The boat pulled out in due time and reached St. Louis. Though young, Vic was quite able to look out for himself. At St. Louis he wandered around, took in the sights, and went where boys should not have been allowed to enter.

After a week he went to the steamboat landing and secured passage for New Orleans. No steam was up as the boat was not scheduled to leave until noon the next day; so he retired after getting a berth.

During the night, a steamer next to the one Vic was on caught fire from an overturned lantern. The steamers, of which there were seven, were cast loose from the dock and allowed to drift with the current so that they might not be destroyed. Of course there was only part of the crew and a colored family on the steamer Vic was on. The colored family consisted of an Uncle and Auntie, their married daughter and her family, which was several, and a large pack of coon dogs. It was a still night but intensely dark. In less than ten minutes, the dry woodwork and the pitched ropes of the doomed vessel were a mass of flames. The colored family got excited and jumped overboard except one bright little girl who was afraid to get wet, or so she said. They forgot to throw anything over to support themselves, and Vic and the little girl watched them from the deck, as they struggled with the dark water, until they sank one by one.

Flames were rapidly consuming the vessel, and Vic picked up a plank from off the deck and threw it overboard. After a rough and tumble fight with the colored girl, who still wished to keep dry, he pushed her overboard and quickly followed. After somewhat of a struggle, Vic got her onto the plank. Paddling with a piece of board, he was soon away from the burning boat. The mate of the boat drowned, as did three of the deckhands. Vic paddled out into the current and was soon picked up by a rowboat. The girl was taken care of by the authorities, while Vic shifted for himself.

The next day Vic, with another boy about sixteen years old who said his name was Jimmie Tubbs, secured a skiff and started down the river. One week later they camped at night twenty miles above New Madrid, Missouri. Setting the fishline they had, they caught two large catfish for supper. Before midnight it started to rain. As they had no shelter, they started along the shore to a habitation they had passed about a mile back. When they were within hailing distance of the place, some vicious crossbred hounds attacked them. Vic climbed a small tree near the hen house, while Tubbs ran back and climbed a tree about one hundred yards from him.

Some of the hounds camped under Vic's tree, while the rest of the pack volunteered to keep Tubbs company. A bolt of lightning struck the tree Tubbs was in. By the flash, Vic saw him shoot to the ground with the traditional dull thud. Poor Tubbs and three of the hounds that were under the tree were killed by the bolt. The thunder-shower was soon over, but the remaining dogs kept barking at Vic. Finally, a lanky Missourian with a shotgun appeared near the tree to find what kind of "pesky varmint" the dogs had treed.

Vic, who had seen poor Tubbs fall from the tree, was too paralyzed to speak. The "settler," seeing a dark object about thirty feet up the tree, blazed away, and then Vic found his voice. When the farmer held back the dogs, Vic descended the tree. Mutual explanations followed. Finding that Vic had only three buckshot in the calf of his leg, the farmer said he was half sorry he had not fired the other barrel, as he had no use for a chicken-thief.

They went over to the tree where poor Tubbs and the three dogs lay. Vic was sure he would get the contents of the other barrel then, as the farmer was greatly wrought up over the death of his dogs, claiming the "dawgs" would not have been under the tree if the boys had not been around trying to steal his chickens. He called his boy, a fever and ague tinted youth about fourteen years old with a marvelous growth of tow hair, and they toted Tubbs to the milk house. Then they took Vic, washed his leg, and put a large chew of tobacco (the universal remedy for all cuts, wounds, or bruises in Missouri) over each buckshot wound. After a week of such treatment, Vic was himself again. He still carries the buckshot as souvenirs in his leg.

The tow-headed youth traveled all the next day, notifying the neighbors, who lived from two to five miles apart, of the tragedy. Two days after Tubbs's death, the neighbors gathered. A hole was dug, and Tubbs was enclosed in a coffin made of split walnut slabs two inches thick and lowered into the ground. An aged darky preached the funeral sermon which, only for the solemnity of the occasion, would have been extremely humorous. At the funeral, Jeff Gumm (the man who shot Vic in the leg) blubbered like mush a-boiling over but whether for the dogs or poor Tubbs Vic was not sure.

Gumm took a liking, or as he termed it a "hankerin yearnin," to Vic and insisted on Vic making his home with him. Vic remained with Gumm two years. As Jeff put in most of his time hunting possum, bear, and deer, Vic became an expert in the chase. The canebrakes were full of wild razorback hogs, which were more to be feared than any bear. The pack of hounds that Jeff Gumm owned were expressly for bear and wild boars.

On one occasion after Vic had been with Gumm a year, they paddled upriver for about three miles and struck out toward a ridge where there were plenty of pecan nuts and also wild boars. Soon they heard the grunting of hogs, and Vic spied a nice looking porker about six months old. He fired his rifle and broke its back. The excited mother of the pig quickly saw the smoke of the gun. Seeing her crippled young and hearing its cries, the sow charged the hunters, followed by seven other sows and boars.

In his anxiety to get out of reach of the enraged animals, Vic dropped his gun as he climbed a scrub oak. Fortunately, Jeff had a strap on his rifle. Slipping it over his shoulder, he easily shinned up a tree out of harm's way. Two of the boars were old residenters with enormous tusks. The hogs could not be induced to leave the tree, and Jeff was obliged to kill all of them. They cut off all the best portions of the hogs and carried them to Vic's boat (or dugout commonly used in those days, made by trimming a log and digging out the center), which was filled to capacity.

When all the pork was loaded, they started down the bayou for home. As Vic's dugout passed some trees that were leaning over the water, a large moccasin snake fell from an overhead limb midway into Vic's dugout. Spying Vic, the snake immediately started toward him. Vic struck at the snake, and the boat, being loaded to the guards, easily turned over. Soon the water, which was about fifteen feet deep, was filled with snake, Smith, and razorback pork. The snake made directly for Vic. If Jeff would not have pulled alongside and killed it with a blow of his paddle, the snake would have certainly bitten Vic. In the water the snakes are very swift, and a bite from the yellow moccasin is considered almost certain death.

The ensuing fall, Jeff and his family, with Vic and the dogs trailing along, attended a dance at a place called Goober Bottom, some ten miles distant. The cemetery there contained forty-eight graves, of which forty-one of the occupants died with their boots on and a gun in their hands, or they were killed in ambush. The word liar was not tolerated in good society. If a person made use of those terms, the killing commenced then and there with no postponement on account of the weather. A funeral was invariably the next day due to the warm climate, and as all hands went armed to church or to the cemetery, it was frequently necessary to give notice of another funeral or two.

But to return to the dance—all were happy: men in cowhide boots and jeans, ladies in linsey-woolseys,[6] the younger ones barefooted, dogs lying around underfoot, and as birth control was not practiced there, every woman had a baby or two. About two in the morning, when the moonshine tanglefoot[7] and corn-rye (the kind that will make a rabbit walk up and spit in a bulldog's eye) were circulating, Abe Jensen stumbled over one of Jeff Gumm's dogs that was lying on the floor. Abe and his lady Miss Pussy Brown were hopping around the room at the time and both came to grief on the puncheon[8] floor. Jensen quickly arose. Stung by the loud laughter from the crowd, he kicked the dog, who resented the familiarity by fastening his teeth in the calf of Abe's leg. When the dog refused to loosen up at Abe's request, Abe pulled a large dirk knife,[9] commonly called a gut ripper, and disemboweled the canine.

Now Jeff, who overlooked an insult to his wife during the evening, could not stand an insult and calamity like that to his "dawg." He drew his knife and slashed Abe in his jugular vein. Bill Morley, a friend of Abe's, drew his revolver and plugged Gumm dangerously near his solar plexus.

Friends on both sides drew their weapons. When the smoke of the battle cleared, four men were dead and three wounded. Miss Pussy Brown received a bullet in the fleshy part of her anatomy as she crawled under a bed in the next room to get out of the danger line, but she recovered (it was only a flesh wound) and lived to be in at several more deaths. After nearly every dance, a new headboard would be erected in the cemetery.

Whitewater Adventures

After two years with Jeff Gumm, Vic had made remarkable headway in the use of the rifle and was well-posted in the art of hunting and trailing game. Having read Bonneville's *Adventures in the West*,[10] he longed to reach the "Land of the Buffalo." When he finally landed at St. Paul, Minnesota, he took the cars to St. Cloud. There he drove a team for a freighter as far as Alexandria. Then he jumped the outfit and hoofed it to the home of his parents, about twenty miles distant.[11]

He remained home for one year, hunting deer and moose. Game was very plentiful, and there were no restrictions on the sale of venison. Although a mere boy, none of the old hunters could shoot any better or kill more game than Vic.

He was wonderfully fleet of foot and very strong, it being an actual fact that he ran a yearling deer to death in six inches of snow. However, it is doubtful the deer was perfectly healthy at the time.

His parents concluded to sell their ranch and move to Chicago. Vic, with his brother Bill,[12] a year younger than Vic,[13] determined to go on a trip to Minneapolis. Being shy on ducats, they concluded the water route was the most feasible and least expensive. A light skiff was decided upon, and one Monday morning the two boys hitched up the cayuses[14] to a wagon and started to town for the necessary lumber and nails to build a craft.

While returning with the outfit, and about five miles from home, they met an old black she bear and two cubs that had climbed an oak tree close to the road. When the horses were within twenty feet of the tree, the bears started to descend. The bears broke holds on the tree and jumped to the ground, a habit all bears are guilty of. The team took fright and ran down into a small lake, where one of the plugs[15] drowned. After extricating the remaining horse, removing the harness, and hitching onto the rear of the wagon, the boys pulled the vehicle ashore.

Vic then went about three miles to a neighbor's to borrow an ox team to take their load home. He found that the neighbor had a sick ox, so he borrowed the well one. Leading the ox back to the wagon, he harnessed it up with the cayuse and managed to get home. His brother, who had remained with the wagon while Vic went after the ox, said that the bear came back on the other side of the lake. Smelling the dead horse, she and the cubs swam out to the carcass. The cubs climbed onto the carcass, and the old bear towed the outfit ashore on the opposite side of the lake. After making a meal off the dead horse, they shuffled into the timber.

After a week of patient labor, the boys had a very credible boat ready to launch. About the last of May, they boarded the frail craft and paddled out into the current, their parents bidding them a tearful goodbye. They floated leisurely down the Long Prairie River, the weather being ideal.

On the third day, they sailed into the Crow Wing River, near where the Chippewa and the Sioux once had a bloody conflict, in which the Sioux Indians bested the Chippewa and took twenty-one scalps and twelve squaws.[16] The Sioux made their way back to the Big Missouri River, where the older squaws were used in a most atrocious manner and finally scalped alive. The young squaws were used as concubines by some of the Sioux, and their lot was worse than death.[17]

At that season of the year, when their adventures entered the Crow Wing River, lumbermen were running down pine logs for the different mills at St. Paul and below there on the Mississippi. About twenty-five miles below the confluence of the Crow Wing and Long Prairie rivers, where the river was about a mile wide, the boys spied a large black bear swimming. A rope that was around the bedding was quickly removed and a slipknot tied.

Vic, meanwhile, paddled with all his might to lessen the distance between them and bruin. When they finally caught up with the bear, Vic rose, threw the rope over the bear's head, and gave it a yank that tightened it. Mr. Bear, with a snarl, whirled around and after two or three strokes was alongside the craft. The bear reached a hold of the gunwale. At the same time, Bill, who was a very good guitar player, smashed the guitar on the bear's head, converting the guitar into kindling wood. This angered the bear more, and he quickly capsized the boat. As luck would have it, they were near the shore on the shallow side where the water was not more than four feet deep, just up to Bill's chin. The bear swam ashore, and Vic caught the boat and saved most of the provisions, while Bill clung to the guitar that was in a silk sack. The bear disappeared into the brush, and with it went the vision of fifty dollars that the boys thought the bear would bring at some menagerie.

At the next village, Bill glued the instrument together. One day later they were out of the Crow Wing River and into the Mississippi. When near Little Falls, the roar of the falls was startling. Rae [Bill] was for going ashore and letting Vic paddle the craft over the falls; but Vic quieted his fears, and when they reached the falls they went over about a 25-foot drop. Vic cleverly steered the craft between two huge rocks that towered upward at the foot of the falls. Their boat submerged for a brief period, then shot upward, and came to the surface without capsizing, with Bill still clinging to his guitar. The boys slid into the water and swam ashore, towing the boat after them.

When they arrived at St. Cloud, the river was full of logs. The log drivers had a boom[18] across the stream and were guiding the logs through an opening in the boom. When the skiff shot through, a red-shirted log driver hooked his picaroon[19] into the craft and cried out "halt." Vic threw the picaroon off and paid no attention to the man. As the log driver shouted, "You will be crushed to death," the craft was steered among the seething mass of pine logs. Quite frequently the logs would shoot up from beneath, nearly their full length out of the water, and fall back again, barely missing the frail craft.

The bridge was lined with people, who fairly held their breath to see the perilous position the boys were in, and when the danger was passed, the people gave them a hearty cheer as they floated down the river. When they arrived at Minneapolis, Vic insisted on shooting

St. Anthony Falls, which meant certain death. He certainly would have done so if Bill (still clinging to the music box) had not reached out and caught one of the bridge braces. They then abandoned their craft. Bill went to Pine City, Minnesota, while Vic went up to White Earth Reservation, Minnesota.

Indian Tales

A good many years before Vic and his brother's adventure at St. Anthony Falls, as the story runs, the Sioux and Chippewa Indians were on friendly terms. A handsome young buck[20] of the Sioux tribe had won the admiration of Dreaming Eyes, the pretty daughter of the proud Chippewa chief. Her parents forbade the union, but after some pressure by White Tail, the Sioux buck lover, the maiden consented to elope with him.

At midnight, Dreaming Eyes stole to the banks of the river where White Tail awaited. Getting into the birchbark canoe, they silently paddled down the "Father of Waters."[21] The girl was soon missed. Since some of her belongings were gone, her parents were certain she had eloped. Fifty Indians struck across the country to the Falls to head them off, if they had gone that way. The Indians hid in the bush.

Shortly after daybreak, the canoe with the two lovers came into sight. There were Indians on both banks. Seeing they could not escape and knowing that capture meant certain death, the lovers stood up in the canoe. Singing the death chant, they took the fatal plunge with their craft into the swirling falls, which never gives up its dead.

At the reservation, Vic joined forces with a well-educated Indian whose father was hanged at Mankato, Minnesota, for murdering eighteen white women and children in the Minnesota Massacre in 1862.[22] They hunted together for two years, and it did not take Vic long to gain a fair degree of proficiency in the Indian dialect. At the Agency was an aged darky named Bungo, who was married to a squaw named

Fishbone. She had several children by him. He claimed he was the first "white man" that ever trapped on Lake Superior.

It is related of Bungo that one cold winter while he was trapping on the Great Lakes, his daughter, a fine-looking girl about eighteen, who unfortunately was afflicted with St. Vitus's dance[23] and in consequence was shy about thirty percent mental, wandered away from the lodge and froze to death. It was several days before old Bungo could locate her remains.

He then discovered that the martens, minks, and fishers had made great inroads on her body with their voracious appetites. Being of a thrifty turn, he concluded to leave her in the rushes where he found her and use her for bait. As the weather lingered around forty degrees below zero, she lasted a long time, and he made a record catch of furs off the remains. The "Gentleman from Africa" then amputated one limb from the trunk. Trailing it about three miles on the ice, he scented it with beaver castor and caught three silver-gray foxes, for which he received seven hundred dollars.[24]

The Northern Pacific Railroad was just being graded then, and Brainerd, now a beautiful city, had but few houses. They were built of logs, while the rest of the people lived in tents. One of the houses was the city bastille.[25] At a small country schoolhouse about five miles away, the teacher, a young maiden, well-educated and handsome, taught the settlers' children. As is usual in the country, she "boarded round." She had to walk two miles to her home after school.

There was a meeting at the schoolhouse one afternoon, and the trustees were on business. She left for home, not thinking of danger, as she could easily make home before dark. Two half-breed brothers, twenty and twenty-two years of age, lay in wait for her and forced her to accompany them into the woods a mile back from the trail. Until daylight she was compelled to submit to their hellish passions. They held her, cut her throat, put her on a brush pile, and cremated her.[26]

As she did not appear for school the next day, the scholars returned home, and the settlers sent out searching parties and found her remains partly consumed. The home of the half-breeds was about four miles from the scene of the murder, but they were not even suspected. About two months after the murder, the breeds got drunk. Their mother, a full-blooded Chippewa squaw, heard them discussing the crime, and she immediately reported it to the sheriff. They were arrested and confessed, giving all the particulars of the crime.[27]

They told how the young lady cried and begged for her life, promising never to divulge their names or deeds if they would spare her life, but one cruelly held her hands, while the other one cut her throat. Showing no remorse at their deed, the brothers were locked in the log jail at Brainerd. A crowd of railroaders, headed by Blinkey Jack, assembled at the jail. When the jailer said he had lost the keys, the crowd quietly but energetically hitched a rope to one of the logs of which the jail was built. After pulling out a log, they extracted the half-breeds. Throwing one end of the rope over a limb of a stately pine tree and the other over Baptiste's neck, he being the older brother, they slowly hoisted him into eternity.

His hands were not tied, as the crowd was too intent on "delivering the goods" for any chance of escape. When the rope tightened on Baptiste's neck, he grasped it and overhanded to the first limb with the agility of a wild cat. Seating himself on a limb, he crowed all the same as a rooster. Charley, the younger brother, looked on apparently unconcerned and joked with Baptiste and told the crowd, who were pulling their guns, they could not hit a squirrel. Quickly throwing the noose from his neck, Baptiste grasped the trunk of the tree. Amid a shower of bullets, he climbed among the branches and continued crowing until he was in the top of the tree. Although he had been hit several times, his vitality was such that he did not fall until Bill Chadwell raised his rifle and dropped him from the tree. (Chadwell was afterward killed at Northfield, Minnesota, while a member of the Jesse James gang in 1876.)[28]

Baptiste's body no sooner struck the ground when the crowd demanded the life of Charley, the younger brother, who showed the same bravado as Baptiste did by climbing the tree and crowing. He joked with acquaintances he saw in the crowd below. Before he could throw the noose from his neck and repeat the performance of his brother, he was perforated by bullets and fell from the limb. The mother of the boys looked on with the stoicism of the Indian race.[29] After the hanging, she laid the bodies side by side, covered them with her blanket, and slowly walked away. Vic made a mental note of the whole performance, which he filed away in his brain for future reference.[30]

PART II

INTRODUCTION
TO THE
FRONTIER

Carrying the Mail

The following spring, Vic went to old Fort Ransom on the Sheyenne River in North Dakota. Vic remained there for a while shooting beaver while the water was high. He averaged five beaver a day for thirty days. Their skins were worth seven dollars apiece.

There was a young man driving team for the sutler named Billy Preston. The river that ran by the fort had no bridge but had a good ford. Preston usually rode on the backs of the oxen across the stream, which was about five feet deep at that season of the year. One morning he asked Vic to ride behind him on the ox while they forded the stream. The bank had washed away to quite an extent, making a steep pitch for the bulls to go down. Vic readily agreed and climbed on, facing the tail and hanging onto the same. In going down the steep pitch, Vic's tail hold slipped, and he shot backward onto Preston. Both went over the oxen's heads into the water.

Preston, who had a very quick temper, smashed Vic in the face. In the roughhouse that ensued, Preston came near to losing his life through strangulation and would have except Vic pulled him ashore. In about a half-hour, Billy was himself again and dove into Vic. This time they fought to a finish. That scrap cemented their friendship, and they struck up a partnership and supplied the post with wild game for a year.

Then Billy went north to join forces with Louis Riel, the half-breed who was causing the Canadian government a great deal of trouble. After Riel was hanged and his followers scattered, Preston returned.[1] The following winter he and Smith wintered forty miles above Brainerd, Minnesota, at a station called Aldrich, where there was splendid hunting and trapping. A man named Costello kept the section house there.

The following spring, Vic went to Leech Lake after an Indian who had stolen a bale of wolf hides from their lodge. During Vic's absence, a drunken Indian came to Costello's house demanding whiskey. As Costello had never given the Indian any booze, he told the Indian he did not drink himself or keep any booze in the house. This angered the redskin, who pulled his rifle from the scabbard, thrust it into Costello's face, and pulled the trigger.

Costello grasped the muzzle of the rifle at the moment of its discharge. The bullet took off one of his fingers, passed through the door, and penetrated the brain of Mollie Costello, the handsome daughter of the house. As she fell dead, her brother Bob picked up a rifle and put two bullets through the body of the fleeing redskin, but it didn't stop him. Bob had no more cartridges, and the Indian gained the safety of his camp one mile away.

One hour afterward, Preston heard of the murder and sent word to the sheriff at Brainerd to come immediately. That evening the sheriff and posse arrived. After dark Billy Preston, as guide, piloted the party to the Indian camp, which in the meantime had moved about two miles back into the timber. When within three hundred yards of the camp, the sheriff got cold feet and refused to go any farther. Billy threw off his coat and administered a good thrashing to the sheriff and took away his revolvers. Preston could find but one nervy man in the posse. Together they searched all of the lodges but found no trace of the murderer. It was learned from the Indians that he eventually died from his wounds after suffering for nearly two years.

Bob Costello died with his boots on near the Black Hills in '77 on Alkali Creek for participating in a number of holdups.[2] Bob Costello's brother-in-law Shang Stanton killed Dan Shumway, a notorious tough at Moorhead, Minnesota, and received a reward of three hundred dollars for doing so. This was two years before Bob's summary taking off. It was in that section where Vic caught two young calf elk that Dr. Carver,[3] the great rifle shot, afterward bought and broke to harness.

The following May, Vic bought a horse and saddle from a Catholic priest on Wild Rice Creek in North Dakota. The priest was doing missionary work among the half-breeds. His Holiness had come into possession of a well-broken bull elk that would whirl him over the prairie in the summer in a half-breed cart. In the winter the priest, wrapped in his buffalo robes snugly tucked in his elk-drawn tobog-gan, would easily cover seventy-five miles a day. With motor power like that, he had no use for a measly cayuse.

Vic went to Fort Abercrombie on the Red River of the North. Finding that a couple of packhorses were necessary, he hired to the government to carry mail until he had enough money to purchase the needed outfit. His route was from Fort Abercrombie to Fort Totten at Devils Lake, North Dakota. The distance was 160 miles, and there were but two places the entire distance where there was enough wood to build a fire; this was at the crossing of the Maple River and the upper Sheyenne.[4]

There was only one settler on the entire route, and he and his family were afterward murdered by Indians, except the oldest girl who was about eighteen years old. She was kept in captivity by the redskins and subjected to indignities and rare brutality that only Indians could devise and put into execution.[5]

In the summertime, the mail was carried in a Red River cart, made by half-breeds without a scrap of iron. The tires were made of buffalo bull hide, and buffalo tallow was always used as a lubricant.

The vehicle was drawn by a half-breed horse, a cross between an Indian pony and an American horse. The harness was also made of buffalo hide.

In the winter, three dogs were hitched tandem-style to a toboggan eight feet long by two and one-half feet wide. The dogs, a cross between large buffalo wolves and imported Esquimaux dogs, weighed about ninety pounds apiece and had great endurance and considerable dog sense. If necessary, they easily could make seventy miles per day over the hard snow. Their dispositions were morose and savage.

The driver always kept his weather eye peeled for trouble and always hung onto a ten-foot trail rope. Uphill the driver ran, hanging onto the trail rope; downgrade or on the level, he rode. The dogs were guided by the whip or voice. Frequently, when a wolf or coyote was sighted, the team would take off in pursuit, but the sting of the lash on the sides of the leader would soon bring the dogs back to the trail. Fact is, there was no trail, only mounds of sod six feet high and three hundred yards apart.

One day when Vic was about fifty miles on the road, he saw a blizzard coming. He turned the sled over in a coulee. Then taking the side poles, which were hickory and about ten feet long, he ran them through the rings of the canvas and had an improvised shelter up before the storm reached him. The shelter was only about three feet high, but he tied the dogs in under the canvas with him. Being in a narrow coulee and his "windbreak" low, the storm could not blow it away very handily. Within ten minutes, the "windbreak" was deeply covered with drifting snow. The dogs soon nestled down for a snooze, but before retiring one of them managed to snatch and swallow the lunch Vic had put up for his dinner.

The blizzard raged for three days. Luckily the weather was not cold, and the warmth of the four bodies in the limited space kept the temperature of the bungalow quite comfortable. By the third day, the dogs and driver were in a fighting mood through hunger, as they had nothing to eat since the morning they left the fort. Vic would give all the dogs a few raps with the butt of his whip to insure peace. Then all beings would curl up for another snooze, until the fighting of the dogs would arouse everybody into action.

On the evening of the third day, the storm broke, the sky became clear, and the air was very cold. Hitching up the dogs and grabbing the tail rope, as there was a half-mile upgrade for a starter, the outfit took off. Mail dogs are never fed in the morning, and they well know grub awaits them in the evening at the end of the day's journey. Consequently, they are always eager to finish the day's travel. Next morning they arrived at their sod station. The way man and dogs devoured dried fish and bacon was surprising.[6]

Large packs of wolves were common in those days. One cold day at the crossing of the Sheyenne River, Vic encountered a large male wolf and his consort. She was a splendid specimen of the wolf family, about eighteen months old and apparently just making her debut in society, while he was a magnificent animal weighing about a hundred pounds. As a rule, Vic's team would pay little or no attention to the vagrant bands of wolves they saw daily. However, this time, his full-blooded wheeler[7] dashed toward the couple, dragging sled and all. They were eagerly met by the enemy. They mixed, and in the struggle that ensued the wheeler freed himself from the harness. Vic held the other animals back by the tail rope attached to the sled.

The fair "Delilah" sat on a knoll about fifty yards away with a demure look that plainly said, "the best wolf takes me." (Vic's team consisted of one full-blooded wolf and two half-breeds.) The animals fought with the same ferocity that humans fight over females of their own race, with the charmer looking on all the while. They cut and gashed each other with their razor-like fangs until the wild wolf, weakened from loss of blood and not having his meal served regular (while the team wolf dined on fish and pemmican each evening), slunk away. Then the team wolf proudly trotted away with Evelyn. He looked back at Vic as much to say, "To the victor belong the spoils."

The Indians around Devils Lake were the Santee Sioux who

slaughtered the settlers in Minnesota in '62 and '63. However, since that trouble, and remembering the trouncing they received at the hands of the whites, they remained fairly quiet.[8]

Smith Averts Hanging

Vic carried the mail for about two years.[9] Then drawing his voucher from the government, he started for Winnipeg across the Canadian border. He traveled on horseback along the bank of the Red River, with his packhorse following, until he arrived about where Grand Forks now stands. The camp, called Wolftown, was home to a number of professional wolfers. These men wolfed, loafed, gambled, drank, and fought for four months out of every year, and the other eight months were devoted to the chase.

Vic remained with the rollicking wolfers for a week. During that time, a stranger dropped into camp who seemed to be fairly strong financially, as he was not backward in producing a fat roll while playing a sociable game of draw with the boys, where the ante was a dollar and their pile was the limit.[10] Hanging on in the camp was a dissolute fellow known as "Brocky." He was tolerated because the wolfers did not want to kill him to get rid of him.

When the stranger came to camp, one of the boys saluted him with, "Hello, Stranger," and that was all the name he got, as no one asked his name, and he did not take the trouble to tell them. The "Stranger" had been in camp four days when "Brocky," who had been making himself particularly obnoxious, was requested to pull his freight. In a half-hour he had saddled his horse and left, saying that he was headed for Winnipeg across the line.

Three days afterward, the "Stranger" started west for Fort Totten, while Vic pulled out for Winnipeg. "Brocky" had attempted to lead the men astray as to his destination, as he merely had gone on the old Fort Totten trail and awaited the coming of the "Stranger" to rob him. At any rate, two days after the "Stranger" left, a well-known frontier character known as "Jimmy from Cork,"[11] one of the best-known dog team drivers in the west, came to the wolfers' station and said that while about thirty miles out, he had been attracted by the presence of buzzards to a buffalo wallow. On riding to the spot, he found the body, or rather the skeleton, of a man who had recently died. He described the clothing, and they all agreed that the "Stranger" had met his fate.

Their suspicions fell on "Brocky" as the one who assisted him into the next world. Ten men immediately saddled up. Taking "Jimmy" with them as guide, they rode west until the circling buzzards gave notice that they were near the scene of the murder, for such it proved to be. On examination of the skeleton (the birds had picked the bones clean), a bullet hole was found through the skull, the bullet having entered the back of the head and emerged through the eye. They soon dug a hole and buried the remains about twenty yards from the trail.

A large buffalo skull bleached white from long exposure to the elements was used as a tombstone. The shaft of an old broken-down cart nearby was driven into the earth at the head, and the buffalo skull was slipped on securely. Date and "Stranger" were laboriously cut into the skull with a knife. A spoke from a wheel did duty at the foot of the grave. The party then divided to find the murderer, if possible.

The day after the murder, as Vic was jogging along slowly, he was surprised to have "Brocky" overhaul him and banter him for a trade. "Brocky" was riding the "Stranger's" horse, which was a very fine animal, and leading his own. Vic didn't recognize the steed, as the wolfers all had good horses, and the horses all herded together. "Brocky" offered Vic twenty-five dollars and a revolver to boot in the horse trade. Vic accepted and unwittingly became the victim of the most damaging circumstantial evidence, as the horse and pistol both belonged to the "Stranger." They then separated.

At sundown, Vic unsaddled his horses and cooked his supper of coffee and bacon, with a couple of prairie chickens he had shot. He had camped near the deserted sod cabin of some wolfer and had just finished his repast when a half-dozen wolfers rode up. They did not seem sociable, merely answering Vic in yes or no. Vic told them if they were hungry they could help themselves to the grub if they felt disposed to cook. The men laughed outright and said, "You have got your gall with you, young fellow." Then they told him they knew he had killed the "Stranger," as he had both the revolver and the horse of the dead man. Vic vehemently denied the accusation and said he had traded his horse to "Brocky" and had received in return the horse, the revolver, and some money.

The shack was built of sod, and there were no trees nearer than three miles, just large willows and brush. If there had been trees handy, they would have hanged Vic then and there, as the evidence was all against him. They had been searching for "Brocky," as they felt sure he was the murderer, but when they discovered the "Stranger's" horse with Smith, they thought he was the guilty one. They kept Vic in the cabin with them and sweated him thoroughly while their supper was cooking. The wolfers then bound his hands behind him, tied his feet together, and tied him to a stake outside the door for the night, while they took turns guarding him.

It was the refinement of cruelty and wholly unnecessary. Vic suffered greatly during the night, both mentally and physically. At daylight they found him nearly unconscious. The thongs sank deep into the flesh, and his limbs were greatly swollen. They poured some whiskey down his throat, which revived him somewhat, and then removed the ropes. After breakfast they saddled their horses, intending to take Vic about three miles to where there were some elm trees and snuff out his lights.

Just when they were in the act of mounting Vic on a horse and starting the funeral procession, some wolfers came along. Among them was a man who had come down from Fort Abercrombie. After hearing the story, the man said that two mornings previous he had seen a man who fit "Brocky's" description, and the horse that Vic now had was then in "Brocky's" possession. This statement was largely in Vic's favor, and a large wad of hope filled his bosom.

They held a short powwow, and then all hands headed for Wapiti Creek, twenty-five miles away, the direction that "Brocky" took when last seen by the newcomer. A travois[12] was improvised, and Vic was laid thereon, being too sore to sit in the saddle.

It took some time for the two men who were with Vic to get ready. When they finally got ready, the rest of the gang was three miles away and barely discernible with a glass through the hazy atmosphere. Vic and his two comrades arrived at Wapiti Creek at seven in the evening. They found the party encamped near a large ash grove where there was a fine spring of cold water. "Brocky" was in their company, securely tied. His horses had pulled their picket pins the previous night. While he was hunting for them, the wolfers discovered and gathered him.

Some of the party went to find the horses and finally returned with them. Immediately all hands recognized Vic's horse and knew that "Brocky" was the assassin and that Vic was not guilty. A drumhead court-martial was held.[13] After Vic and the man from Abercrombie had testified, "Brocky," who had wolfish courage, said he would tell the whole truth if they would take him before the proper court and let him have a square deal. To simplify matters, the wolfers agreed to do so.

"Brocky" then said he had met the "Stranger" where his body was found and that he had offered the "Stranger" fifty dollars between horses. The man wanted seventy-five dollars. Then they agreed to settle the difference with a deck of cards. While the game was in progress, a dispute started, and the "Stranger" arose and started for his gun that was lying on his saddle twenty feet away. Realizing it was death for one or the other, "Brocky" fired and shot him through the head. Instead of turning back and notifying the wolfers of the man's death, he headed for Fort Totten and excused his action by saying he intended going before the proper authorities to tell his story and knew he would be exonerated.

He could not satisfactorily explain why he had traded horses with Vic and had not informed Vic of the "Stranger's" death. His story was so manifestly false that a vote was called, and "Brocky" was unanimously condemned to die. There were two trees about ten feet apart that were forked twelve feet above the ground. A pole was pushed through the forks of the tree, and a good scaffold was secured.

When the prisoner saw all hope was gone, he braced up and showed that he was not afraid to die. "Brocky" uncorked the vials of his wrath on the crew for going back on their word, in not taking him before a civil court. A rope was thrown over the beam. He was somewhat averse to seeing himself suspended from a limb, so he quickly slid from the horse's back and disappeared into the brush.

Horsemen quickly surrounded the thicket, while two men looked through the brush and finally discovered him snugly cached behind a log in the hazel brush. When unearthed from his hiding place, he laughed and said that if his hands had not been tied behind him he could have jerked the rope from the hands of the man who held the horse and escaped, as that horse was fastest nag in the outfit. He was remarkably cool for a man who was about to meet death. "Brocky" never let up scorning his captors until death cut short his speech. He was again placed on the horse. A man on each side of him held his legs so that he would not attempt to get away again. There was no hitch this time when the noose was slipped over his head and the other end fastened to a sapling.

He was asked if he had anything to say. His eyes were not bandaged, and in a clear voice without a tremor he said he had shot the "Stranger" for his money and confessed to two other murders that until then were mysteries. As the horse was led out from under him, his last, almost inarticulate, choking words were: "I'll see you all later, you lying band of strangling coyotes."

Vic was an interested spectator of frontier justice. As he gazed at the slowly strangling form of "Brocky," he thought only for a lucky chain of circumstances[14] he would have adorned a limb himself. "Brocky" gave an exhibition of tenacity of life that was startling. He squirmed and kicked until one of the men grabbed him by the shoulders and pulled him down. Soon "Brocky's" soul went up the spout. A grave was dug and the body interred, but no headboard or inscription was left to mark the last resting place of this wandering spirit of the Red River of the North.

Early Buffalo Adventures

The main herds of buffalo were west of the Big Missouri River. As Vic had not been fortunate enough to see any of that noble game yet,[15] he longed to be in touch with them. When a party of friendly Santee Sioux came along, he joined them. The following week on Mouse River in North Dakota was where he saw his first buffalo. There were only a few scattered bands, the main herds being about two hundred miles farther west. Scouts of the party came in and reported a herd of about one hundred buffalo five miles away.

By seven o'clock the next morning, twenty-five bucks, mounted on their horses and leading their "buffalo runners," were followed by a dozen squaws with packhorses and travois. Arriving near the herd, the horses were left with the squaws, while the bucks mounted their swift "buffalo runners" bareback. A lariat around the jaw was used for a bridle. The horses' tails were bedecked with eagle feathers, and the bucks were adorned with paint.

Within ten minutes, thirty-five buffalo were slain, and the squaws were skinning and cutting up the meat. About dark the bucks and squaws got back to camp smeared with blood. A royal feast was held, each individual trying to outeat the others. Feasting and singing were indulged in until after midnight. Vic remained with the Indians until

October, the hides being good then. The Indians were killing all the cows they could for the skins, which were far superior to the bulls, but the price was ridiculously low for the skins. A finely furred, hand-painted cow buffalo robe would bring only $1.50 to $2 in trade at the trading store on the Big Missouri.

The meat was converted into pemmican, which was made by drying the meat in strips, mixing it with bull [buffalo] berries and marrow, pounding the mass all together, and sacking it into raw buffalo skin sacks of about one hundred pounds each. It would keep for years and was a staple article of commerce in the northwest. A plentiful supply of hair was mixed in, too.

About the 12th of October, Vic went west to the Missouri River and up to Fort Buford, which is opposite the mouth of the Yellowstone. He disposed of his horses and bought a large Mackinaw[16] about thirty feet long that would carry a large load. He purchased a quantity of fine, hand-painted buffalo robes from the Indians before he quit them on Mouse River. Vic secured the services of a half-breed named Charbonneau to go with him to pull the Mackinaw with oars as far as Sioux City, promising him a good horse and a first-class rifle.

Twenty miles above the mouth of the Yellowstone is a tributary called Charbonneau Creek, named after the husband of Sacajawea, the Nez Perce[17] woman who was of great assistance to Lewis and Clark on their journey to the coast in 1804 and 1806. [Charbonneau] had trapped on the stream the year before Clark secured his and his wife's services. The Charbonneau who accompanied Vic down the river claimed that Sacajawea's husband was his uncle.

It was a very pleasant fall, and the trip down the river was fraught with danger, as there were plenty of hostile Indians. Beaver were very plentiful, and every day about four o'clock the men would make camp where there were lots of beaver signs. One would go upstream on foot, and one would go downstream. They would get several beaver every evening. The animals were so tame that three or four would be shot in succession before they would jump into the water from the bank.

A beaver generally sinks when shot dead. As soon as a beaver was shot, a long light pole with a four-inch sharp hook attached to the end was used to hook and pull the beaver ashore before it had time to sink. At the mouth of the Heart River, opposite of where Bismarck, the capital of Dakota, is now, they found six trappers from Fort Benton, who were repairing their Mackinaw, it having run on a snag, badly smashing the craft. A hole nearly three feet in length was the consequence.

Vic and Charbonneau camped there overnight and then resumed their journey with the trappers, who had come from the head of Navigation in their boat. When opposite of where Fort Lincoln was erected years afterward, they were greeted with a volley of bullets from a party of hostiles cached in a point of timber. An ounce bullet, called a trade ball and fired from a shotgun, went through the trappers' boat and through the leg of one of their men.

Both boats ran for the opposite shore and hugged it until far enough away to be fairly clear of danger. No Indians were seen; they kept well-hidden in the timber. A number of bullets struck the boats, but no more damage was done. A tourniquet made from a large bandana handkerchief effectually stopped the flow of blood from the shattered leg of the wounded man.

Seven miles farther downstream, the boats were pulled up into the mouth of a creek, which came out through a heavy point of timber. There the party camped for the night, as the wounded man had to be attended to. Some blankets and robes were laid down, and a large canvas was spread down, and the man was placed thereon. His leg bone was badly shattered, and amputation was necessary. As there was no chloroform to be had, the poor fellow was held down and told to take his medicine like a man.

One man had been a nurse in a hospital and had acted as assistant to a surgeon at a military post. A handsaw was brought out, and the "surgeon" caught up the large veins and arteries with an improvised wire hook and a pair of pliers. He tied them with a thread made from a buffalo sinew. The flesh was slit up the leg, the bone was sawed off, and the lacerated flesh was cut away. Then the saw was heated and applied to the stump, which effectually seared the arteries and prevented the further flow of blood.

The suffering of the poor fellow was terrible, but he was firmly held by his companions until the operation was over. The "surgeon" was a genius at lopping off limbs and amputated the leg with zeal and efficiency. While the "surgeon" sharpened his skinning knife on a butcher's steel, he remarked how he sure disliked to trim up a fellow without the proper tools. But as Vic lamped the look in his eye, he opined that the "surgeon" was delighted at the opportunity to show his skill.

At daybreak the next morning, the party was out on the dirty bosom of the Big Missouri, with the wounded man doing as well as could be expected. Near noon that day, a small herd of buffalo was sighted near the riverbank, and Vic was put ashore to get one of them. Skirting down the bank of Antelope Creek, which emptied into the river here, Vic's approach was screened by the heavy growth of willows, which enabled him to get within 150 yards of the herd. He picked out a fine, fat two-year-old heifer, and a bullet behind the ear dropped her in her tracks.

The boats ran ashore, and a generous portion of the animal was stowed away in the boats. About sixty miles below Standing Rock Agency, a party of Indians rode up to the riverbank and motioned to the travelers to come ashore. The current set in from the opposite bank. While parleying, the boats drifted farther away from the Indians and soon drifted in close to the bank. Vic and one of the trappers sprang ashore and commenced firing at the Indians, who, before they could make cover, left two horses and one of their number dead. Five miles farther on, the party went into camp but kept two men on sentry until midnight. Then sliding into their boats, they resumed their journey.

At old Fort Yates, Ketchum, the wounded man, was left at the hospital where he recovered in good shape. After getting well, he caught some young buffalo and a Sioux squaw, the daughter of old Chief Buffalo Chip,[18] and went to raising full-blood buffalo and half-breed children. When last heard from, he had quite a herd of each.

When Sioux City was reached, the party beached their boats, and Vic disposed of his robes and furs. Besides the horse and rifle that he purchased for Charbonneau, Vic gave him a pair of revolvers and twenty-five dollars. That evening one of the trappers got into a quarrel at one of the dance houses and was shot through the heart, but while falling he managed to draw his gun and kill his adversary with the ever-ready gun. It seemed that the aim of every man in those days was to kill a man and establish a standing in society.

On the morrow, bidding his friends adieu, Vic gave Charbonneau ten dollars, as the fellow had blown all of his money and had sold his revolvers and field glasses and was broke. Vic boarded a train, to which he had been a stranger for years, and broke for Chicago to see his old mother. His parents had long mourned him as dead, not hearing from him in years. In due time, he reached Chicago, hired a cab, and gave the driver the address and five dollars. A western man is always generous while his money holds out. On reaching the house, he bolted in and gave his mother a hug and a kiss that more than surprised her, as she did not recognize him at first. His brother Bill, of the guitar episode, then came in and called "breakaway."

His mother caught her second wind and said she would like to see the color of the $50 that Vic had disappeared with years before. He dug down into his buckskins and handed his mother $250. At this show of generosity, she gave him a kiss and another motherly squeeze and said, "Vic, with all your shortcomings, you are my darling boy yet." She gave him two more kisses and renewed the interrupted sweeping.

Although Chicago was a western town, a genuine plainsman was seldom seen there, and Vic, with his handsome features, well-proportioned frame, and beaded suit of buckskin, was admired by all who saw him.[19] His father, who was a master mechanic on the Chicago Northwestern Railway, wanted him to remain in the city and forego the strenuous life he had been leading, but Vic answered that he could not think of living in a country where prairie chickens were called big game.

When Vic tried to get his brother to come west with him, he answered that he did not wish to live in a country where dried apples were called fruit. Tiring of city life in three weeks and feeling "the call of the wild" pulling at his sleeve, Vic said so long to his parents and brothers and pulled his freight for the West.

Conversion Through Immersion

At St. Cloud, Minnesota,[20] Vic hired to old Captain Anderson, who was an officer in the army during the Minnesota Massacre, to drive a beef herd to Fort Buford on the Big Missouri, opposite the mouth of the Yellowstone River. There were twenty-five men in the party, with teams belonging to Anderson, who were sent along to put up hay for the government at that post at forty dollars per ton. About fifteen miles a day was accomplished. No incident occurred worth mentioning on the route, except one night the Indians tried to stampede the herd. The two night herders fired at them and succeeded in killing one horse and a beef.

The coulees and lowlands were full of deer, the bluffs full of elk and mountain sheep, and the prairies liberally spotted with antelope, while forty miles west, the plains were black with buffalo.[21] On arriving at Fort Buford, Vic gave the herd to the quartermaster and bought two good packhorses and a good saddle animal from old "Napoleon," the chief of the Gros Ventre Indians, who in his day was a great warrior, whose "coup stick" was covered with many notches, representing Sioux Indians he had killed in battle.

As the beef herd was inadequate to supply the required amount of meat for the garrison and too thin from the long trip, the quarter-master employed Vic to furnish game for the troops. Vic also contracted with Anderson's hay camp to keep it in meat. As there were plenty of elk, deer, antelope, mountain sheep, and bear, Vic had very little trouble in filling his contract.

Riding his saddle horse and leading his two packhorses, Vic would go down the valley about eight miles, swim the Big Missouri, and go into camp. That same evening would see him with enough meat to pack his horses. He would then construct a raft from a few dry logs and load the meat that he had packed to the bank with the horses. Next he would drive the animals into the water and paddle the raft over himself. The horses would swim across fairly straight, but Vic would drift about a mile, after which he would get the horses, load the meat, and hike for the fort.

One day in June when the river was very high, he arrived at the bank and drove in the packhorses. They swam across and wandered upon the bench about a mile from the river. Vic rode his saddle horse out until deep water was reached. Then quietly dropping alongside the animal, he swam for about a half-mile, or about the middle of the river. Being a trifle tired, he dropped back and clung to the horse's tail, letting the animal tow him along. In a few moments, the cayuse commenced to strangle and turn in the water, trying to strike Vic with its front feet. Being a Mary Jane cayuse, it was naturally contrary. Vic dived under the water. When he came to the surface, the horse was struggling violently about twenty yards downstream. The horse soon strangled to death and floated like a cork on the surface.

Vic had used precaution and had divested himself of his clothing and had fastened them to the saddle. Being in light swimming order, he struck out for the opposite shore. It was still a half-mile to land, and Vic was nearly exhausted from his exertions and swam slowly. He found himself growing weaker and weaker. Then his thoughts turned to God. He promised if the Lord would pull with him and enable him to make shore, he would never lie or use profane language again and would live an upright life.

His prayer was answered and coming to the throne of Grace gave him strength to renew his struggles. At that period, he was a past master in the use of profanity. Knowing his weakness, he promised the powers above he would never, never use profanity again if his life was spared. (When the devil was sick, a monk would he be; when the devil was well, the devil a monk was he.) As his feet touched the opposite shore, his good resolutions were forgotten, and he remarked, "G-d d-d, if I ain't lucky."[22] He calls that episode a "conversion through immersion."

By this time, the drowned horse was a half-mile downstream, and the pack animals had wandered out of sight. Steve Scott's woodyard was three miles downriver. Vic knew he could get there quicker on foot than trying to find the pack animals. He started on a run down the bottom, which was thick with cacti. When two-thirds of the distance was accomplished, he entered the timber, which was full of rose brush about six feet high. His feet were full of cacti, and his body was scratched badly by the thorn bushes.

When he arrived at Steve Scott's woodyard, he made a dash for the house to ask "French" George (who afterward was killed at the Big Muddy by Indians) if there was a skiff at the landing. Vic thought Scott and his wife were at the fort. Waiving all ceremony, he plunged open the door and sang out, "Say, George," when his eyes encountered Mrs. Scott. Without apologizing for his lack of raiment, Vic turned and fled for the riverbank. Finding a bull boat[23] at the landing, he jumped in and paddled out to the dead horse as it was passing the landing. He untied his clothes, detached the saddle, glasses and gun, transferred them to the bull boat, said goodbye to his faithful steed, and pulled for shore. He purchased another bronco and kept at the meat business.

Smith Takes His First Scalp

Vic had built a good shack near Steve Scott's woodyard, which was about ten miles from Fort Buford, which he intended to use for his hunting lodge for the winter. Living with Scott was an ancient, fossilized dominie[24] named "Deacon" Hemmenway. He and Scott were cutting wood for next year's run of steamboats. In those days, there were no railroads or telegraph lines in that country. Freight by boat was at almost prohibitive prices. Although the prices were high, they had to have wood.

Early one morning, Smith, who was supplying the fort with wild meat, observed an Indian sneaking up on the "Deacon," who was cutting wood. Smith thought it was a friendly Gros Ventre Indian intending to kill the "Deacon" for luck, as they frequently did to change their "Medicine."

Vic took his rifle. Keeping a large cottonwood tree between him and the Sioux (as it proved to be), Vic approached unobserved within one hundred yards.

The Sioux had his coup stick with him, a willow with three forks to stretch a scalp on. When the Indian was within about seventy-five steps from the woodchopper, the Indian rested his rifle across a stump and was about to shoot. But Vic drew a bead on the redskin and said in the Sioux language, "What are you doing?" The Indian, startled by Vic's voice, turned and ran. Vic, still thinking it was a friendly Gros Ventre, did not shoot.

When the Sioux was about seventy-five yards away, he turned and shot at Vic but missed. Then spreading his blanket to effectually screen himself, the Indian ran at full speed in zigzag jumps to divert Vic's aim, but Vic, the champion game and running shot of the west in those days,[25] planted a bullet over his hip, which exploded one of the cartridges in the Indian's belt and enveloped him in smoke. Vic, knowing that his shot had surely reached a vital spot, watched the Indian run about one hundred yards and sink behind a stump.

Scott, who had been a quarter-mile below piling up cordwood, heard Vic shout "Indians." He ran to his house and told his wife to keep the stockade doors closed and to let no one inside. He ran back up to the opening toward Vic with rifle in hand. A few minutes after the Indian fell, and while Vic stood behind the tree, two Indians came out of the timber within 125 yards of Vic and deliberated for a minute. Then one of them dismounted, walked over to where the Indian lay, picked up the rifle of the wounded Indian, came back, mounted his cayuse, and disappeared into the timber with the other Indian.

Vic said it was the only time in his thirty years' experience on the frontier that he ever heard of Indians leaving their dead in the hands of the enemy when there was a chance to remove them. Vic still thought they were friendly Indians wishing to change their luck, and he did not attempt to kill the two Indians, which he could have done easily.

When Scott came up, they went to where Vic had seen the young Hunkpapa Sioux fall. There he lay looking plenty mournful, but he would not talk a word. Vic threw his gun down on him to put him out of his misery, but Scott interposed and said, "No, let him suffer." The Indian was a splendid specimen of an aborigine not over twenty-two years old. They left him alone in his glory and followed the trail of the Indians to the edge of the timber.[26]

It was the fore part of September, and a light snow had fallen during the night, and tracks were plainly visible. About a mile from the edge of the timber on a knoll, the Indians could be seen plainly with the field glass that Vic carried. There were eleven of them. They were Hunkpapas from the camp of wily old Chief Sitting Bull, located on Charbonneau Creek about thirty miles away. The Indians were singing their death song, while two others were rounding up stock belonging to Smith and Scott.

As a smooth strip of territory lay between the Indians and the men, it was impossible to approach them without being seen and probably killed. Consequently, the men went back to Scott's house and found that ten of the Indians had been hiding in the brush, waiting for the Indian to kill the "Deacon." Then they would have rushed to the house. However, when Smith fired and shouted "Indians," they ran back into the timber, mounted their horses, and started for the bluffs, where they were seen by Smith and Scott.

Vic went again to the clearing where the Indian lay and found him in the throes of death. On going back to the house, they heard someone shouting on the opposite side of the river. Scott took the large skiff, rowed over, and brought back a teamster who wanted to hunt. He was a mule whacker for Uncle Sam, and there was a detail of eight soldiers with him. When Scott came back, they all went up to where the Indian lay, now a good Indian. Smith scalped the redskin and afterward presented the scalp to Colonel Moore[27] of Fort Buford. Castle, the mule skinner, cut off a portion of the Indian's anatomy and stretched it over the horn of his saddle.[28] It was reported that Vic went to the Agency to try to draw the annuities of the dead Indian, but the story was generally discredited.

The "Deacon" then took refuge and grub at Scott's house for a space of six weeks, never venturing outside the stockade during that time. Then one crisp morning, the "Deacon" thought he would go split up the tree that he had cut into cordwood lengths when the Indians made the hostile raid. He had split for about two hours and was cribbing the wood. After every stick he would crib, the "Deacon" would cast his eyes toward the brush. As he raised a stick, he observed two Indians pointing their guns at him. He quickly jumped behind the crib just as two bullets struck the crib. He grabbed his gun, fired into the air, and broke for Scott's house.

Vic arrived from the fort a half-hour afterward with a team, intending to take up five elk he had killed the day before. Scott reported the Indians to him. Together they took up the trail, following it nearly to Charbonneau Creek, where Sitting Bull's camp was still located; but the Indians had too much of a start. Fearing they would be met by a large party of warriors, they returned.

Shortly after Christmas, a unique character known as "Wood Hawk John," a white man, went to work for Scott. During the winter, he conceived a violent love for Mrs. Scott, a handsome woman and true to her husband. John, while never pushing his affection to the obnoxious degree, would sigh and follow her with his gaze until Mrs. Scott informed her husband that he would have to discharge John. It was the last of March, and John knew his time was limited, as he had been informed he would have to vamoose as soon as the river broke. Shortly afterward the river broke, and trees, large cakes of ice, and dead buffalo came down. It was a grand sight to witness the breaking up of the river.

John deliberately walked out to the bank of the stream, which was now a mile wide. He took off his coat, vest, watch, and pocketbook, laid them on a stump, and shouted to draw attention. When Scott and his wife appeared at the door of the cottage, John said so long. He threw Mrs. Scott a kiss and projected himself off the bank to his death amid the crushing, roaring, rumbling ice packs of the Big Missouri that seldom, if ever, gives up its dead.

One day as Vic was leaving the fort to get some venison for the command, Hank Bloom,[29] a scout, asked to accompany him. At the crossing of a creek below Scott's woodyard, they saw an otter push its head through the ice. Vic fired and the otter sank in the stream. In a few minutes its body came to the surface and was secured. One mile farther, they saw two white-tail deer feeding. The ground was frozen, and there was a knoll between Vic and the two bucks. When within seventy-five yards of the game, he heard them running, their hoofs pounding the frozen earth as they fled. Jumping from his horse, Vic ran around the knoll and fired at them. The deer were running broadside at full speed, and a bullet went through both deer in the exact same spot and came out on the opposite side the same, a most remarkable shot. After hanging up the deer, the men went up the valley.

Between two high bluffs, Vic rode up on a knoll and saw a white-tail buck running at full speed, off about three hundred yards. Quickly dismounting, he fired and saw where the bullet struck the alkali and kicked up dust and ricocheted up into the stomach of the deer, killing him instantly. On returning to the lodge, Smith and Bloom went through a heavy body of cottonwood and found two large bull elk engaged in mortal combat. Their horns were locked together in a deadly embrace. One elk was lying on the ground too exhausted to rise and not far from death. The ground, torn up for about two acres with saplings knocked down, showed that they had been at it for at least two or three days. Vic shot the elk that was on his feet. Since the other one was unable to rise, he cut its throat. That was a most remarkable day's hunt: one otter, three deer, two elk, and all in the expending of only four cartridges. Vic gave the elk heads to George Grinnell, a typical frontier character, who will be discussed later.

An Indian Love Story

Two miles above Fort Buford was old Fort Union, which was abandoned in 1866 when Fort Buford was built.[30] The old Fort Union cemetery was being continually encroached upon by the current of the Big Missouri, and nearly all the graves were washed away. Catfish were, no doubt, nibbling away at the bones of some of those now buried in the bottom of the river. The river was nearly a mile wide at that point.

Vic and George Mulligan, an Indian interpreter, wished to cross the river to kill a large buffalo bull that was feeding on the other side. They attached ropes to two coffins that were overhanging the water and ready to cave in at any moment. Using a pole, they loosened the coffins, which fell into the river. Towing the coffins to a sandbar, they opened them, dumped the contents, washed out the coffins, and made them watertight with clay. They made paddles from the headboards and got started. Midway across the stream, Mulligan's coffin capsized, but his gun was safe as it was strapped across his shoulders. Being an expert swimmer, he got across sometime before Vic did and wounded the buffalo bull badly, which ran down the riverbank and jumped in just as Vic was nearing the shore. Vic barely escaped the rush of the bull, but waves from the animal upset his coffin into four feet of water. Vic shot and killed the animal, which floated a short distance and grounded on a sandbar. Tying some dry logs together with green willows, the men made a raft. After cutting all the meat from the carcass, they loaded it onto the raft and pushed the raft into the stream. Swimming beside the raft, the men pushed it as best as they could until they landed about two miles downstream.

The following fall found Vic below Fort Rice on the Big Missouri, shooting beaver and poisoning wolves. In January when he was about one hundred miles below Fort Rice, Vic started again for the Yellowstone country. The second night out, he camped with a party of Oglala Sioux in a point of timber near the riverbank.

In one of the lodges that night, an Indian recounted to Vic how twenty years before that same camp of Sioux had murdered a family of whites on the border, tortured the men, outraged the women, and murdered all but one child, a boy of five years.[31] They brought him up in the ways of the aborigine. He was adopted by Chief Bull Tail, who named the boy O-pah, which means elk. Chief Bull Tail had a two-year-old daughter named Wee-no-nah, who became O-pah's constant companion and playmate until he was about eighteen years old. They fairly adored each other. Exposed to the weather and sun with no covering for his head, he acquired nearly the same complexion as his sweetheart. His habits and ways were as the Indians, and except for a lighter color and finer features he would pass anywhere as a native.

Wee-no-nah, the Indian maiden, had classical features and far above average intelligence for an Indian. She was straight and well-proportioned, worshiped by her father, and was the belle of the village. Wee-no-nah was admired by all the young bucks and some who were old enough to know better, but she had eyes for no one but O-pah.

The young bucks of the village were jealous of O-pah and made it so unpleasant for him that he decided to leave the camp. He consulted with Wee-no-nah, who promised to wait for him until he would return and steal her from her people. Both knew full well that Chief Bull Tail never would allow his daughter to marry a paleface. O-pah quietly left camp that night, taking three of the best horses that belonged to the jealous young bucks.

The next morning, anger and excitement ran riot in camp. Chief Bull Tail was angry at the ingratitude, as he expressed it, of O-pah. A party of braves and some of the best trailers in camp were soon after O-pah. For three days, they followed his trail and finally came up to O-pah while he was cooking his supper. They had orders from Chief Bull Tail to capture O-pah, if possible. He would have had to suffer at the stake if he were caught and burned alive.

With demonical yells, the Sioux dashed toward O-pah and told him to surrender. Knowing his fate if captured, he fired at the Indians, killing two of them. Mounting the fastest of the three horses in his possession, he dashed across the prairie with the foe in swift pursuit. He soon outdistanced them, and they gave up the chase. O-pah went north and lived for five years on the Yellowstone River with the Crow Indians, inveterate foes of the Sioux. Twice during his absence, the Indian agent from the Crow Agency had business at the Standing Rock Agency on the Big Missouri River. Each time O-pah sent verbal messages to Wee-no-nah by the agent, who faithfully performed the task reposed in him and brought back loving messages from Wee-no-nah to her lover.

Chief Bull Tail was angry that his daughter would not accept the advances of any of the young bucks of the village and attributed it to the affection that she had for O-pah. When O-pah parted from the maiden, he promised he would return for her in five years and would take her from her father's tepee. The five years had expired the same night that Vic was camping at Chief Bull Tail's village.

Vic had seen Wee-no-nah that day and conversed with her. She had ripened into a perfect Indian Venus, but an icy one as far as Indian adorers went. Her affections were open for only one and that was O-pah. That evening about two inches of snow fell. O-pah, with eight Crow Indians, had been many days on the trail and was already in the vicinity. O-pah had induced the Crows to come with him, ostensibly to steal horses, but really as a reinforcement in case he was successful in getting away with his sweetheart who was waiting for him.

Five years before this, the lovers had rehearsed how O-pah would get her when he came. At midnight, the double howl of a coyote was heard, and Wee-no-nah knew it was her lover who had come to take her away. She stole out of her father's lodge and went west four hundred steps and into the arms of O-pah. They embraced and exchanged fervent kisses.

O-pah led her to a large tree a half-mile away. Leaving her there, he started for the horse herd to secure horses for their return in swift order. When O-pah and the Crows attempted to steal the horses, the dogs scented them and set up such a howl that the camp was alarmed. O-pah, fearing a surround and believing it was impossible to get the horses, returned to where Wee-no-nah anxiously awaited.

Indians on a horse-stealing expedition invariably go afoot, and this party was no exception. Being afoot, they can more readily escape detection and will never return without horses they have stolen. Sometimes they are gone for six months on a horse-stealing raid.

While thirty miles away the day before, O-pah's party observed a small camp of Sioux. There the party started back, hoping to secure mounts to escape on. They traveled fast. When daylight came and it was found that Wee-no-nah was gone and the trail of the Crow horse-thieves discovered, a party formed to follow them. Vic was invited to join the chase, which he gleefully did, but secretly wishing that if O-pah had stolen the girl, as he suspected, the lovers would escape.

But the fates decreed otherwise, as the party was headed by a nemesis in the shape of Chief Bull Tail, who had blood in his eyes and murder in his heart. The fugitives kept up the river on the ice and had covered twenty miles when discovered. The Sioux located them with a field glass. Making a long detour, the Sioux got within a half-mile of them. The timber was too far away for the party to reach, there being nothing but sandbars and willows for a mile.

Wee-no-nah was the first to discover their pursuers. She quietly turned to O-pah and said, "We are lost." Using the quirt on their horses, the Sioux dashed at full speed along the frozen sandbars after the Crows. Now according to the Indian belief, losing your scalp will prevent your entrance into the happy hunting grounds. That is why the Indians, when one of their number is slain, use every endeavor to get away with the dead to prevent them from being scalped.

A large whirlpool seemed the only avenue of escape for the doomed to the happy hunting grounds. By this time, the Sioux were within three hundred yards of the Crows. Mounted on their barefooted ponies, the Sioux whipped and urged them to their utmost speed. Vic's horse was sharp-shod, and when his horse struck the ice he easily left the Sioux, while their ponies slipped, fell, got up again, and fell down again on the slick ice.

The Crows turned their guns loose at the enemy and succeeded in killing three and wounding seven. Vic, by this time, was within seventy-five yards of the Crows. They, one after another, deliberately walked into the whirlpool, thereby saving their scalps. Wee-no-nah and O-pah were the last ones to go. Clasped in each other's arms, they took the fatal plunge. As the waters closed over their heads, a handsome, fancily beaded otter skin cap with a long tail of eagle feathers worn by O-pah floated on the surface, supported by the air inside the cap. When Vic arrived at the whirlpool, he reached out with his gun and captured the cap, a memento he kept for years.

The dead Sioux were strapped on the horses and the wounded put on travois, and in this manner camp was reached. The lamentations of the squaws and relatives of the dead and wounded were pitiful. Squaws took off their skirts and donned breechcloths (same as buck Indians do). With a sharp knife, they gashed their legs from above the knees to the ankles at a depth of a half-inch or more and walked about barefooted in the light snow until the place looked like a slaughter pen.

A father of one of the dead warriors showed his intense grief by having a knife run under the muscles alongside the backbone. Then he inserted a buffalo thong and tied the other end to four buffalo skulls, which he dragged through camp for three hours. Finally the resisting power of the bull heads caused the sinews to give way, and he was released from his penance.

For three days and nights the wake was kept up, and if anyone slept it was not Vic. He saddled his horse and followed by his packhorse struck upriver. He had previously disposed of his pelts and furs to a trader at a good figure. At Standing Rock, he fell in with a party of wolfers bound for the Black Hills and joined them. For, to tell the truth, it mattered little to him where he went. He would often arise on a morning with no determined destination in view, saddle up and go with the wind, whichever way it was blowing.[32]

Dodging Danger in the Black Hills

It was safer to travel in the winter, as there was less danger of encountering any Indians while the weather was cold, the grass dead, and their horses poor; but in the springtime, about the first of June when their horses were fat, the Indians' thoughts lightly turned to love and slaughter of the whites.

Vic and his party found wolves so numerous in one section, they concluded to camp for a while to poison and shoot them. They built a dugout in the side of the hill, split pine puncheons for roofing and doors, and scraped antelope skins very thin for windows. Soon they had a very comfortable house about twenty by thirty, well-propped up with timbers and a roof covered with dirt. After two weeks of very successful wolfing and no signs of Indians, one wolfer came in at night and reported seeing two Indians skulking among the hills about ten miles away, trying to cut him off.

Of course, everyone was on the lookout then. Next day all hands left camp except Vic, it being his turn to watch camp and cook. About noon he was about a quarter-mile from camp and espied two persons about a mile away. By their movements, he was soon able to recognize them as Sioux. He cached himself. When they were within one hundred yards of him and entirely in the open, Vic halted them with a shot that dropped one. Before the other one could make cover, his spirit wended its way to join his companion in the happy hunting grounds. The weather was extremely cold. Vic scalped the two Indians and laid them side by side. He scanned the surrounding country for the rest of the day, but discovered no more Indians.

When the wolfers straggled in that evening, they were greeted with the bloody scalps hanging over the door. The next day, one of the men threw the body of one of the Indians on his shoulder (the body being frozen solid), packed it to the dugout, and used it for a prop to the door. They stood the other body close by to do duty as a sentry.

The party had great success getting wolf skins, frequently averaging between fifty and seventy-five wolves a night. About three weeks after the Indian episode, about 9 A.M., when two wolfers were leaving the dugout for their baits, a war party cached a short ways from the cabin opened fire and killed both men. The rest of the men were in the dugout. When they looked out, they were greeted with a volley of bullets. They closed the door quickly.

The Indians thought they had the wolfers trapped, but when the wolfers had built the dugout, they had foreseen possibilities of trouble and had dug a tunnel back to a distance of sixty feet. An opening at the farther end was behind a big log in a thicket, well-covered so that it would not be noticed. The entrance was in the back part of the dugout. The remaining wolfers entered the tunnel. Crawling back to the opening, they pushed aside the cellar door of brush and sticks, arranged themselves behind the logs, and watched for a minute or so.

The Indians were on top of the dugout and supposed they were safe from any fire from the whites. They had scalped the two wolfers and had the bloody trophies dangling from their coup sticks. There were thirteen Indians in the party. Each white man picked an Indian. Vic picked one who he supposed was the leader or chief, as he wore a handsome warbonnet. Vic called "pull" and down dropped four Indians. Two more were downed before they could make the shelter of a patch of brush about one hundred yards away. The redskins were cut off from their horses, which fell into the hands of the whites. When the Indians broke for the brush patch after the first volley, one Indian snatched the headdress of the fallen chief and carried it with him to the shelter.

The boys watched the timber until nightfall, but the Indians were too cunning to expose themselves. During the night, the Reds sneaked in after the horses that were corralled, hobbled, and tied. Two men on watch discovered the Indians and fired on them. The next morning a trail of blood for one hundred yards showed where one of the marauders had been wounded. Knowing their scalps would be safer in Deadwood than where they were, the boys packed all their furs in as small bales as possible and resumed their journey to the Black Hills.

They encountered no Indians on their way but ran into some terrible blizzards, which were nearly as bad. In crossing Alkali Creek, thirty miles east of the Black Hills, a herd of buffalo dashed down over the bluff at the crossing and swerved to the right, barely missing the packhorses. When the buffalo struck the ice, being under great headway, they slipped and floundered on the ice to the degree that the packhorses stampeded. It took the men three hours to round them up, gather the packs, and get the outfit underway.

At Deadwood they realized good prices for their furs. At Spearfish and Deadwood, they took in the sights and trailed the Elephant to his den.[33] On the 10th of June, Vic received $250 to carry a private dispatch to Bismarck. On the head of Heart River, Indians gave chase and followed him nearly ten miles. They pressed him so close that he was obliged to take shelter in a clump of quaking aspen. His packhorse, which was following behind, was cut off and captured by the Reds. The Reds charged Vic's stronghold, but he succeeded in wounding two of them and killing three horses. It was after dark when Vic eluded their vigilance and escaped.

At Medicine Creek he passed "Shang" Procter, a noted character, who was a combination of scout, gunfighter, and prospector. Procter had a handsome half-breed girl with him and two splendid elk heads and meat on his packhorses that he was taking to Fort Lincoln for sale. In 1886, Procter started a wild west show. While at St. Paul, one of his buffalo that he had purchased from Vic got out of the corral and wandered down the highway to Fort Snelling, where a shavetail lieutenant saw it coming across the parade grounds. Supposing the main herd was just outside the fence, the lieutenant shot and killed it. In 1898, Procter was killed in a landslide near Spokane, Washington. In a buckskin pouch found on his person were some very rich nuggets of gold, but the place where they came from never could be located.

That winter Vic supplied Bismarck and Fort Lincoln with wild meat. At that time, the country was full of hostile Indians, who were killing many people on the trail to the Black Hills. Over three hundred prospectors and settlers were killed in two years.[34] At the fort, General[35] George A. Custer was in command, and Vic frequently accompanied him on hunting excursions with the famous Custer pack of hounds.[36]

Vic and a hunter named Dick Stone went thirty miles up Heart River after meat for the fort. They killed six elk the first afternoon. Then each took separate routes for camp. It was a bright moonlit night, and Vic ran into a very large silvertip bear at less than seventy-five feet distant. Throwing up his rifle, he planted a ball in the bear's shoulder. The animal instantly charged and kept so close to Vic's heels that he dared not turn to shoot. For over two hundred yards Vic imagined that the bear was not more than a foot and a half, maybe two feet, behind and steadily gaining. When Vic reached the bank of the river, he jumped in, and the bear, sadly hampered with a broken shoulder on land (luckily for Vic), was more so in the stream, and gave up the chase.

When Vic got back to camp, he found Stone there but was informed that Indians had sneaked up during their absence and stolen the horses. The hunters walked to Fort Lincoln that night, and Custer let them have a span of mules and an escort of soldiers to bring in the meat and the wagon. Stone and Smith said they did not require the escort, but the General said he was afraid the boys would forget to return the mules if the escort did not accompany them, as government mules were looked upon as public property in those days.

A Horse Raid with "Red" Mike

Mike Welch, better known as "Red" Mike, was a scout for Miles also. He was a fearless man, a dead shot, and a good hunter. In the summer of 1884,[37] Vic took a trip with Welch to the Musselshell. When they got to Lodge Pole Creek, they camped to let their horses rest for a few days. They had traveled for days through vast herds of buffalo, and the prairie was covered with antelope. Elk were plentiful in all timbered coulees, and every day they saw several large cinnamon bear and some grizzlies. They were making the trip just for the excitement it afforded, and to get back some horses the Indians had stolen from them, and to bring along any bunch that happened to belong to the enemy. Welch and Smith were seeking the camp of Black Moon, chief of the Hunkpapas. They had seen Indian sign that was quite fresh the day before on the creek. Consequently, they were on the alert, as they well knew that if they were seen they would have a strenuous time. The men camped in a dense grove of quaking aspen. During the day, they let their horses graze in the timber. At night, they put them on the picket line outside the timber where there was luxurious bunchgrass.

Game could be seen any time of day, and the big buffalo wolves and their cousins the coyotes let their presence be known after sundown. The day after they made camp, Welch went to a high bluff two miles away, where he could command a view of the surrounding country. About 3 P.M., as Vic was on the creek about a mile from camp, he saw twenty-one Indians coming up the creek. As luck would have it, they were on the north side of the stream, a mile from camp and at the edge of the prairie. The boys' camp was on the south side; otherwise the horse sign would have been discovered and their camp located.

Vic watched them for an hour until they passed up the creek out of sight, and he felt their camp was not far away. Mike came back about dusk with the news that he had located the camp, with the aid of the field glass, three miles distant. Vic had caught a fine mess of trout just before sundown. Their appetites, sharpened by the excitement of the trip, made the heaped tin plates of grub look like thirty cents when the repast was over. At 11 P.M. they curled up in their robes. Soon the outlandish airs of the coyotes and the dismal howling of the large gray buffalo wolves sang them to sleep.

Break of day found them awake, and soon they had a repast before them and an appetite Rockefeller would give a million for. They hobbled the horses for a few hours on the rich buffalo grass, while they kept watch from a butte a half-mile away. About 10 A.M., they tied the horses in the densest part of the grove and followed a fork of the Lodge Pole to within three miles of the Sioux camp. Then they climbed a very high butte, which was undoubtedly used by the Indians for a lookout, judging from the fresh signs thereabouts; but as the day was cloudy and indicated rain, no Indians had come out that day, which was fortunate. With the aid of good field glasses, the boys from the eminence could look down on the camp and note every particular.

The Indians were engaged in trying out some warriors. The boys could hear the noises of the tom-toms borne on the breeze quite plainly and could see three young embryo warriors swinging on a long pole supported by buffalo thongs that were run through the muscles of their backs. What interested the boys most was the herd of horses, among which were several fine mules.

Vic had brought along a generous lunch, which had been disposed of, and again they were hungry. Vic went back to camp, while "Red" Mike kept vigil on the peak. When Vic arrived at camp, he found a large cinnamon bear and two cubs about as large as a wolf just commencing to destroy things in search of eatables. He dared not fire at mamma bruin, as it might betray their camp to the enemy. Climbing a narrow bank within thirty feet of the bears, he threw a rock that hit the old bear on the leg, which caused them all to run up the creek. He then watered and picketed the horses in a big opening, for as it commenced to drizzle there was not much danger of any stray Indians coming along. He carried the camp plunder about one hundred yards, cached it, took a coffeepot and some grub, and went back to "Red" at the head of the fork.

Before he started to climb the peak, he made the coffee, as both were ravenously hungry again. There on the butte, the hot coffee and lunch, in spite of drizzling rain, put them in the best of humor. "Red" said the Sioux had hobbled about one-half of their horses. At dusk when he could scarcely see, even with the aid of the glasses, he noted they were driven up within the confines of the camp, hobbled, and let go.

They knew that by ten o'clock at night, the herd would be a half-mile from camp. The boys agreed a campfire would be all right for an hour or so. Clambering down in the main Lodge Pole, they built a small fire in a dense thicket and dried their clothes, which being buckskin were disagreeably clammy when wet. Then they struck out for the herd of horses. Meanwhile, the clouds had partly drifted away and objects could be seen quite plainly. With very little difficulty, they found the herd of horses.

The testing of the young warriors must have been a success, judging by the singing, drumming, and racket that floated from the lodges while the boys rounded up the herd. The men approached the herd gently in order not to stampede them, and they threw their ropes over a couple of squaw horses. These they mounted and drove the bunch to the camp where their saddle horses were. Saddling their horses, they cut the hobbles from the Indian horses, mounted them, and drove the herd down the valley. They made about thirty miles before daylight and ate a light breakfast of coffee, slapjacks, and cold buffalo tongue. Smith and Welch had such a start that the Indians never got within sight. Two days afterward, they landed the herd at Bill Norris's ranch, a short distance above Fort Peck on the Big Missouri.

In the winter of 1885,[38] "Red" Mike made his last shuffle in the game of life. After a limited number of bouts with "Norris Germicide,"[39] he and a wolfer named Doyle[40] engaged in a quarrel. Before Welch could get his gun in the corner of the room on his blankets, Doyle fired and killed him. Doyle expressed regret at the deed, shook hands with the corpse, mounted his horse, and left.[41]

Buck Marsh's Puppy Love

That fall, Vic and a man named "Buck" Marsh hunted on Burnt Creek, ten miles above Fort Lincoln. Marsh was of a religious turn of mind, but, as it afterward proved, a trifle inconsistent. He always said his prayers at night and said grace over the mulligan. He likewise exhorted Vic to change his ways. Marsh would kneel before the campfire in meekness and humility and supplicate the Great Spirit to make his "medicine" strong in the hunt and enable him to steel himself against pitfalls of sin that he was prone to bump up against while in the towns.

Marsh was a guerrilla and had served under Mosby during the war.[42] While sitting around the campfire, he would relate how his bushwhacking companions would pot the little naked niggers[43] with a ball and three buckshot[44] while they were fleeing to shelter.

He also told a story of his first love that was interesting. Marsh said he was born and bred in old Texas and that he and his siblings wore nothing but a long homespun endowment robe until they reached the age of fourteen, and all ran barefoot. One night he went to a dance when he was fourteen years old, and there saw his undoing in the shape of a pretty and clever girl of fifteen, whose parents were well-to-do. The girl espied young Marsh with his bare feet, tousled hair, and one "gallus"[45] to support his jeans. In the spirit of sport, she dragged him on the floor. As the tipsy fiddler sang out, "Salute your pardners," Marsh was borne away among the hilarious dancers to the air of "Arkansas Traveler." He stumbled over his own feet and fell, dragging his laughing companion to the puncheon floor with him.

At daylight next morning, the "crow hop" broke up after one man was placed *hors de combat* from a shot intended for another. The girl made Marsh promise to come to see her the following Sunday. Marsh was in the seventh heaven of bliss and neither ate nor slept during the week. He explained matters to his mother. To see her boy cut a good figure, she made him a pair of buckskin pants that his brother had tanned. His father "expanded" and bought him a pair of brogans and a straw hat. Thus togged, he impatiently awaited the coming Sunday morning.

After breakfast, he saddled and mounted his father's mule and started for the home of his charmer sixteen miles away. A heavy thunderstorm came up when he was three miles on the road, and his clothing was thoroughly soaked. When about eight miles on the way, the sky cleared, and the sun came out very hot. Marsh had occasion to dismount. To his dismay, he found that his buckskins had stretched until they were about eight inches too long. (A peculiarity of buckskin is that when it is wet, it tends to stretch.)

A dampness could not dampen his ardor, and he cut off the offending garments at the ankles. He rode slowly after that so that his clothes might dry, and his appearance would be presentable to the girl. Arriving at the domicile, Marsh alighted. To his dismay, he found that the hot sun had shrunken his buckskin pants to the degree that they just reached the top of his calves. His thin legs with no stockings stuck in his brogan shoes made him look ludicrous. He would have mounted and fled, only at that moment the girl appeared and insisted on Marsh coming into the house.

Her father, who had an exaggerated tummy and tipped the beam at 350 pounds, said, "Bubby, I will have Jim stable your critter." The girl was pretty and well-raised, and her training would not allow her to notice the laughable figure that Marsh cut. When dinner was announced, Marsh resisted all entreaties to sit up and dine, as his humiliation was great. He sat the meal out, with his feet curled up under the chair and his finger in his mouth. Buck pleaded a headache and would not eat, though ravenously hungry.

The day passed and at suppertime, Marsh, who was sitting with his back to a shelf on which rested a skillet, put his hand behind his head. Feeling the skillet there, he absentmindedly worked his little finger through the hole in the handle. By this time he was nearly all in from hunger. Having lost his appetite for a week, it now returned tenfold. At the call of supper, he found that his finger would not come out of the skillet hole; yet he was too bashful to get up and pull the offending member from the skillet. He again pleaded a headache and would not eat until breakfast time, having concluded to remain overnight at the earnest solicitation of the old man and the girl. After supper, the finger slipped out of the skillet by itself.

The sleeping apartments of the hired men were about one hundred yards from the house and formed part of the corral where the cows were kept at night. At bedtime Marsh was assigned a bed there. At his side the chinking had fallen out, and a six-inch space was the consequence. As the wind blew in quite chilly, he, upon retiring, stuffed the crack with his abbreviated buckskins.

Being weak in body from his long fast, he did not wake until the head of the house came and disturbed his slumbers at six in the morning. On reaching for his trousers, he found only a hole where they had been. Looking into the corral, he saw that two heifers had pulled them from the crack. Each had swallowed a leg up to the seat; the salty buckskin apparently appealed to their taste. He drew the attention of the girl's dad to the situation, who got him a pair of his own. As the old man weighed about 350 pounds and Marsh only a featherweight and very skinny, the picture he presented was more excruciating than when he was encased in the buckskins.

The men had gone to work, and the girl's father had gone away. As Marsh saddled his mule, he espied the girl going toward the barn with the milk bucket. Leading the mule to the gate, he tied the animal on the outside of the hitching post. Buck went into the milk house, stood on a crock, and grasped a pan of milk as the quickest way to appease his hunger. When he had disposed half of the pan, the girl stepped in. Marsh, in his confusion, turned over the crock and spilled the pan of milk over himself. He broke for his mule, mounted the animal, and never returned, living happily ever afterward.

After giving Vic some good advice, Marsh went to Fort Lincoln the following spring. There he stole seventeen government mules and struck out for the British possessions, with a squad of soldiers in hot pursuit. He easily eluded them, and the following spring he was preaching to the benighted Canadians at Alberta.

Rollicking with Joe Taylor

Vic and Joe Taylor,[46] the following spring,[47] started from Painted Wood on the Big Missouri in North Dakota for Mouse River to secure some buffalo calves. Taylor was a unique character. He had been an editor of several papers and a soldier during the rebellion. Joe was the shrewdest trapper the West had produced in many years.

Fur-bearing animals were very plentiful when Taylor came West. When he quit trapping after thirty years of trap extermination, he said that he alone had killed over 12,000 beaver, otter, and mink. He wrote a book called *Twenty Years on the Trap Line,* but he said very little about the slaughter he did among the flat-tails. Joe was of the old school, and his latchstring always hung on the outside of his wind-break.[48]

Taylor was a splendid cook and could have graced the cafe of Delmonico.[49] He was an expert at cooking flapjacks, and he did not spit into the frying pan to see if it was hot, as other frontiersmen have done, but he did keep the ground coffee in a German sock, and to save untying the same, he let it filter through a hole in the toe that had been worn out the previous winter. Taylor could cook a skunk in such a manner that only an epicure could detect the difference between that and a badger. It was little wonder that Vic glued to him for a few months. Joe always considered badgers and coyotes a nutritious special.

Joe preached that a person should not change his shirt but once in six months, a rule he religiously observed. The first day out they made thirty miles and camped in a draw just below a heavy growth of timber. It rained heavily for an hour before they got to camp, and quite a stream of water was running down the coulee from which they dipped the water for supper and breakfast.

Saddling and packing up after breakfast next morning, they rode through the grove and found that it was the burial place of the Sioux. Many trees were fruitful with bodies of Indians on scaffolds made of tepee poles and lashed to the branches. Some of the lashings had decayed with time and the elements. The bodies had fallen into the coulee, and the bones and skulls were washed clean with the water that Vic and Joe had cooked their meals with and smacked their lips over the coffee.

The next day on the head of the White Earth, they met Charley Reynolds (who was afterward killed in the Custer Massacre)[50] who said the Indians had driven all the buffalo from that locality. As Charley was never given to the use of the "long bow,"[51] his word was accepted as final, and Vic and Joe turned toward Heart River. That evening, three Mandan Indians came to their camp and remained overnight. When asked where their tribe came from, the Indians related the following legend that had been handed down for many generations.

They said their tribe originally lived underground. Once while traveling about in the bowels of the earth, they espied a hole above them and a grapevine hanging down from where they could see daylight. One venturesome buck climbed the vine until he got to the surface and saw the prairie covered with buffalo and antelope. He shouted down, and his squaw climbed the vine, and another buck and another squaw, and so on, until half the tribe had ascended. When a large squaw attempted to go up, the vine broke under her weight, and so half the tribe is yet underground. Since then they called themselves the ha-a-wak-took-taes, or "where are they—the wandering tribe."[52]

At daybreak next morning, Vic heard a racket and stampede among the horses. Slipping out of bed, he ran out just in time to see a large cinnamon bear drag down and kill a fine yearling colt. He shot and killed the bear. All hands woke and helped skin the bear, and they soon had a goodly portion of his bearship basting before the fire. Vic gave the carcass to the Mandans, the only tribe that eats bear meat.[53]

Leaving Taylor and the Indians, Vic went upriver to old Fort Berthold. The post trader there was named Packineau, a famous footracer, who had been a trader there for over forty years.[54] Packineau related how thirty years before, when he was on the opposite side of the river from the fort after some venison, a small party of Sioux jumped him and killed his horse. When he went down with his horse, his gun fell on a rock, and the flint was lost. The Indians were on foot and thought victory was easy; however, they reckoned without their host, as Packineau was the fastest man on the river in those days. It was lucky for him that but one Indian had a gun, and that was a flintlock. The rest were armed with bows and arrows.

He dashed through a clump of brush, while the enemy ran around it. Thus he gained on them and was soon about eighty yards in the lead; but eighty yards is too far for arrows to be very effective. It was three miles of a slope to the river, and he said that a small mare buffalo jumped up and challenged him for a race. He grabbed it by the tail and steered it a mile straight for the fort. The speed was too great. When the calf flagged, Packineau passed it with the Indians in hot pursuit, but losing ground. A short distance farther, he scared up a black-tail deer that struck straight for the river. To his dying day, the old man said he kept up with that deer and patted it on the back, urging it to greater speed. Seeing the man acting pacemaker to a deer was too much for the Sioux, and they gave up the chase. Packineau made the river safely and swam to the fort.[55]

PART III

SCOUTING

Ambushed in the Black Hills

The first of May [circa 1875] found Vic on the road to the Black Hills with Tip Simmons and Charley Sampson. Vic had private dispatches with him, for which he was receiving good money for delivering. At the second crossing of the Owl River, they camped for the night. Not seeing any Indian sign, they were a trifle careless and camped under a cut bank that was about fifty feet high.

After supper, while sitting around the fire, they were startled by a volley from above. Vic and Simmons grabbed their guns and jumped into a cave in the cutbank, which extended back about forty feet. As the cave had curves, there was no possibility of the bullets hitting the men, who were being fired on by the Indians. However, poor Sampson was shot and fell a few feet from the fire. The Indians did not attempt to shoot again but left him in his agony.

It was ten o'clock at night when the Indians jumped the boys, and from the top of the bank one of them, who spoke fair English, said, "Come out boys. Me no hurt you. Me good Indian." His invitation remained unheeded while the boys watched Sampson writhing in his agony, begging the boys to put him out of his misery. The campfire was burning brightly. His sufferings were so agonizing to behold that Vic, at his entreaties, raised his rifle to his face and said, "Goodbye,

Charley." He would have fired, but Simmons struck the rifle up and begged Vic not to shoot. Vic demanded to know the cause of the interference. Tip, who was horrified at Vic's cold-blooded but humane attempt, said, "If you finish Charley, and I ever get out of this place alive, I will have you arrested for murder." Vic brushed him aside and would have ended Charley's sufferings, except that again Tip grabbed the gun and begged so hard, and with such dire threats of vengeance by the law, that Vic desisted. For three long hours, they were obliged to listen to the sufferings of poor Charley, while the Indians above jeered at his writhings. About two in the morning, the spirit of the boy fled and his sufferings were over.[1]

A storm was brewing and the night became intensely dark. The campfire had gone out sometime before. The boys came out of the cave, groping to where the body lay. Vic threw it on his shoulder, while Tip carried the guns. Downstream about four hundred yards, they dug a grave in the sand with their hunting knives and buried Charley. There was no stone to mark his last resting place. Instead the boys covered him as secretly as possible so that the Indians could not find and mutilate the remains.[2]

Since the Indians captured their horses, the boys were obliged to hoof it back to Bismarck.[3] After a sojourn of three days, Vic again started for the Black Hills with a good saddle horse and a packhorse that would follow without leading. This time he took as companion his friend Billy Preston.

In 1867, Preston's father was scout and game provider for a force of 260 Fenians that left St. Paul and invaded Canada with the intention of capturing that fair country and bringing it to America. Loren Fletcher of Minnesota, who afterward was Secretary of State,[4] also Colonel O'Leary of Anaconda, a lawyer of sterling repute,[5] were along to help free Ireland. They cut across the country until they reached Fort Abercrombie on the Red River of the North. Then that stream was followed to Fort Dufferin in Canada. They captured the place without the loss of an Irishman. The "force" remained in Canada until

Uncle Sam heard of the invasion and promptly sent a small detachment of troops to order them back where they belonged.[6]

When Vic and Preston got to the Grand River crossing, they traveled upstream three miles and went into camp, as the buffalo had eaten all the grass below. Near where they camped that night, they found a wagon with the spokes all cut away and the bodies of a man and woman ripped open and otherwise mutilated. A few steps away, the Indians had driven two stakes into the soil. About four feet from the ground, they had sharpened the stakes to a point. They had taken the two children, a boy and a girl, about three and four years old, and while the children were alive, the Indians had inserted the stakes into their little bodies and left them to untold sufferings, suspended between heaven and earth on a sharp stake. The men buried the bodies as well as they could. The victims had been dead about three days.

On arriving at Deadwood, they took in the sights and squandered their money at faro[7] and "sich." In Deadwood, Vic made the acquaintance of a female shorthorn named Miss Jenny Buckley,[8] generally called "Calamity Jane" for short.

She often acted as a scout for the government against the Indians. Where the capture of a woman by redskins meant worse than death, she knew not the word fear. She was held at about thirty-five percent discount morally, but she was generous with her money and many a busted prospector she had grubstaked.

When Vic saw her, she was fair to look upon and not over twenty-five years old, although she had been exposed to the vicissitudes of frontier life such as scouting, prospecting, drinking poor whiskey, etc. She was at home on the wheel mule of a government six and equally dexterous with a sixteen-foot bullwhip over the backs of ten yokes of bulls, hitched to a freight of three heavy wagons loaded high above the guards.

After the Black Hills became settled and towns sprang into prominence, Calamity Jane, dressed in a beaded buckskin suit (pants, shirt, and moccasins), would mount and ride any bucking cayuse brought to her. Jane was handy with the six-shooter and would shoot on the least provocation or without any at all. Once the editor of a Deadwood paper published an article about her reputation, which she resented. Donning her war paint from a bottle, she armed herself with a Winchester rifle and skipped up two flights of stairs to the office of the publisher. Jane opened the door, but before she could draw a bead, the whole force jumped from the window of the sanctum and fled up the street, only too thankful to escape the wrath of an outraged woman. Left to herself and monarch of all she surveyed, Jane shot up the office and converted everything that she could draw a bead on into pieces.[9]

In 1880, Vic saw Calamity Jane in Billings, Montana, dressed in men's clothes and a soldier's overcoat, driving through the streets with a load of pole wood. Poor Jane, led astray in her youth by a smooth-tongued villain, she fell by the wayside as many a sister has done before. When outside of a half-dozen highballs, she was reckless. Sometimes she would sit and ruminate over the time when she was a happy, innocent girl. Tears would spring to her eyes, and she would forsake the primrose trail for months at a time and accept any honest labor that she could perform, no matter how menial. Her money or her help were always at the beck and call of the needy, and she never asked any favors in return. Many a time she bandaged the wounds of men shot by Indians or in sociable quarrels and nursed them back to health. Poor girl, she went to her reward a few years ago.[10] On her deathbed she said even though Christ preached forgiveness, she could not forgive the villain who had made a hell of her life.[11]

Smith Just Misses the Little Bighorn Battle

Generals [Lt. Colonel George A.] Custer and [Alfred] Terry were to start for the Upper Yellowstone May 5, 1876, to compel the hostile Sioux to come to the reservation on the Big Missouri, or to wipe them out, root and branch. Since Vic had promised to accompany Custer on the trip, he and Preston saddled their horses, and, followed by their two pack animals, started for Fort Lincoln. The second evening, they camped on Clay Creek with a party of emigrants and freighters of about thirty wagons arranged in a circle. The horses were placed inside the wagon corral at night so that the Indians might not stampede the stock.

It was just breaking day when the men started to turn out their stock, hobbled to graze for an hour before being hitched up. While the men were cooking their breakfast, one man, who was more lynx-eyed than the others, observed an Indian peering at him over a bank. He gave the alarm, and the horses were nearly all corralled before the Reds could get action. The Indians captured only five horses and lost three of their own from the fire of the whites. Those Indians who were unhorsed jumped onto the backs of horses ridden by their comrades and scampered to a place of safety.

A half-hour after daylight, about seventy-five Indians dashed out of the shelter a half-mile from the wagons and ran at full speed in Indian file past the camp on the opposite side of their horses. Discharging their rifles at the camp, the Indians went by like the wind. They repeated their tactics three times, until the men got a line on them and succeeded in emptying three saddles. Then the Indians drew off and were seen no more. The party concluded to stay another day. Vic and Billy remained with them until midnight, when they slipped out and struck for Fort Lincoln by the stars.

About fifteen miles from there, they saw a number of Indian campfires, which showed the Indians were getting ready for an early morning raid. It was about two in the morning when the boys unexpectedly ran onto five good horses that were hobbled and had strayed nearly a mile from the Indian camp. After the horses were promptly appropriated, the boys jogged along a little faster, bearing more to the left. The next day at four o'clock in the afternoon, they struck the Cannonball River, about fifty miles from Fort Lincoln.

Smith and Preston camped there for the night, as their horses were very tired. About two hundred yards from camp, they found two grinning skulls and a few bones, all that remained of people whom the Indians had punctured. Next day, when about ten miles from Fort Lincoln, Smith shot and killed two fat cow elk. The boys loaded all the meat they could onto the saddle and pack animals and rode bareback on the other cayuses to the fort.

On the 5th of May, the expedition, under the command of Generals Terry and Custer, got underway, heading for the home of the hostiles on the Bighorn. Preston joined Custer's command in the capacity of herder, while Vic was sent with dispatches to Fort Buford, about two hundred miles up the Big Missouri.

At the crossing of the Little Missouri on May 15th, the expedition was caught in a three-day snowstorm, in which three feet of snow fell. When the storm was over and the weather cleared up, the country was almost impassable for the heavy six-mule transportation wagons. The expedition crossed the Yellowstone, where Glendive now stands, and proceeded up the bank of the river until opposite the mouth of the Tongue River. There the group rested for four days. At the expiration of that time, or to be more explicit, June 22 at noon, the Seventh Cavalry under General Custer left the mouth of the Rosebud after being reviewed by General Terry and Colonel Gibbon.

Custer had about fifty Ree and Crow scouts with him, a few white scouts, and Mark Kellogg, correspondent for the *New York Herald*. Mitch Bruguier was interpreter for Custer and Fred Girard for Terry. Seventy-three miles from there, the cavalry found the camp of the hostiles on the Little Bighorn commanded by Sitting Bull, Gall, Black Moon, Crazy Horse, and Rain-in-the-Face. Custer split his forces into three parts. He gave three companies to Captain [Fred] Benteen, three companies to Captain [Thomas] McDougall, in charge of the pack train, and took the remaining five companies himself. Smith, who was of a quiet, unobtrusive disposition, who wore his hair short, caught up with the command at dusk. After changing horses, he was immediately sent back to Fort Buford with dispatches, about three hundred miles.

Smith was at Fort Buford when the *Far West* came down with the wounded, and he had no chance to enter the fight. As the command ascended the ridge and looked down the Little Bighorn Valley, their eyes caught an Indian village that extended for two miles down the slope. [Major Marcus A.] Reno moved his forces down along the riverbank, with Custer on his right. All of the scouts, except the interpreter Bruguier and Bloody Knife, a full-blooded Sioux and great friend of Custer's, remained with Reno.[12]

A short distance down the valley, as Custer disappeared over the ridge, he waved his hat enthusiastically and never was seen more in life by human eyes, except by the Sioux who annihilated his command. The strength of the enemy was estimated at nearly three thousand warriors. It was only a few weeks previous that these same Indians had whipped [General George] Crook on the headwaters of the Rosebud, and they believed their "medicine" was strong enough to scalp the universe.[13]

Reno dismounted his men on the banks of the creek as the Sioux threw their weight against his left flank, which was supported by Indian scouts, who, by the way, were weak sisters who flew the coop and never stopped until they arrived at the Powder River. The troops were easily beaten back into the timber. At that time, Reno had lost only a few men and according to military critics should have stayed in the timber where he was. There he was well-sheltered with trees and an abundance of good water, where he could have stood off thousands of Indians most effectually.

The command remained in the timber one half-hour when Reno, most lamentably rattled, sounded a retreat to the bluffs, an action of a lunatic. Lieutenant [Charles] DeRudio,[14] scout [William] Jackson, interpreter Fred Girard, and a buck soldier were concealed in the willows bordering the stream, their horses having been killed.

DeRudio said when Reno led the retreat, which had degenerated into a fleeing, frightened, panic-stricken mob, he and his companions were obliged to remain, being without horses. Just then Charley Reynolds, a scout who had been with Custer in many an Indian fight, came up. Reynolds had gained the sobriquet of "Lonesome Charley" through his modest demeanor, for as conversationalist his strong suit was silence. Dismounting, Reynolds said, "Boys be quick and take a drink out of this flask, as I am going to catch up with that command if possible." They hastily accepted the offer. Then quickly mounting his horse, Reynolds flew after the thoroughly frightened soldiers, who were three hundred yards away.

DeRudio said that when three hundred steps away, a bunch of Indians swung alongside Reynolds and shot down his horse, but before they could get action on him, he killed four of them with his Winchester. There perished the Davy Crockett of the Bighorn, honorable, truthful, generous, and fearless. (Mrs. Custer speaks of Lonesome Charley in her book *Boots and Saddles*.)

In the retreat, Reno lost about forty officers and soldiers. DeRudio states that from his vantage point in the willows, he saw most of the dead knocked from their saddles by the Indians with war clubs. No resistance was offered except by a couple of officers who drew their revolvers and fired at the enemy. DeRudio and his companions succeeded in reaching Reno's entrenchments on the bluff the second night. While in the willows, they saw several squaws around a wounded soldier, whom they tortured most horribly before the breath left him.

Major Reno remained on the bluff where he had entrenched himself for two days, all the time striving to keep the Indians from annihilating the command. For several hours of the first day, Reno could hear the firing between the Indians and Custer getting fainter and fainter until it ceased entirely. On the 27th of June, Terry and Gibbon arrived, the Indians fled, and Reno's command was saved.

There were nearly four hundred[15] soldiers and scouts killed in the battle between the opposing forces. All of the dead were scalped and mutilated. One dead officer, who wore dundrearies,[16] had his face scalped in addition to his head.

All told, the losses of the Indians were but eighty-three dead and wounded. Bruguier and Bloody Knife were among the slain. Custer reposed great confidence in Bloody Knife, who, for wrongs done to his mother by a party of Sioux years before, swore eternal vengeance against the tribe.[17]

"Yank" Brockmeyer Is Killed

Colonel [Major Orlando H.] Moore, of the Fifth Infantry under General Terry, was encamped at the mouth of the Powder River on the Yellowstone. While the commands were getting in shape for another go at the Indians, scouts Vic Smith, Bob Jackson, and "Yank"[18] Brockmeyer were assigned to Colonel Moore to keep their weather eye peeled for Sioux. Vic put in a month hunting and scouting for the camp.

On the 25th of July [1876], Colonel Moore sent Vic to Deadwood, South Dakota, with important dispatches. He arrived there August 1.[19] The next day he watched a poker game in a saloon between four men, one of whom was "Wild Bill" Hickok, champion of champions with a six-shooter. (As an annihilator, "Bill" was a heap reliable with either gun or knife.) Opposite of "Wild Bill" at the table sat Captain Massie, a retired steamboat man. While engrossed with their game, a man named Jack McCall entered very quietly, drew a heavy .45 revolver, and shot "Bill" behind the ear. The ball passed through Hickok's head and entered Captain Massie's wrist, where it lodged.

McCall was tried by a jury, "tried and true," of his friends and acquitted, but a nemesis named Charley Utter, a friend of Hickok's, was on his trail. Utter followed McCall to Yankton, caused his arrest, and saw that he was promptly hanged.[20] Ten years afterward, Vic met Captain Massie at Bismarck, and the bullet was yet in his wrist. Massie said that he had a hunch he would pass in his checks before long and said he had a clause in his will that after his death the bullet should be extracted and sent to Vic. He died all right, but Vic never got the bullet.[21]

Three days later, Vic was back to the mouth of the Powder River with dispatches for his Colonel. On August 10, Colonel Moore had orders to march his troops to the Rosebud to cooperate with Generals Crook and Terry. Being short on transportation and the river low, he was compelled to leave 100,000 pounds of oats and corn behind in sacks on the bank of the river. When forage for the horses ran short, Grant Marsh, captain of the government light-draft steamer *Far West*, and Colonel Moore, with one company of troops, were sent to bring up the grain. Vic and Brockmeyer accompanied them in their capacity as scouts.

When the steamer arrived at the mouth of the Powder River, where the grain was left, the men found that the Indians had carried away all the corn, cut open the oat sacks, scattered the oats upon the ground, and had taken the sacks. Soldiers and deckhands were soon employed in carrying the grain in boxes, blankets, or any old receptacle. As soon as they landed, Vic and Brockmeyer took their horses ashore to scout back in the hills. They rode about three miles and climbed a high bluff. With their glasses, they discovered a large camp of Indians up the Powder River Valley, nearly twelve miles from the steamboat.

The men came back to report. When about one mile from the boat, Vic discovered six Indians sitting on a knoll three hundred yards away. One Indian got up and leisurely followed the boys at a safe distance, to within three hundred yards of the landing, and dared the whites to come out and fight. Vic wanted to kill him, telling the Colonel that he would waste but one cartridge, but the Colonel said it was a friendly Indian merely doing a little bluffing. Finally the Indian made a few indecent gestures, and the Colonel sat up and took notice.

The cannon was run off the boat, and the Colonel sighted it and fired a shell at the Indian. The Indian fled. Colonel Moore refused to let Vic go back to the bluffs after he had discovered the camp of

Indians; so Vic went into the cabin, lay down, and fell asleep, although the heat was almost unendurable. Dave Campbell, the pilot of the boat, awoke Vic and asked to ride his horse into the hills with Brockmeyer and the herder.

After the men had gone about two miles, the six Indians that Vic had discovered rose from a coulee and chased the men, who broke pell-mell for the boat. The doughty Colonel again trained his cannon on the Indians and fired another shell, which struck just right. Two Indians were seen to fall, and one horse went down to rise no more. Three of the redskins took back to the bluffs, while one (the one who had followed the scouts to the boat in the forenoon) followed in hot pursuit after the fleeing whites.

Vic awoke when the cannon discharged. Taking the situation in at a glance, he grabbed his Winchester rifle and ran down the stairway to the lower deck. Untying the halter that held Colonel Moore's thoroughbred horse, he mounted without saddle or bridle. Guiding the horse with the halter, Vic dashed out on the gangplank, in spite of the soldiers, who, at the Colonel's orders, tried to stop him. Colonel Moore was afraid that his favorite horse might never get back again.

When within three hundred yards of the party, which was rapidly coming toward him, followed by the Indian, Vic noticed the Indian throw up his gun and take a chance shot at the men. The bullet struck Brockmeyer's horse just under the backbone. The horse fell, and the gun dropped from "Yank's" hands as the horse fell across it. There was nothing for "Yank" to do but to run, as his comrades had run away and left him. The Indian quickly caught up with Brockmeyer and sent a bullet from his Seventh Cavalry carbine (captured at the Custer fight) through his body and "Yank" dropped.

The Indian kept coming toward Vic, who was riding to meet the foe at full speed. Not more than two hundred yards separated them when Vic fired at the Indian. After a few more shots from Vic's Winchester, and when not more than fifty yards separated him from Red Bull, a bullet passed through Bull's heart. When peace was declared, the Sioux said he was one of their bravest warriors. Just then the Colonel again turned the cannon loose a few times, and the exploding shells mussed up the shrubbery and sagebrush something extensive. Then the captain of the boat Grant Marsh and the crew of deckhands came out to find Brockmeyer. Since the sagebrush was about two feet high, it took about fifteen minutes before Brockmeyer was found. He was not dead. The Indian was quickly found and scalped.

Meanwhile, Brockmeyer's horse had got up and was walking toward the boat. Vic caught the horse and removed the saddle blanket. "Yank" was tenderly laid on the blanket and carried to the boat. His horse was later sold at an auction after recovering from its wound. After a few hours of suffering, "Yank's" soul went aloft to meet its maker.

About twenty miles upriver next day, the body of poor, unfortunate "Yank" Brockmeyer was laid to rest on an island in the middle of the Yellowstone River so that the Indians might not find and mutilate the body. Lieutenant Woodard[22] of the artillery rendered an impressive funeral service, and it was not until the steamer had landed at the Rosebud's mouth and the soldiers had mingled with their comrades that the memory of the occasion was partly effaced.

After Custer's cavalry was annihilated, the command under General Terry had orders to march up the Rosebud, and on the 15th of August Vic accompanied them again. With him were scout Jackson and interpreter Fred Girard. Strict orders were given that no shooting be allowed other than at the enemy; however, Vic could not restrain his penchant for shooting and kept ahead, frequently shooting deer, antelope, or elk and leaving them on the trail for the command.

After a three-day trip up the Rosebud, they came to the trail where the Indians had crossed the stream after the fight with Custer. The trail was leading east toward the agencies and was fully a half-mile wide and eight inches deep, plainly showing that Custer had a formidable foe to deal with. Ten miles beyond where the trail was crossed, the command of General Crook was sighted coming down the stream. When first sighted by the big clouds of dust, it was supposed that the enemy was going to deal another round, but General Crook's head scout Frank Gruard[23] rode into camp and said that Crook was coming.

Vic and Fred Girard were the first scouts to ride into Crook's command to inform him that Terry's outfit was a few miles away. There Vic made the acquaintance of Frank Gruard, Crook's chief of scouts. Gruard's father was a missionary in the Sandwich Islands, and his mother was the daughter of a Ka-na-ka chief.[24] He was the best scout and trailer that ever saw the Indian country. Crook said Gruard was the boss of them all, and as Crook was the best Indian fighter he ought to know what he was talking about.

That evening after dark, Vic was sent back alone with dispatches to Fort Buford on the Big Missouri (a 450-mile trip). After several narrow escapes from the Indians, Vic reached the river. Having lost his horse in his last encounter with the Indians, he threw a dry log into the river, and with all of his clothes on he swam the stream, which was nearly a mile wide. It was now September, and most of the Indians had separated and gone to their different agencies, followed by different commands.

General Miles had orders to keep his eye peeled for Indians and later on to build a cantonment at the mouth of the Tongue River on the Yellowstone. Miles gathered around him a band of old-time frontiersmen as scouts that filled the bill to a nicety. There was "Liver-Eating Johnson" (Jack Johnson), George Johnson, Vic Smith, Tom Cushine,[25] Bob and Billy Jackson, Bat Shane, George Fleury, and Milan Tripp.

The cantonment was commenced, and one day Vic and Bob Jackson were sent out after some elk meat. In a slough a mile out, they discovered two half-grown otter swimming about. Vic, who was the champion shot of the frontier, bet Bob that he could crease both otter without killing either one. Bob took the bet, and at two shots both otter lay motionless on the water. Jackson rode out into the slough, picked up the two otter, and found that though neatly creased across the neck by the bullet they were not mortally hurt.[26]

Bob promptly paid the bet. Then he put them into a sack that was behind his saddle to prevent them from escaping. That evening wagon boss Hank Blum[27] paid $50 for them. Soon getting well they made great pets. An officer bought them and sent them to his wife in the states (called states because Montana was a territory then).

Colonel [Elwell] Otis, with his command, was escorting the mule and bull trains that were hauling the supplies for the cantonment at Tongue River, which was to be called Fort Keogh, in honor of Captain [Myles] Keogh who was killed with Custer. The supplies came up the Missouri River by steamer to Fort Buford and then were freighted to their destination by teams.

Delivering Dispatches—A Dangerous Duty

On the 10th of September 1876, Smith, Al Geddy, Jim Slue, and Bill Turner[28] were sent with dispatches down to Fort Buford. At the crossing of Bad Route Creek, Turner jumped off his horse to shoot an antelope. At that moment, a band of Indians, concealed behind the ridge about seventy-five yards away, opened fire and killed Geddy and also the horses of four scouts. A retreat to some thick brush was the order of the day, and there the boys stood off the Sioux until midnight, without losing any more of their number.

On the 18th of October, Miles and his infantry started for the head of Cedar Creek, where he thought Sitting Bull was cached. He dispatched three scouts: Vic Smith, Kelly,[29] and Billy Cross to the mouth of Bad Route Creek to pick up the trail and follow it until they had run it into a hole. On reaching the mouth of Chokecherry Creek about dusk, they found that Sitting Bull had moved camp that day, as the embers of the campfires were yet aglow. They counted where one hundred lodges had stood. The men found where the Indians had left the scalps of two white women hanging in a tree, which had been forgotten. One was auburn and the other blonde. The scouts followed the trail over to and up Cedar Creek. Just before dark, Vic shot a fat mountain sheep and tied a goodly portion on the saddle for their supper and breakfast.

Traveling three miles after dark, they went into camp and feasted right royally on the sheep. At two o'clock in the morning, a herd of buffalo stampeded through the camp, taking the packhorses with them. Their saddle horses were picketed, while the pack animals were allowed to roam. Shortly after daybreak, the scouts saddled up and resumed the trail. Soon with the aid of a field glass, they could see the command actively engaged with the Indians about five miles away. Eager to join in the fray, the scouts urged their horses along at a stiff gait. Since the Indians had burned the prairie, it was only when the wind had cleared the smoke away that the combatants could be seen. The Indians were getting decidedly the worst of the argument and were fading away until all had disappeared.

The scouts had no difficulty getting within three hundred yards of the command. However, when the troops resting on the slope of a hill saw the scouts, they opened fire, mistaking them for the enemy. About two thousand cartridges were expended in their endeavor to annihilate the scouts, but they failed to connect. The Indians were dropping sore-footed ponies along the route, which Miles ordered shot. A number of the Seventh Cavalry sore-footed horses that had fallen into the hands of the Indians during the Custer fight were picked up. For these, the quartermaster gave a reward of thirty dollars apiece.[30]

The main body of Indians retreated across the Yellowstone, while Sitting Bull, with a handful of warriors, easily eluded the military and went north across the line into Canada. Miles sent Vic and scout Kelly from Fort Keogh to old Fort Peck on the Big Missouri River to look for the hostile camp.

The first night they camped at a large spring, but the water was so strongly impregnated with the filth of the buffalo that it was hardly drinkable. From the hoofprints in the mud, they scooped up a mixture of water and buffalo chips sufficient to make slapjacks and liquid nourishment for supper and breakfast.

In the morning on waking up, they were greeted with the sight of at least one hundred wolves sitting around them at not more than seventy-five yards away. The scouts had camped on the headwaters of the Redwater, and on looking down the valley they could see large herds of buffalo as far as the eye could reach. It was the rutting season, and the buffalo emitted a steady roaring and bellowing that sounded like a storm on the ocean beach.

On the head of Elk Prairie Creek, they discovered the camp of Black Moon, chief of the Oglalas, a most bloodthirsty villain, who cut a leading figure at the Custer Massacre. They examined the camp with a field glass, the said camp being two miles away. They found that to whip the Indians where they were was a huge task, as the camp had natural fortifications about it, making it a veritable Gibraltar. From there the boys went down the creek, crossed the Big Missouri, and camped for a week at Fort Peck, which was nothing but an old trading post. Fort Peck was built by Durfee and Peck fifty years before, but when Smith and Kelly were there it was a reservation for Yankton.[31]

At Fort Peck, Vic ran across his old friend Cap Healy, who was deputy marshal. Healy was there in the interest of people who had lost stock by the Indians. All stock other than Indian cayuses were taken from the Indians and placed into a large corral. At that time, Healy had confiscated over four hundred American horses from the Indians. Many were Seventh Cavalry horses, for it must be remembered that many of these same Indians were in at the death of Custer.

The Sioux had a system of heliographing[32] with looking glasses, equal, if not superior, to any other nation in the world. By this method, the news of the fight on the Little Bighorn was known the next day at Fort Peck, over five hundred miles. The day after their arrival, a heavy electrical storm raged. As an Indian, whom Healy had despoiled of a handsome mare, was running from the trading store to his wigwam, a bolt of lightning struck and killed the mare and knocked the Indian down. Some Indians in the trading store observed him fall, ran out, picked him up, and brought him into the store. Restoratives were applied, and "Spotted Fish" was himself again. Through the interpreter, he said the Great Spirit looked down, saw him, mistook him for the marshal, and struck him down. When he fell on his back, the Great Spirit saw his upturned face, noticed the mistake, and did not finish him.

Vic rode a high-strung horse that he wished to trade to an Indian for a fine horse that the siwash[33] rode. Vic's horse was well along in years. When the Indian looked into the horse's mouth and noticed its age, he would not trade. Not wishing to give offense by saying, "Your horse is old," the Indian softened it by saying, "My friend, your horse has heard it thunder a great many times," and of course he broke off all further negotiations.

Smith and Kelly left there and went to Poplar Creek Agency, swimming the river by hanging onto the horses' tails. Then they struck south for Tongue River on the Yellowstone. Their route took them over a rolling country covered by countless thousands of buffalo. Nothing very rushing was done for a while except scouting around the country and guarding the train that was hauling supplies for building of the Keogh cantonment. Now and then a brush with the Reds would enliven the monotony of the trips, but most of the Indians were returning to the agencies, where their dear old Uncle Sam would feed them until spring and give them annuities in the shape of red blankets, etc.

McCormick's Hair Turns White

During the holidays that winter, General Miles sent Vic up the Yellowstone to the old Crow mission with dispatches for Captain [Charles] Hargous. The weather was very cold. Paul McCormick, one of the foremost citizens of Montana at the present time, also a member of the legislature for several sessions,[34] was at Fort Keogh and asked Vic if he could accompany him, as it would afford protection.

McCormick being a man in every respect, Vic willingly accepted his company. They left Keogh at midnight so that the Sioux, who were ever looking from the bluffs with field glasses, might not see two lone men leaving the fort. Their destination was near where Livingston [Montana] is now. The second day out, they saw the trail of three enormous grizzly bears in the snow, which was about four inches deep. Vic remarked that in all of his experience he had never seen bears out in such bitter cold weather before. When they reached Pease Bottom, a few miles from the mouth of the Bighorn, they camped for the night, and Mac gave the history of the place as follows:

Two years before, Mac and Major Pease[35] left Bozeman early in the fall with ten wagon loads of provisions, blankets, calicoes, beads, etc., to start a trading post at Pease Bottom. Eighteen hardy frontiersmen accompanied them in the capacity of wolfers, as wolves and coyotes were very plentiful in that section, they never having been hunted there before. They found the Indians were also on hand to do business with them.[36]

Plans for the buildings and stockade were laid within fifty yards of the Yellowstone River, and erection commenced on the same. Before they completed the buildings and stockade, Indians killed five of the party and stole one-half of their stock. After the post was finished and ten more wolfers had joined the gang, the boys would go in parties of five or six to kill buffalo for bait and put three to five bottles of strychnine in a carcass. In a day or two, they would go with a wagon and haul in the dead wolves and cord them up until a chinook thaw came. Then they would skin and stretch them. Eagles were a great menace to the dead wolves, as they would tear and destroy the skins if they got at them. Eight or ten men would accompany each team when they went to haul in the wolves. Every few days the men would have a brush with the Indians.

One very cold day, the Indians sneaked up on two wolfers who were warming themselves at a campfire after skinning a lion they had shot. The savages killed one, and the other escaped into the brush and cached himself. The Indians ran up to the fire to warm their hands, preparatory to scalping the dead wolfer, when his comrade in the brush fired and dropped two Indians at one shot. They happened to be in line, and the 120 grain Sharps rifle would pass easily through a half-dozen men. One Indian, whose back was broken, fell across the fire. The other Indian grasped him to pull him away, when the wolfer shot him dead. Before they could collect their scattered senses, four of them had dropped dead. Thinking the Lord was pulling with the whites, the Indians fled. The wounded Indian lying across the fire gave no evidence of pain, but stoically bore his sufferings with the fortitude of an aborigine. His wound was such that he could not move. The wolfer took a sardonic pleasure in watching the suffering Indian for a few minutes. Then he stole down the riverbank and made his way to the post. When he returned with a packhorse and several friends, they found that the Indians had scalped and mutilated their comrade.

The most thrilling incident in the history of the trading post occurred in January. There was a high butte one mile from the post, and every morning two men would go on horseback to the summit. With a field glass, they could scan the surrounding country for Indians and buffalo. On this particular morning, McCormick, accompanied by a man named Devine,[37] went out to the butte. They had a well-defined trail through the sagebrush, which was about three feet high. In this sagebrush were seventy-five Indians. The savages were hidden on each side of the trail and allowed the men to proceed to the bluff, thinking that more men would come from the post. The men ascended the butte and started on the return to report "nothing doing."

When the men passed where the Indians were concealed, the Indians suddenly arose from the sagebrush and poured hot fire into them. Devine fell, riddled with bullets; McCormick's horse fell, shot through the body, but immediately arose with Mac clinging to the saddle. Mac righted himself in the saddle, and amid a shower of bullets the maddened horse flew for the post. A number of Indians had to jump aside to avoid being trampled upon by the seized animal. It was a miracle how Mac escaped. His clothing, riddled with bullets and powder burns in several places, showed how close the Indians were to him. When the horse with its rider reached the gate, it sank to the ground never to rise again.

Within a week McCormick's hair turned snow white. By this time, Pease and he concluded that a trading post on Pease Bottom would not pay and was a little too strenuous; therefore, they loaded all they could onto their wagons and packhorses and pulled for Bozeman. Their loss in three months was thirteen men killed and most of their stock killed or stolen. They had thirty-nine Indians to their credit.[38]

That evening, as Smith and McCormick were ready to turn in, a small detachment of troops came downriver and camped overnight at the stockade. They were a scouting party going upriver in a few days. McCormick threw his lot in with the soldiers, as visions of good grub, a good bed, and more protection loomed up before him. Vic only wished he could do the same. They separated the next morning and never have met since. McCormick rose to wealth and distinction, while Vic still flits from bush to bush, a veritable bird of passage, as it were. After breakfast next morning, Vic bid adieu to all hands. Climbing onto his horse, Vic pulled out for the mission, 150 miles farther upstream.

Fifty miles from there, Vic met Archie MacMurdie,[39] a husky, young Scotsman, who was on his way to Tongue River with dispatches for the Diamond R. Vic and McMurdy, who had not seen each other since the hanging of the half-breeds at Brainerd years ago, dismounted, made a fire, and smoked the pipe of peace, as it were. Archie then related how three lodges of Crow Indians had left the old mission three months ago to hunt buffalo and never returned. He stated he saw a human head hanging in the bushes about five miles back that indicated to his practiced eye that the hunting party had found their finish in the neighborhood.

They had coffee and Archie produced some fine buffalo hump that when roasted before the fire was a feast fit for the gods. Each man then resumed his way. Vic, determined to solve the mystery of the missing Crows (who were always friendly to the whites), soon arrived where the ghastly Indian head was hanging by an ear to the limb of a small cottonwood tree. After a short search in the willows that fringed the borders of the Yellowstone, he found where the Crows had cleared away three spaces of willows to erect their lodges.

The cut willows were piled in two heaps. On each heap lay the nude body of a young Crow woman, one apparently about seventeen years old and the other about twenty. Their limbs were spread-eagle and their bodies frozen stiff. An old piece of blanket was thrown over their faces. When Vic removed the blanket, he saw two remarkably well-featured young women. Besides the indignities to which all captives are subjected, the small end of a tepee pole had been inserted in their bodies and pushed through lengthwise, until there was two feet of pole protruding from their mouths, all of which evidently had been done while they were alive. The limbs of the trees were hung with ghastly ornaments in the shape of arms, legs, and heads of the unfortunates that comprised the three lodges of Crows. There were fifteen in all, among them were four young women of marriageable age.

Wolfers Versus Sioux

In due time, Vic arrived at the mission and delivered his dispatches. While there, he ran across his old friend Frank Woody,[40] who was a splendid specimen of the frontiersman, six feet, two inches in height, manners agreeable, and totally unacquainted with fear.

It was in the fall of '71 that Woody and two other wolfers, Cox and Hubbell,[41] took twelve packhorses loaded with grub, ammunition, traps, and camp equipage, and went up Pryor Creek, which empties into the Yellowstone near where Huntley [Montana] now stands. They were looking up hunting and trapping grounds for the season, beaver being the animals they mostly sought. After building their house and stockade, they planned to settle down for the winter. It was then about the first of September. Camped fifty miles upstream, about two miles back from the timber on the prairie, they were disagreeably surprised to see seventy-five Sans Arc Sioux riding leisurely toward them.

Realizing the jig was up, the boys dropped the horses, and a friendly washout afforded them shelter. The washout was shoulder-deep, ten feet long, six feet wide, with six inches of water in the bottom. They took in plenty of ammunition, a sack of bread, and some boiled buffalo hump, knowing full well that flight would avail them nothing. The boys concluded to sell their lives as dearly as possible.

The Indians came within a hundred yards of the washout and dismounted to make "medicine" according to their custom. Sitting down in plain sight, they smoked their pipes and conjured up the assistance of the Great Spirit to help them destroy the hated paleface. Their council ended after an hour, with the belief that their medicine was strong enough to kill the whites with clubs and save ammunition.

When all were ready, a portly savage about forty years old, well-painted and greased to kill, wearing nothing but a breechcloth and moccasins, and armed with a war club, advanced to slow music by the tom-tom, while his comrades remained sitting on their haunches. When within about forty steps, Cox remarked, "See me hit his belly button," and at the crack of his rifle, the Indian's navel button disappeared. He sank to the ground, where he writhed in agony for a half-hour before death let his spirit go to the happy hunting grounds.

Then the Indians lost a little faith in their voodoo charms and fell back on their rifles. As there was nothing visible but the men's heads, the Indians failed to score. They then changed their tactics. One at a time, an Indian would mount his cayuse, ride pell-mell past the washout, and endeavor to shoot some of the men within, but they invariably met death before they passed the washout. One Indian came at full speed. When within twenty paces of the washout, he was shot and clung to the pony until nearly opposite the men. The pony, shying at the men, caused the Indian to lose his hold, and his body rolled into the washout.

Cox, who was the daredevil type, quickly scalped him and waved the scalp at the Indians. The dead savage was a welcome addition to the boys, as they could stand on his body and keep their feet out of the water. Finally, a fine specimen of an Indian, presumably the chief or head warrior, wearing an elegant headdress of otter skin and eagle feathers and mounted on a handsome horse, came like the wind. He was a splendid shot, as the bullets from his Winchester rifle pattered close to the washout where the boys were cached. His charge was supported by the rifle fire of his comrades. A perfect rain of bullets spattered in and around the hole but failed to connect with the white men's flesh. He fell within twenty feet of the washout when a ball found lodgment in his heart.

Cox climbed out of the hole, made a dash to secure the warbonnet, and got back without being made a sieve of—a miracle how the Indians missed him. The Indians lost twenty-six and quit charging after the death of the chief. It was a dark night, and the men succeeded in escaping to the Crow mission, about forty miles to the west. The wolfers informed the Crow Indians, who came over and found where the Sioux had buried the dead in the trees. According to Indian custom, the Crows pulled down the stiffs and scalped them. The warbonnet was taken to Bozeman, where it was an attraction in a store window for many years.

Three years afterward, Cox and Hubbell were trapping on Skeleton Creek, a small branch of Pryor Creek. They had built a commodious cabin at the mouth of the stream where it empties into Pryor Creek. They had it well-loopholed and well-provisioned for a long siege if necessary. The two men had made a good catch of beaver so far, also many wolves, coyotes, and some bear. They expected to visit the states (Montana was a territory then) in the spring—that being the mecca to which all their thoughts tended. After years of roughing it, visions of a trip to the states in the mind of a western hunter or scout was paradise itself.

One afternoon about four o'clock, Cox went downstream to shoot a buffalo for wolf bait, having spotted a small herd. Meanwhile, Hubbell went upstream to bring in some pelts that they had left the night previous. Hubbell related that when he was a mile from Cox, he heard the report of Cox's gun, followed by the reports of about fifty more. He said when he ran to the edge of the willows to look, a party of Indians commenced firing at him. He then ran back into the willows. Assuming that Cox was killed and knowing that they could not hunt there after being discovered, Hubbell waited until dark and struck out for Bozeman, 150 miles distant.

Hubbell told his story and how it all occurred. Prompted by curiosity, a dozen wolfers and hunters went to the camp the following spring, guided by a map that Hubbell had drawn. They found Cox propped against a tree, dead. His rifle was lying across his lap, and two cartridges were in his hand, but there was no sign of Indians. A bullet wound through the head told the cause of his death. The mystery of his death will never be solved this side of the Great Divide.[42]

Woody later guided eastern parties on hunting trips for many years after the Indian troubles had ceased. He also guided Theodore Roosevelt on a bear hunt in Wyoming.[43] Woody finally passed in his checks at the Yancy Ranch in Yellowstone Park in 1902.

End of the Indian Wars

Vic left the [Crow] mission the last of January '77 and returned to Fort Keogh. He quit scouting for a while and went wolfing with Jack and George Johnson about twenty-five miles from the fort in February and March. Tom Keefe went along, and in six weeks they had more than six hundred wolves. Ninety-four were killed in one night at the carcass of one buffalo.

Keefe, a butcher by trade, accompanied Smith to Dog Basin one day after antelope. The snow was deep, and the antelope had bunched together in great numbers, all the same as sheep. Vic killed fifty that day. At one shot he killed six antelope, which shows how thick they were huddled. They took off all the skins that day, each worth ninety cents, and left the meat for the wolves. A present day hunter would stagger at what he would denominate as hoggishness when he hears of such slaughter, but he must remember there were thousands of antelope, buffalo, deer, and elk then. A man who was an expert with the rifle in those days and able to stand at the head of the class with his gun was looked upon as "Big Medicine" by both whites and Indians.

General Miles had 250 Crow Indians at the post that he fed for what little services they rendered. One day the Cheyenne Indians, who had harassed the post all winter, sent four members to the fort to ask Miles for coffee, sugar, and tobacco, for which they agreed to abstain from stealing any more government stock before spring. Not knowing the Crows, who had just arrived, were in the vicinity, the Cheyenne rode up, bedecked in all their finery of bear claws, eagle feathers, and elk teeth, and painted in the latest style. Some Crows, seeing the Cheyenne coming and knowing their mission was of peace, as they carried white flags, ran between them and the stockade, while some other Crows cut off their retreat.

Smith and Johnson were coming into the post at the time on horseback and had a fine view of the skirmish. Three of the Sioux[44] were speedily hemmed in and slain, but the fourth, mounted on a splendid mustang, came near making his getaway. It was a thrilling chase, and the sympathy of the two scouts went to the weaker side, although they had been fighting these same Indians for years.

About sixty Crows were in swift pursuit, all firing in hope that a fluke shot might bring down man or horse. The remaining Sioux was steadily pulling away from his lifelong enemies, when a Crow about seventeen years old, who was herding the ponies near the bluffs, saw him coming. The herder, lying down at the time, was not observed. When the fugitive was within about sixty yards, the boy shot him dead. The other Indians came up and scalped and mutilated the body and did the same to the other bodies.

During the winter of '76-'77, General Miles went with his command up the Tongue River to the Wolf Mountains and encountered Crazy Horse, a noted Sioux chief, and his camp of Indians. A skirmish ensued and the scouts, headed by "Liver-Eating Johnson," captured a buck and a squaw. Several soldiers were killed, and after the war was over the Indians admitted they had lost only one man, Big Crow, the Medicine Man.[45]

In May '77, Johnnie Bruguier and George Fleury discovered Lame Deer's band of hostiles up the Rosebud. (Johnnie Bruguier was the half-breed son of Mitchell Bruguier. Mitchell was one of Custer's interpreters who was killed with him at the Massacre on the Bighorn in '76.) Bruguier and Fleury returned and reported to Miles. Being short on transportation, Miles secured Morgan Williams's bull train of ten six-yoke teams. With his infantry, he started after the Cheyenne.

About 240 Indians were in camp, probably about 50 of which were warriors. When within ten miles of the Indians, the command camped and rested until 11 P.M., when the command was put into motion. At daylight, the command was within a mile of the village. Nine scouts, including Jack and George Johnson, Bob Jackson, Smith, and several more, led the way. The scouts rode between the tepees and the big herd of ponies that just had been turned loose to graze. It was just break of day, and the scouts were abreast of the lodges, when an old Indian came out with his gun and shouted, "Turn back or I will shoot."

George Fleury shouted in Sioux, "Shoot away." The Indian fired, killing Bob Jackson's horse. Fleury reined in his horse, and Jackson jumped on behind, and in a twinkling the herd was driven down the valley. Meanwhile, the soldiers were coming up as fast as possible.

The Indians, cut off from their mounts, took to the high bluffs. While two scouts remained with the herd, the others rode back quickly to tackle the Indians in the bluffs. Lame Deer and Iron Star, the two chiefs, stopped at the lodges and did not attempt to escape. The fact is, they did not want to fight anymore.

Miles shook hands with Lame Deer, and just then a buck soldier rushed up. The chief, thinking he was to be murdered, prepared to sell his life dearly. Raising his gun, he fired point-blank at Miles. Although only a few feet away, Lame Deer missed his aim and killed Miles's camp aide.[46] Bob Jackson, who had just come up to interpret, threw his Winchester down on Lame Deer and killed him instantly. Then turning quickly, Jackson snuffed out the life of Iron Star. Drawing his sheath knife, Jackson had both Indians scalped in a twinkling, greatly to Miles's disgust.

The troops lost four men and had a number wounded, while the scouts killed fourteen Indians and a squaw. "Antelope Charlie," a scout whose parents were killed in the Minnesota Massacre, killed and scalped three Indians and a squaw in a hand-to-hand encounter. The Indians lost, by capture, nearly a thousand ponies, which they stole back two months later. The scouts brought in fourteen scalps, which they hung up in their tepee by the post. The scalps hung there for a day or two and then were thrown aside, as the men knew more could be obtained any old time.[47]

Jack Conley, who was afterward sheriff of Deer Lodge County [Montana] for two terms,[48] captured a squaw and was having a strenuous time with her. He was slowly dragging her toward the brush, but she, being a husky dame, was putting up a vigorous resistance. Witnesses said Jack intended getting her into the brush out of sight and scalping her alive, but Jack denied that tale and said that was not his intention. Miles was anxious to capture some Indians, and Conley wanted to have the credit of making the capture. It was not until "Antelope Charlie" came to Jack's assistance that they were able to handle her. Charlie threw her on his back, while Jack held her hands, and they carried her to headquarters in the field. Conley tried to get a medal from the government for distinguished valor in connection with the capture of the Amazon but failed.

The Sioux war was then practically over. In fact, the Indians had never wished to fight after the Custer Massacre. They were willing to rest on their laurels and also feared that they would be called to account for that slaughter. Of course, the Indians would lay out a scout now and then or massacre a few settlers and carry away the young women, but the large organized killings in which they used to participate were over.

Delivering Mail

In 1877, Major Pease, an old-timer and gentleman of the old school, who was with McCormick in the Pease Bottom wolfing station in '74, took the government contract to carry the mail between Fort Keogh and Fort Buford, two hundred miles. He secured the services of the best two men he could procure, one of them being Vic Smith and the other Tom Keefe, who had scouted for General Terry in '73 and '76. The Indian troubles were practically over, and the two hundred dollars per month Vic got for carrying the mail looked good to him and was far better than scouting for ninety dollars.

The first trip Vic made with the mail for Major Pease was the first of May. Seven miles below Fort Keogh is Sunday Creek. The night before, a pack mule train with an escort of soldiers was coming to the fort, intending to make it there by ten o'clock. "Tex" Fountain, a handsome six-footer in charge of the train, had some words with packer Horace Johnson during the day. At the crossing of the creek, sometime after dark, Johnson slipped behind "Tex" and shot him through the head. The ball came out his mouth, knocking out several gold-filled molars. Johnson fled, and, though followed for several days by a squad of soldiers, he was never captured. While the pack train went on to the fort that same night, Johnson went into the mountains.

Next morning at daylight, Vic was on his way with the U.S. mail on two packhorses. At the creek, he saw blood in the road where "Tex" had fallen from his mule. Vic stopped to examine the scene, not knowing of the tragedy the evening previous, as he had left Keogh quite early. Looking around, he found three gold-filled teeth from the mouth of poor "Tex." He gathered them and put them in his pocket. When Vic arrived at Bad Route Creek, where Geddy[49] was killed the year previous by Indians, he found coyotes had dug up the remains, and the skeleton was strewn around the prairie. Vic gathered all the bones he could find and put them back again, except one shoe with the foot inside. This he took with him to Fort Buford, his destination. After losing several games of billiards,[50] he tendered the gold-filled teeth and the skeleton in the shoe as payment. Fred Figley kept them behind the bar for several years as relics.

Geddy's grave was marked by a stake driven into the ground and a piece of cracker box nailed thereon with the universal epitaph cut deep with a knife: "A good fellow but out of luck." Vic was later told that Geddy's bones were gathered with the buffalo bones by bone haulers and sold to be used as fertilizer or for the refining of sugar.

At the crossing of Cedar Creek on Vic's return, Indians jumped him, took his horses and all the mail, and besieged him in a natural fortress for two days. When they raised the siege, Vic walked into Keogh. He made another trip and tendered his resignation, as he could make more money at something else.

Catching Brockmeyer's Horse

Shortly before Brockmeyer the scout was killed, he and Vic were running some buffalo on Squaw Creek. "Brock" had a magnificent horse, for which he paid three hundred dollars. While running the buffalo, his horse stepped into a badger hole and fell, throwing "Brock" over his head. The horse could not be caught again. "Brock" remarked to his horse, when he found he could not catch it, "Never mind, old fellow. I'll get you this fall." Little did anyone know that two months from that day his life would be snuffed out by Indians at the mouth of the Powder River.

That fall, Vic gave another character named "Glendive" Smith fifty dollars to help him catch the horse. They found the horse up Squaw Creek. Vic crept up within seventy-five yards and creased the animal by shooting it through the neck above the bone. As it fell, his partner, who was mounted and knowing full well that the horse would soon recover, dashed from the timber skirting the creek and threw the lariat about his neck. "Glendive's" horse settled back on its haunches, and there was no escape. Vic saddled and mounted "Comanche." After ten minutes of stiff pitching, the horse surrendered and quietly carried his rider to the cantonment. Vic kept the horse for years in memory of Brockmeyer.

"Slippery Dick"

The Indian campaign of '76 and '77 brought out many peculiar characters; among them was Richard Ream, better known as "Slippery Dick." He had been "rooster"[51] on a Missouri River packet[52] for Captain Dave Marler. In the early days he scouted for Miles, and after the Nez Perce fight he volunteered to go to Sitting Bull's camp across the Canadian border with a dispatch for Sitting Bull to surrender to Miles. On his arrival at camp, he presented himself to "Bull." The wily old warrior expressed his wonder in a series of Indian grunts how a white man could have escaped the observation of his warriors. Dick was rash enough to make some uncomplimentary remarks on the nonvigilance of his warriors.

A council was held, and Dick was to be stripped and whipped. The sentence was carried out to the letter, and Dick was unmercifully lashed. They were about to fasten him on the back of a wild cayuse and turn the animal loose, when a Yankton brave, whom Richard had once divided grub with, interceded for him, and Dick was turned loose. A thin pony was given to him but no saddle and no clothing except his trousers and moccasins. He was told to go, which he did, and he came back safely to the command on Milk River five days later. He subsisted on the carcasses of buffalo that had been dead for over a month. Dick was complimented on his bravery.[53]

Two years afterward, Dick was murdered by a Frenchman on a creek the Sioux called "the creek where the bull floats down." They quarreled over a bunch of horses, and the Frenchman paunched him with a 45-caliber bullet. Dick died the next day. They planted him close to where he fell. The murderer escaped, of course. A slab hewed from a cottonwood marked his resting place, and the universal epitaph was cut on with a jackknife: "A good fellow but out of luck."

Chief Joseph

Milan Tripp was a scout under Miles in 1876. On the Marias River in Montana, where Chief Joseph of the Nez Perce Indians fought his last fight with the soldiers, Tripp took a most active part in the battle. It was by his rifle that Chief Joseph's brother and Chief Looking Glass bit the dust.[54] These same Indians were victorious in all of their fights with the soldiers, but they invariably got the worst of it when they met the hunters and trappers from the time they left the Pacific slope, until they made their final stand on the Marias River.

Seeing they were hopelessly surrounded by soldiers and citizen scouts, nearly all of the warriors escaped in the night across the Canadian line. Of those who surrendered, only fourteen were warriors; the rest were women and children. They had dug rifle pits to protect their wives and children. The Nez Perce killed thirty-three soldiers and four scouts and lost twelve bucks and two squaws. It was acts of injustice and the encroachment of the whites that compelled them to abandon their homes and farms in Oregon and take to the warpath.[55]

The Nez Perce had sent letters to the government, protesting the injustice done to them and gave a set date for their wrongs to be redressed. When no attention was paid to their request, the Nez Perce threw aside their agricultural implements and engaged in the simple pastime of killing soldiers and citizens from Oregon to the Canadian line. The average man does away with all simpering sentimentality when the Indian question is broached; yet one and all admired the manly way that Chief Joseph and his band of Nez Perce stood up for their rights.

"Liver-Eating Johnson"

"Liver-Eating Johnson" was a noted character in the West. He also scouted for Miles and Terry and had undoubtedly killed more Indians singlehandedly than any other man in Montana. He was broad-shouldered, powerful, and had a hug like a grizzly bear. Jack was a stranger to fear and strictly on the square. Johnson had innumerable fights with the Indians and always came out on top. He was a splendid shot, and Vic once saw him kill a cinnamon bear at half a mile, on the opposite side of the Missouri River.

In '74, Jack and George Johnson headed a party who searched the Bighorn country for gold. Their party fought the Indians every day for nearly three months. The outfit lost only one man, while the Indians were 150 shy at the end of the game. George, one of nature's noblemen, drowned in the Musselshell River in '78 while scouting with Jack, who was afterward one of the most efficient deputy marshals Montana ever had.[56]

The Scalping of Jennie Smith

At the mouth of the Musselshell River, Montana, Captain Clemming[57] kept a trading post, where he would trade with the Indians coffee, sugar, and calicoes for furs and robes. In those days, an Indian tanned and painted buffalo robe was worth only $2.50, while a wolf skin was worth $3.50. Many adventurous frontiersmen followed the business of wolfing in the winter and loafing in the summer around a trading post, where they could enjoy themselves. They were always welcome for the protection their presence afforded and also for the money they kept in circulation.

On the 8th of May at Clemming's trading post, Frank Smith and his comely wife, a white woman, had charge of the place during Clemming's absence upriver. (In those days nearly all men kept a squaw, generally called a "sleeping dictionary," for the sole purpose, they said, to enable them to grasp the Indian language more readily.)

One lovely day, Mrs. Smith, "Jennie," as she was called, accompanied by a squaw, the property of a wolfer named Bradley, went about three hundred yards from the stockade after sarvis berries,[58] the bushes being laden with that luscious fruit, when a Sioux war party opened fire on them. One bullet went through the muscles of Jennie's neck, and she went down and out for the count. Jennie's companion "Natooka" received a bullet through the thigh, a flesh wound, and ran screaming for the fort. Hearing the firing, the wolfers ran from the fort in pursuit of the Indians, who had already scalped Jennie and were in full retreat. The Sioux removed Jennie's scalp, about the size of a small slapjack. She was unconscious during the skinning and knew nothing of the exquisite pleasure to be derived from having one's scalp removed by main strength and long practice.

Among the wolfers were four of the best Indian fighters of the day: George Grinnell, "Liver-Eating Johnson," Johnnie Cochran, and Ben Greenwood.[59] All of them had spent most of their lives on the frontier, hunting buffalo and fighting Indians. These four men, accompanied by five others from the fort, followed the Indians down the river until the Indians cached themselves in a washout. When the boys got onto their little game, the Reds soon found they were the ones trapped. The washout was about twelve feet deep, eight feet wide, and thirty feet long. The mouth opened against a slough, and the Indians held up their coup sticks on which was Jennie's scalp lock.[60] The boys, who were within twenty feet of the washout, amused themselves by shooting off the coup stick that held the scalp.

There were seventy-five Indians in the hole. They dared not look out, and the boys dared not look in. As sunset approached, the boys looked for a means to dislodge the enemy, knowing full well when darkness came the Indians would escape. At the direction of Johnson, Smith,[61] Grinnell, and Jimmie Deer[62] walked down the bank for three hundred yards and waded the slough. The slough was in reality the Musselshell River. Screening themselves behind the willows, they got directly in front of the washout. Only seventy-five yards away, they found that the Indians had put poles across the mouth of the washout and barricaded it with blankets and shields of bull hides.

Their shields were similar to ones Zulus used in Africa, but this flimsy barricade could not withstand the rain of bullets that belched from the Spencer rifles in the hands of Deer and Grinnell. The men were all armed with Hawkins-Spencer rifles, while the Indians were armed with old-fashioned muzzle-loaders, and those with shields had bows and arrows. As the bullets came through the barricade, the Indians, realizing the desperate strait they were in, commenced to sing their death song and to climb out of the washout.

While the Indians were clambering out, the wolfers succeeded in killing thirty-two of them. After the remaining Indians had disappeared and the boys were congratulating themselves on getting off so lucky, an Indian sat up and said, "Me good Indian," in order to save his life, both of his legs being shattered with bullets. He claimed that the other Indians, who were all bad, compelled him to go on the warpath with them. Jimmie Deer pulled his revolver, a cap and ball affair, and told him he was too good to live. He snapped the gun in the Indian's face, who shut his eyes and dodged backward. Six times, Jimmie deliberately snapped the gun in the face of the savage. Each snap was a living death to the victim. As it was a rainy day, the gun had got wet and would not explode.

Johnson then said, "Take this old man," and shot him through the head. The bodies were then quartered the same as beef and piled. Mr. Johnson, who until then was known as just plain Jack Johnson, picked up a fine quivering liver of one of the Indians and said, "Who wants some liver?" Several reached forward and said, "I'll take some," but after Johnson had eaten about a pound of liver, they backed out. Since then he went by the name of "Liver-Eating Johnson."[63]

Jake Leader was the only white man killed in the fight, and Ben Greenwood was wounded. It rained all the time the boys were around the washout. As many of the Indians had bows and arrows, their bowstrings got thoroughly soaked, making their arms of little service.

The wolfers took the scalps off and carried the heads to the fort. The flesh was boiled from the heads, and the grinning skulls were placed on a stage landing for passengers on the steamboats to see. A few weeks later a steamboat stayed up there one night, and one of the wolfers[64] swiped the whole outfit of skulls and scalps. He took passage to the states, and through exhibiting and lecturing on them he amassed quite a competency.

The buxom Jennie recovered. A few years afterward when her husband died, she again tackled the horrors of matrimony by leading to the matrimonial hitching post a champion bronco rider named Tucker.[65] Their home was on the Big Hole River, Montana, and the latchstring always hung on the outside. She facetiously referred to the hair-lifting episode as "the rape of the lock." She passed over the range at Wisdom, Montana, in 1911.[66]

A few days after the fight, a steamboat landed, and an English tourist hopped off and announced his intention of killing some big game. He engaged "Liver-Eating Johnson" to guide him, as he wanted a trophy to take "'ome to Hengland." They saddled up and rode about seven miles when Johnson pointed out a bunch of elk. The tourist shot a fine one. While Johnson was skinning out the head, some Indians sneaked through the brush and fired a volley at the men. One bullet killed Johnson's horse and passed through Johnson's leg. The horse, in falling, rolled over and pinned old "Liver-Eater" to the ground. Meanwhile, the Englishman mounted his horse and flew for the fort.

When the Indians rushed up to finish Johnson, he shot and killed five of them. He lay pinned down by the weight of his horse until the wolfers at the post, apprised of his predicament by the thoroughly scared Englishman, came pell-mell on horseback and rolled the horse off his leg. In a few weeks Johnson was himself again and afterward scouted for Generals Terry and Miles and was in several perilous places with "Yellowstone Vic" after that. Johnson was city marshal at Billings, Montana, when the Indian troubles were over and the country filled with railroads and "sich." He was laid to rest at Los Angeles in 1905.[67]

The Bewitching Rosa

Two scouting companions of "Yellowstone Vic's" were Bat Shane and George Fleury. They were well-educated half-breeds, thoroughly versed in the Indian language and ways. After the Indians had quieted down, both acted as interpreters and scouts at Fort Buford. There was a well-developed and pretty Spanish-Mexican girl there. She was the daughter of a government employee named Rafello. Rosa Rafello was much sought after, but the most devoted and persistent admirers were Aleck Ayotte, a deputy sheriff, George Fleury, and Bat Shane. The fair Rosa wavered between them and finally married the deputy sheriff as he had the most ready money.

After the marriage, the deputy discovered that the fair but fickle Rosa entertained a very pronounced feeling for Shane, and he secured a separation. She then married Shane. Shane objected to his wife going to the military balls and expressly forbade the fair Rosa to dance with the soldiers during his absence. One day he was sent with important dispatches to Poplar Creek. Love and jealousy prompted him to return in haste. He rode up in one day, sixty miles. After changing horses, he arrived back home at six o'clock in the morning, only to hear that his wife had disobeyed his instructions and had attended a dance the evening before. After putting up his horse, Bat entered his house and woke up fair Rosa, saying he was hungry. She reluctantly arose and started cooking breakfast. Soon another scout's wife came in, and then Shane charged his wife with attending the hop. She acknowledged the corn and said she would go as often as it suited her.

At the time she was cooking slapjacks, and Bat drew his revolver and shot her through the jaws. The ball went clear through to about where the molars are located. Stubborn, willful Rosa, according to the testimony of the woman who was present at the tragedy, did not even stop turning the flapjacks. Just then, the sergeant of the guard, who was making his rounds, heard the shot, opened the door, and stepped in. Bat, fearing arrest, placed the revolver to his own head and fired two shots, falling dead.

The field was now clear for Fleury, and before grass could sprout on Bat's grave Rosa had become Mrs. Fleury. George had a more or less strenuous time keeping the admirers of the witching Rosa at a proper distance. One evening at a ball at the fort, Rosa was insulted by a soldier, or at least George was, as he overheard the remark. He promptly knocked down the "Swattie,"[68] while the band played on. At midnight at the fort, all revelry ceases, and the participants must retire. The soldier that George Fleury knocked down went to his quarters, sneaked out his needle-gun, went to Fleury's home, and awaited his coming. Soon Fleury and Rosa were at the door of their home. Before Fleury could enter, the "Swattie" arose from behind a large rosebush and shot him through the heart—a most cowardly murder. The soldier was sent to Bismarck, North Dakota, for trial,

91

where he was found guilty and condemned to hang.

On May 6, 1886, Vic finished his tour of the states, giving exhibitions of artistic and accurate shooting through the principal cities. He left St. Paul in time to arrive at Bismarck, expecting to see the "Swattie's" execution. Vic was greatly disappointed on arriving to find that by some chicanery of the law and lawyers that the "Swattie's" execution had been postponed. Three months later he was pardoned and returned to the post where he had committed the murder. He served out his unexpired term as a soldier, despised and shunned by his comrades and acquaintances.

Humiliated by the Sioux

Vic, who was well-shaped and as supple as a panther, was looked upon by the eligible red maidens (many of whom were really handsome) with goo-goo eyes, any one of them more than willing to jump the broomstick (marriage), as it were, with him.[69] One day at the head of Poplar Creek, north of the Big Missouri, Vic ran across a dozen Sioux whom he knew by sight, all young bucks between twenty and twenty-five years. They had all experienced jealousy over the smiles that the dusky maidens had bestowed upon Vic and saw the chance to humiliate him.

They had killed a large fat dog and were stewing him in a large kettle, hair and all. When Vic came up, he dismounted, and sat down to smoke. As he was ready to go, he was confronted by all the rifles at full cock. One young buck acted as spokesman and ordered Vic to eat the dog, well knowing the aversion whites had to eating the animal. Vic, being discreet because he could not help himself, fell to and gingerly devoured a few mouthfuls; but at the urgent request of his entertainers, he gorged himself, for it would have been folly to resist. All this time, the Indians were circling about him with guns at full cock, emitting the most demonical yells. Vic thought his chances for death were good but kept a cool head and a bold front.

The Indians stripped Vic and tied him on a horse Mazeppa-like[70] and ran the horse (what was called a squaw plug) all over the prairie. Most of the lashes supposedly intended for the horse landed on Vic's bare body. When the pony tired, Vic was released and allowed to lie down and rest for a half-hour.

Shortly after Vic was unpacked from the cayuse, about sixty Indians, including squaws and children, appeared over a knoll. They came and pitched camp. When informed of the sport, they readily agreed to assist in the entertainment. All of the Indians were agency Indians, mostly Santee Sioux. In the winter they lived at the agencies supported by the government and drew their annuities. In the spring they would again go on the warpath. They did not dispatch Vic because they were so near the agency that they feared being found out and their rations cut off.

When the tepees were all pitched, Vic, who was still in "undress parade," begged to be allowed a loincloth, as his modesty and bashfulness were causing him more agony than the pain that had been inflicted on his bare back with the whips. In the camp were several Indian maidens who had cast wishful eyes on him at the agency, but not the veriest fig leaf was given to him. His hands were tied behind, and with the plain welts across his back from the lashes, he was marched throughout the village, subjected to the gibes and taunts of the grown Indians and squaws, the tender looks of the maidens, and the blunt arrows of the smaller fry.

After he had entertained his captors for about three hours, Vic was put in shape for running the gauntlet, not intending to kill him, but to furnish more diversion for the Indians, who were nearly wrought up to the killing point. Before the gauntlet was run, a happy thought struck one of the Indians who had seen Smith some years before on the Milk River shoot swallows on the wing and also light matches by grazing the head of the match with the bullet from his rifle, while held in the fingers of a comrade.

There was a young squaw about nineteen years old in camp who was exceptionally handsome for an Indian. She was married to Bull Horn, an extremely homely Indian at least fifty years old. He had purchased her from her father for twenty horses. The night before, when Bull Horn had awakened and did not find his wife in the lodge, he proceeded on a still hunt and found her in the arms of a handsome young buck. He ruthlessly dragged her out by the hair and clubbed her severely. A council was held, and she was condemned to die. The idea that hit the Indian was to tie the faithless wife to a tree and have Vic pin her to the tree, as it were, with bullets. Vic said he would try it on the condition that if the young woman was not killed with his bullets, she should be liberated after the affair was over. Bull Horn agreed, as he thought he would compel Vic to shoot so close to the body of the girl that some of the bullets would end her life.

A large buffalo bull skin, with the hair removed and the hide scraped white and stretched dry, was fastened between two trees and made a most admirable target against which the woman was tied. She was nude except a loincloth, while Vic lacked even that. Her arms were stretched out and tied fast. She had a bright eye and showed no fear. She thought the white man was to shoot her, as her husband had told her.

Vic, the acknowledged chief with a rifle over the whole frontier, stepped off thirty paces and commenced at the top of her head. The first bullet plowed through her hair, and the successive ones were placed about three inches apart from the top of her head to the sole of her foot. The dry white bull hide showed clearly where the bullets were striking, none of them missing the flesh more than an inch. This did not suit Bull Horn, as no blood had been drawn yet. When Vic started to shoot the other half of her body, the Indian insisted Vic shoot closer. Vic was compelled to draw blood five times, but not more than an eighth of an inch did any of the bullets cut into the flesh.

She was then released, and they were both compelled to run the gauntlet. There were forty bucks and squaws lined up, and Vic and

94

the woman ran through the line at their best speed. They were both unmercifully switched and then turned loose. Vic and the girl arrived at the old Fort Peck Agency the next morning and went into the lodge of "Medicine Beaver." Vic prevailed on the Indian to get them a blanket apiece to cover their nakedness.

With majestic stride, Vic wended his way to the store. He stood off the keeper for a suit of hand-me-downs, while his dusky partner in sorrow went to some lodge and borrowed a string of beads. She then came over to the store. Seeing Vic, she "stood him up" for some duds. Again the storekeeper took the "finger" for several dollars worth of dry goods for the woman and charged them to Vic. Vic felt chagrined over the affair and did not mention it for a long time.

PART IV

BUFFALO DAYS

Buffalo Exploits

The following month, Vic and [Frank] Muzzy went out on the range to capture some buffalo calves.[1] On the Redwater slope, they saw a bunch of about six hundred head lying down near the head of a draw. After turning out their horses, they pitched the tents, ate lunch, and then saddled their buffalo runners and started to approach the herd. Muzzy remained in the valley, while Vic rode out around the head of the coulee and appeared above them. He was only about seventy-five yards away before they became aware of his presence.

The weather had been very dry for a couple of weeks, and the ground was very dusty, but there were indications of an approaching thunderstorm. The herd was lying in a V-shape with the tip of the wings at the top of the slope. The soil was alkaline, and ditches several feet deep had been cut by the rains. The calves were mostly in the center of the herd. Vic soon found himself in the V, and the herd rapidly closing in behind him. Soon the whole herd was moving down the slope at full speed. Vic was in the midst and in a cloud of dust so dense that the buffalo did not notice him. He was packed in with them like sardines. They were so close to him that he could lay his hands on their backs.

Numbers of buffalo would stumble in the washouts, fall, get up again, and go on. If Vic's horse would have stumbled and fallen, the excited herd would have ground them into mincemeat with their hoofs. Vic claimed it was the most thrilling excitement he ever indulged in. They ran thusly for about one mile, when the threatened thunderstorm struck, and the dust was laid, and the buffalo spread away from them. They were now at the edge of the valley, and Vic roped a fine buffalo calf. Muzzy, who was cached close by, sailed out and noosed another one. In two days, the boys roped all the calves they wanted. As they had no domestic cows with them, they cut grass and boiled it and gave the juice to the calves instead of water, which nourishment sustained them until the Yellowstone was reached. Buffalo calves at that time were worth fifty dollars apiece. At present, a buffalo is worth about five hundred dollars. A few years afterward, Muzzy went to Alaska and drowned while hunting sea otter.

In the fall of '79, Vic hired Jasper Hults and Don McArthur to skin buffalo for him. He paid them fifty dollars per month and fodder. They always skinned and stretched the hides. From the last day of October until mid-March, Vic killed 4,470 buffalo and many large wolves. Wolf hides were worth $3.50 apiece and buffalo hides $3. The meat was left on the ground, only the skin was taken. Wolves were mostly killed by poison. To the ordinary mind that would seem like slaughter, but before the finish of the buffalo in '83, skilled hunters killed 50 buffalo a day, on an average all winter.

Vic could demoralize or tranquilize a herd of buffalo to the degree that they would not run. He would sit quietly behind a rock or a knoll and kill all of a herd that he wanted, and he generally wanted all of them. If a man made such killings now, he would be dubbed a game hog and no doubt justly. But in those days, when there were millions of buffalo and all kinds of game, a crack hunter or a dead shot was looked up to and bowed down to, the same as any hero of present day. Vic regrets the depletion in the game ranks, but he is optimistic in believing that in less than twenty years, under the present game laws in every state, game will be as plentiful as ever, with the exception of buffalo.

In the winter of 1881, Vic killed over 4,500 buffalo on the Redwater, and he had his men haul the hides to Glendive on the Yellowstone River.[2] He made the largest killing in one stand on record—107 buffalo in less than one hour.[3] The method he pursued was to approach a herd of buffalo, pick out an old cow, and shoot her just in front of the hips. Then he would hit another cow in the same place, always picking the old cows, as their children, grandchildren, cousins, and aunts would stop with the wounded. When shot in that spot, an animal, be it elk, deer, or buffalo, seldom gives more than one or two jumps and stops still, all humped up with pain. After placing about fifteen shots where they were most needed, he had the herd stopped, and the buffalo paid no attention to the subsequent shooting.

That winter of 1881-82, over 400,000[4] buffalo were killed between the mouth of the Bighorn and Sully Springs on the Northern Pacific Railroad route, and their hides were stacked up at different stations. Money was plentiful and times good. You could borrow a few hundred dollars from any man you met in those days, and he would ask no questions, security, or note of hand. It is different now. In this age, he would require a mortgage on your life. Vic made a record killing that winter, but as records made then are frowned upon now, it is as well not to mention them. How easily our government could have extended a protecting hand and saved those noble animals from almost utter extinction.

In the spring of '81, Don McArthur was putting up a corral for Vic at Beef Slough on the Yellowstone. One day he mounted Vic's saddle horse and was bucked off and his ankle crushed. He was taken to Fort Buford, where his leg was amputated below the knee. The next summer the government paymaster Adjutant Arthur Beard stopped overnight at Johnnie Burns's ranch, about ten miles above Beef Slough (now known as Smith Valley and Smith Creek). Next morning the paymaster had a hunch. Instead of putting the safe, which

weighed about eight hundred pounds, in the escort wagon, as he usually did, he transferred it to the ambulance, where he rode with the
mule skinner and one sergeant. In those days, Uncle Sam's paymaster
carried cash instead of checks.

McArthur was knocking around that section with his wooden
peg that season. When the paymaster's six-mule team got a few miles
down from Burns's ranch, four masked men who kept concealed while
the ambulance with the treasure went by confronted them. The robbers
held up the six-mule wagon filled with soldiers. Among the bandits
was a man with a peg leg who demanded the safe. When informed
that the treasure was ahead in the ambulance, about three hundred
yards away and just ascending a heavy short grade, the robber with
the wooden stump, a dead shot, raised his rifle, fired, and killed the
ambulance driver and placed a bullet amidships of the sergeant. He
would have certainly killed the paymaster with the next shot, but the
team just then passed over the brow of the hill.

Meanwhile, Arthur Beard held the sergeant with one hand and
drove the mules with the other at full speed for about seven miles to a
stage station kept by Fred Rounsaville. Two hours after they arrived,
the sergeant died. As everyone recognized the wooden stump of the
killer, he was arrested and tried at Glendive. Since anything belonging to the government in those days, especially treasure, mules, or
ammunition was considered communal property, McArthur was
handed the Scotch verdict: guilty but not proven.

In the fall of '81, a man named Parsons owned the land opposite
of Glendive. As the slaughter of buffalo was at its height, McArthur
asked Parsons if he could build a stopping place for the buffalo hunters
on his land for the winter. Parsons told him to go ahead and that it
would be rent free. McArthur ran a stopping place and saloon that
winter and cleared $10,000. The following spring, Parsons told
McArthur he would allow him to run his place as usual, but he
(Parsons) would start his own place, as there was money enough in
the business for both. Accordingly, Parsons had his men put all the

lumber, sash, shingles, doors, etc., for the house on the ground, all piled up snugly, as the carpenters would commence building the next day.

That night a bouncer named Jensling, who hung around McArthur's place, poured five gallons of coal oil on the building material, set it afire, and completely destroyed it. The next morning Parsons saw Jensling and accused him of burning the property. Jensling sailed into Parsons, beating him up something liberal. Jensling then went across the river to Glendive and saw Judge Olson of the justice court just as the judge was coming down for his morning drink. (By the way, the judge was a great lusher. One day while in a maudlin state, he gave a man twenty-five years for leaving his team unhitched on the street. Of course, that sentence did not stand.) Jensling told the judge that he had a little scrap with Parsons and wanted to pay his fine, as he did not want his "reputation" damaged by being hailed into court. The judge thought a minute and said, "Jensling, I will fine you a dollar and costs." Jensling pulled out a pint of whiskey and said, "Judge, keep this; it's good." The judge, in a burst of generosity, said, "Jensling, I remit the fine," and that settled the case.

When McArthur's case was about to be reopened again concerning the holdup, he fled the country and was heard of no more. Life was held cheap in those days and justice was unknown, unless meted out by a vigilance committee.[5]

On the Trail of "Limber Jim"

In October of that year [1881], Vic had his camp established on a small tributary of the Redwater, north of the Yellowstone. Among his skinners was a man named Dick Rock, whose power of endurance was almost beyond belief. He was an expert buffalo skinner.[6]

One day Vic had killed a bunch of buffalo. Rock, who had just finished skinning a dozen buffalo that Vic killed the evening before, rode across to where he heard Vic shooting. Vic turned in and helped skin until 5 P.M. when the job was finished. While skinning, Vic observed a lone bull performing some queer antics about a mile away. After finishing the bunch, the men rode over to the bull and found that the buffalo, an old one with his horns worn down to a sample, had a man down in a dry ditch that had been formed by the rains. Because the man's body just filled the ditch, the bull could not get a fair swipe at him. Froth from the bull's mouth was all over the man, as the bull had pawed him and tried to rend him with his horns. The bull was quickly killed, and Vic tenderly took care of the man, while Rock rode to camp for a team. His condition was too grave for him to be carried on horseback. Both arms and one leg were broken, and serious internal injuries were apparent.

Rock brought back some whiskey with the team, which revived the man to the degree that he could give a coherent account of the tragedy. He said the bull was all alone, and in a spirit of sport he would run his horse close to his majesty and allow the bull to chase him, just barely keeping out of his way. When the bull was worked up to a frenzy, his horse fell while jumping a ditch, and the rider tumbled over his head. The horse quickly gained his feet and ran away with the rifle, which was in the scabbard. Then the bull turned his attention to his tormentor and jammed him down into the ditch. He had been tortured by the bull for about three hours.

It was dark when they arrived at camp with the wounded man. They would have taken him to the Yellowstone, where medical assistance could have been procured, but they saw he could live but a short time. This surmise proved true, as the man's spirit soared aloft at midnight. The man was perfectly conscious until a half-hour before he died, and he asked that someone pray for him. He said before going West he was a devout member of the church, and that he could not think the Lord would deal harshly with him, as he had never wronged a man in his life. He had three hundred dollars in cash, and he said his horse and gun were worth seventy-five, if they could be found. The man told where in Tennessee his wife and children were and requested the money be sent to them, which was sacredly done with seventy-five dollars for the horse and gun, which were found the next day.

Two of the men were very good singers and sang hymns. Another played an ancient accordion, the doleful sounds of which equaled those of a tom-tom, and thus eased his spirit over the range. He was buried on the banks of the stream the next day. A variegated collection of buffalo hunters composed of whites, Indians, and half-breeds attended the funeral. One of the half-breeds, a graduate of the Carlisle School, preached an interesting sermon.

One week after the funeral, Jack Conley, sheriff of the county,[7] came to Smith's camp and asked about a notorious character named "Limber Jim." Conley said that this gentleman of the highway had stolen two running horses and a very swift mule from a Little Missouri cow camp. Fact is, it was the only known mule that could outrun the swift buffalo cows and would run alongside the ungainly animals without fear. As the aforesaid James had camped two days prior with Vic and had inquired about Sun River, Conley could glean a very good idea where the man was headed.

Next day, Conley deputized Smith to accompany him as his assistant, and Vic had to comply with the request. "Limber James" had lost no time in moving northward, and as Vic and Conley had to smell out the trail, which had been made a day after a rain, their progress was hampered somewhat. On the third day, while on the banks of the Musselshell, and about three miles from the river proper, Conley, with his field glasses, discovered a horseman with three animals, which he rightly divined as the game they were after. Shielding their approach as much as possible, they were able to get within three hundred yards of Jim's camp unseen. He had hobbled his horses and was making his wickiup when Conley and Vic quietly approached. When he turned around with an armful of spruce boughs for his shakedown, he found himself a bull's-eye for the best revolver shot in Montana, Jack Conley.

Jim saw his escape was impossible and with commendable nerve said, "Good evening, gents." Jack put the shackles on James, while Vic finished the shakedowns for himself and one for Jack and Jim, as they slept securely handcuffed together that night. Then Vic turned to and cooked supper from Jim's larder. Jim showed himself quite an epicure, as he had quite a store of dainties that he had stolen from the cow camp. These were in the shape of jellies, sardines, deviled ham, etc., while Vic and Jack's stores consisted of flour, sow bosom, coffee, and buffalo hump. Supper over, they talked on various topics and found Jim a very intelligent and interesting fellow.

After breakfast, Vic saddled and packed the horses, and in two days they were back at Vic's camp on the Redwater. There was a reward of seven hundred dollars on the head of "Limber Jim." Since Jack had dropped five hundred dollars the week previous in one night at Spanish monte,[8] he felt elated to think he would have the where-withal to toy with the coy and fickle Tigress[9] again. Jack felt so pleased with the prospect that he concluded to lay over a day to hunt buffalo.

Next morning, Jack left his prisoner shackled with the cook. Mounting his horse, Conley accompanied Vic after a bunch of buffalo they had seen the evening before upon coming into the camp. They found the herd grazing peacefully in the valley. Screened by a knoll, they approached within one hundred steps before the game became aware of their presence. Before the buffalo were fairly underway, the men were thinning the bunch, Smith on one side and Conley on the other.

Jack used his six-shooters and with twelve shots killed nine buffalo and wounded another that Vic later killed. That is the best work for emptying two six-shooters on record.[10] One of the cows killed had a calf with her that would not run away. Jack thought he could chase the calf off in the direction of the retreating herd, but the calf thought different. When Jack was in hot pursuit, the youngster doubled and ran beneath the horse's belly. The horse stumbled, threw Conley, and ran away. Conley, half-dazed, got to his hands and knees. Then the pugnacious calf came full tilt from behind and butted Jack out completely with his little bullet head and hoofs. The calf probably would have killed him, only for the timely arrival of Vic.

Conley was too badly stove up to ride horseback; so Vic rode to camp and came back with a team and carted Jack in, while one of the skinners remained and peeled the hides from the slain. Jack remained at camp four days before bidding the boys goodbye. Taking "Limber Jim" with him, Conley lit out for the Yellowstone River.

"Dutch Jake" on the Make

Three miles below Vic's camp on the Redwater was the skin tepee of a character known as "Dutch Jake." He was the proud possessor of two squaws, a mother and daughter. Jake came from Utah and was a dyed-in-the-wool Mormon. A Santee Sioux stopped for a few days with Jake and partook of his hospitality and was ungrateful enough to elope with Jake's youngest wife, a brunette of thirty snows. The steal occurred while Jake was temporarily absent from the lodge.

Within two hours of the elopement, Jake was up to Vic's lodge with his little tale of woe. In a mixture of Dutch and Indian, he related his loss. When Vic evinced his willingness to assist Jake in straightening out the eternal triangle, Jake was transported with gratitude and offered Vic his choice of the squaws, which was blushingly declined.

The wife-stealing Indian dared not steal a horse of Jake's, as he well knew that the first time he showed up at the agency he would be arrested; so he mounted his own cayuse, with the squaw behind, and struck out. Knowing full well that the fugitives would strike for the Fort Peck Agency, about eighty miles away, Vic and Jake, well-mounted, started in pursuit and overhauled the couple after a four-hour ride.

When within three hundred yards of the pursued, Jake said, "Vic, hobble me before I break loose and kill that Indian. I cannot trust myself. I will remain here while you go and bring back Suk-e-chinka." The Indian looked back. Seeing that he could not escape with his horse carrying double, the Indian dumped her off in a bed of prickly pear and fled for his life. His speed was accelerated by a string of bullets that Vic dropped all around him from his big buffalo rifle to scare him.

Jake was overjoyed to retrieve his first love. To show his pleasure, he would have given her a sound whipping with his rawhide quirt if Vic had not intervened. Two years afterward, Jake divorced himself from his wives with a club and hied himself to pastures new in Idaho. There he married a husky Mormon woman who had been tenth [wife] to a prominent pillar of the Mormon Church, but she got tired of owning but a tenth of a man and flew the coop with winsome Jake.

Jake took up a ranch thirty miles from St. Anthony, a settlement at the base of the mountains. As there were plenty of fish and game, they were happy. When signs of winter approached and the snow lay a foot deep on the ground, Jake loaded his team with choice elk meat and two bear that he had killed and started for the railroad, promising his superior fraction that he would make the trip on the wings of love. At the railroad, Jake disposed of his meat, intending to start back the next morning for home, but the seductive "Budweiser"[11] was too much for him. He fell by the wayside, remaining on a spree for a week, forgetting all about his wife.

Meanwhile, winter had set in earnest, and the snow was three feet on the ground and yet falling. It was impossible for Jake to get home with his team, and as he had large bunions on his feet he could not wear snowshoes. He concluded to wait until the storm subsided, as he had left two pounds of coffee and ten pounds of flour at the ranch before he left. It stormed almost continually for six weeks and was the worst winter in the memory of the oldest inhabitant.

Then Jake decided to work at a cattle camp for the winter and take chances on "Abagail" surviving the rude shock of a rigorous winter on an unlimited supply of fresh air and moss agates. The following spring, when the snow had melted sufficiently to enable Jake to get back to the ranch on horseback, he pulled his freight. On arriving at the ranch, he was surprised to find his wife yet in the ring, but like the bear that hibernates during the winter, she was somewhat attenuated.

When "Abagail" holed up for the winter, she had laid up several inches of fat on her frame, and her avoirdupois was about 250 in the shade, but now she had shed the surplus and would not pull the beam down at more than 110 pounds. "Abagail" was so overjoyed to see Jake that she forgot to upbraid him. She told Jake the week he left, the bears came into the shed and stole all the meat he had left her. To subsist, she had boiled the hay from the stack and lived on the juice.

Smuggling Whiskey

At Poplar Creek, whither Vic was bound,[12] Jimmie Boyd and Dan Knapp kept a restaurant and general stopping place. Hearing that Vic was coming up during the holidays, they sent him a letter to smuggle up ten gallons of whiskey so that they could have eggnog and Tom and Jerry. Introduction of whiskey onto an Indian reservation called for a penitentiary sentence of ten years standing, but Vic, wishing to accommodate his friends, took the chance.

His business kept him there several days, and while there he boarded with Knapp and Boyd. After supper, a dozen of the elect would congregate in the back room and while away a few hours playing draw[13] and sipping the seductive eggnog. The Indian agent got next to the proceedings through a mulatto employee and sent a squad of Indian police to raid the joint. After dark, while all hands were enjoying themselves, they heard a knock. When the door was opened, in walked the squad with carbines, while the coon swung a big army revolver.

Vic realized the situation. Without any unnecessary hesitancy, he slipped into his buffalo overcoat, pulled the capote over his head, and plunged headlong through the window, carrying sash and all with him. He ran to the stockade, which was ten feet high, scaled it, and then ran toward the timber in the bottom. It was a very bright full moon, and one hundred yards ahead of him he saw a squad of soldiers from the new cantonment coming down to assist in the capture.

Vic pulled his capote over his head. The soldiers thought he was an agency employee, not knowing that the Indian police, in their zeal to make the capture and cover themselves with glory, had sprung the mine a trifle premature. After passing the soldiers, Vic slipped over the bank and down through the Indian burial ground to a patch of rose brush of about ten acres. The brush was about four feet high and very close, so much that a horse could not be forced through it. Vic crawled deep into the thicket and cached himself. On being informed that Vic was the only one who escaped, the agent sent word to the Indian camp a half-mile away that he would give fifty dollars to the Indian who would catch him.

For three days and nights, the hunt was kept up. All this time, Vic lay in the rose brush, with the thermometer about six above zero, not daring to sit up except after dark. His diet was rosebuds straight. Fortunately, he had his big revolver and a half-dozen cartridges in his overcoat pocket when he fled. The third night at eleven o'clock, Vic crawled out and went to the cabin of an agency woodchopper and woke him up for a meal of bacon, sourdough bread, and coffee, and to this day he relishes the memory of that meal. Vic told Rogers to go out and find some Indian horses and come back and report. Rogers moved with the greatest alacrity, as he expected to be hanged, drawn, and quartered if Vic was found in his windbreak.

While Rogers was absent, Vic went to the Indian burial ground, climbed the scaffold, cut the rawhide fastenings, and let down the bodies of two dead Indians. At that period, the Indians built scaffolds ten feet high and laid the dead there to mummify. He then unwound from the bodies two good lariats and several U.S.I.D. [United States

Interior Department] blankets that he needed for bedding and took them back to the shack of Rogers, who soon came in and said that he had located two cayuses.

Vic got the direction and went and roped the "frames," they being very thin. He fastened the blankets on the plugs and passed up the grade within twenty feet of the sentry at the cantonment, who said "good evening," not knowing who Vic was. Six miles farther was the old Indian village of Deer Tail. Before Vic got there, he passed through the main herd of the Indians' horses and appropriated seventeen head of them without consulting the owners. When daylight came, he was surprised to find that two of the horses were his own that had been stolen from him two years before.

At Deer Tail, the log houses ranged on each side of the road for a half-mile, sloping to the river. It was about 2 A.M. as Vic passed along the lane. The Indians were making merry with their tom-toms and their hideous singing, as was the custom at all hours of the night. Luckily for Smith, the Indians did not see or hear him go by. Deer Tail is on a high bench, and after Vic got his herd across the frozen river, he was so sleepy that he could not sit in the saddle. He then tied one horse and let the other ones graze about in the joint grass. Vic then curled up in the ghoulish raiment that he had despoiled from the dead and was soon sleeping the sleep of the innocent.

When he awoke, the sun was nine o'clock high in the heavens. On the opposite side of the river was Deer Tail village in plain sight. He could easily see the Indians attending to their duties and hear their voices. The squaws were chopping wood, and all was bustle about the Indian village. Most men would have been rattled under those circumstances, but Vic's motto was "Don't worry about the river until you get there, and then the chances are that you can wade it."

Fashioning a saddle out of the grave clothes and gathering up his herd, he started for the Yellowstone, seventy miles away. He was in clear view of the Indians at Deer Tail, but they supposed that it was someone who had a right to be there. In Vic's anxiety to separate himself from Poplar Creek, he had neglected to provide himself with any grub at Rogers's cabin. Again the pangs of hunger commenced to assail him after several days of feasting on rosebuds and wind.

He made forty miles that day, changing mounts every two hours. Along about sundown, he saw a large badger on the prairie. As there was neither stick nor stone to kill it with, he fired two shots before he got him. At dark, Vic and the horses were tired, so he turned them out on a creek where the bunchgrass was abundant. The proper way to cook a badger is to roll the whole animal in clay, neither skinning it nor removing the viscera, and then cover it with ashes and coals. But as Vic was ravenously hungry, he could not wait for baked badger. He merely drew the animal and threw it on the fire. After the badger had scorched and burned for a while, he snatched it from the fire and tried to eat it. But since it was poor, old, and tough, he could not eat it except by cutting it into chucks and gulping it down. Then rolling up in his shroud that he purloined from the cadaver, he was soon dreaming of sourdough bread and bacon in abundance.

The next evening he arrived at the banks of the Yellowstone at his cabin. Putting two of the best horses in the stable, he turned the rest loose to graze. The Gros Ventre Indians were camped upriver a few miles hunting buffalo. Before Vic arose the next day at noon, they had come along and swiped the entire herd of horses that Vic had brought from Deer Tail, except the two he had put in the stable. Vic pirouetted around for several days but found no trace of the stock.

A reward of five hundred dollars was offered for Vic's apprehension, as the act of taking liquor on an Indian reservation placed a man among the undesirables. The reward caused many deputies to keep their eyes open for Vic, and they hung about his wickiup to catch him unawares. While he never dodged them or ran away, they never got him, as he always saw them first and averted trouble. One day in Glendive he saw Aleck Ayotte, the deputy marshal from Buford. Ayotte told him there was a new U.S. commissioner appointed at Wolf Point who was unsophisticated in the ways of the country and his duties, and he (Ayotte) could get Vic off free if he would go up with him and give him the credit of arresting "Vic Smith."

They immediately went into the saloon and clinched the bargain with a couple of highballs. Vic agreed to meet Ayotte at Buford in January. True to his promise, although risking his liberty, Vic met him at the appointed time. Ayotte had a splendid team and hired Evan Bronson, son of Lieutenant [Nelson] Bronson of the Sixth Infantry. (Evan Bronson was later hanged by "Flopping Bill's" stranglers, he being purely innocent.)[14]

At Poplar Creek, Ayotte wanted to stop and let the people at the agency know the nerve he had to arrest Vic, but Vic told the driver to go ahead, and Ayotte said no more. Arriving at Wolf Point, Vic played a few games of billiards and then sauntered over to the commissioner's office. He pleaded not guilty to the charge and was acquitted all in five minutes. The commissioner was judge, jury, and counsel. That same week, the commissioner was relieved of his position for incompetence.

The mulatto who informed the agent about the boys having whiskey was found dead one year afterward shot through the head. (Verdict: died of lead poisoning.) Boyd and Knapp were taken to Miles City and tried, but Vic had written to U.S. Marshal Botkin that he alone was to blame for the trouble, and they were turned loose. All the same, their property was confiscated, and Vic's team was also.[15]

Hard Luck at Hardscrabble

In March 1882, "Yellowstone Vic," Frank Muzzy, and Fred Rounsaville each built a light skiff, put them behind their horses on travois, and went south of the Yellowstone, about forty miles, to Beaver Creek, to shoot beaver. They pitched their tents and awaited the breaking up of the stream. Each man was for himself.

In five days the ice broke, and the banks were running full. The day before the stream broke, Vic got a bad bite in his hand from a beaver that he had thought was dead, which prevented him from using his paddle. He offered Muzzy one hundred dollars to handle his skiff for him. Muzzy agreed, as he was an inferior shot, especially from a small skiff and the target a beaver head. Meanwhile, Rounsaville had taken his skiff and horse upriver about twenty miles, so he would not interfere with the boys' camp below.

The first day's shooting netted Vic twenty beaver and two otter. At sundown they found themselves about two miles below camp. Muzzy started to remove the pelts, while Vic walked back up the river after his horses, intending to move camp down to the boat. On his arrival, Vic found that some hungry Gros Ventre Indians had stolen all the grub. Vic moved camp down to where Muzzy was with the skiff. As the water would subside in a week and the beaver shooting would be over, Vic wisely saw they would be obliged to forego the pleasure of meting out a little justice to the thieves.

For a week they lived on beaver and prairie dogs, the prairie dog meat being white and a more delicious flavor than the flat-tails. At the end of 7 days, on counting up the hides, Vic had 125 beaver and 9 otter, which he afterward sold to the trading store at the mouth of the Yellowstone for $617, a fair week's work.[16]

As the water had gone down and the beaver could return to their houses, Vic and Muzzy moved upstream to the old camp and hunted up Rounsaville, who had thirty beaver and one otter. A square meal of Dutch oven bread and bacon from Rounsaville's larder made the beaver-eaters happy. Next day they pulled for the Yellowstone. On their way home, Vic shot a large white buffalo wolf. As it was very fat and close to their camp, they made a mulligan of it and declared that it was superior to either prairie dog or beaver.

In the summer of '82, Vic was camped at a place thirty-five miles above the mouth of the Yellowstone called Hardscrabble. Smith had a sixteen-year-old kid named Jim Aglew herding his horses. The kid had run away from Butte City [Montana] to hunt buffalo and to fight

Indians. Jim was a mischief-loving kid, and his mind was filled with dime novel trash. He longed to do something desperate so that he might be recognized as a pocket edition of Jesse James or "Liver-Eating Johnson."

One day in August, Jack Williamson, who scouted for General[17] John Gibbon at the Big Hole fight with the Nez Perce (and who was afterward murdered by "Flopping Bill's" gang along with Will Close on the Big Missouri in '84),[18] came into Hardscrabble and reported that a herd of buffalo was about twenty miles away. It was summertime, but the buffalo hides were good for carriage leather. Vic hitched up his broncos and hired Arthur Mahoney for twenty-five dollars for the trip. Taking the kid with them, they started over the hills for the herd, which Williamson said numbered about 140. Vic kept ahead on his saddle horse and finally spied the herd. He waited for the team to come up and told Mahoney to remain where he was until he had finished killing. Vic approached the herd and succeeded in killing forty two of them. Then signaling to Mahoney to come on, Vic commenced skinning the dead.

On the arrival of the team, Vic let the kid take the rifle and dispatch several buffalo that were down with broken backs. All hands skinned until dark, and next morning they were at it by daybreak. By 11 A.M. the heat was unendurable, and they were obliged to lie by until 4 P.M. By that time, the upper sides of the buffalos were completely baked by the scorching rays of the sun. Smith would skin the sides of the animals that were not baked, while the kid would sit in the bottom of the wagon box and drive the team. Mahoney would drive an iron pin into the ground and fasten the head of the buffalo to the pin. After he fastened another chain from the scalp to the hind axle of the wagon, the kid would crack up the broncos and off would come the skins.

Near sundown, Vic was skinning a buffalo cow about seventy-five yards away from the wagon. While stooping over, he heard the report of a rifle and the ping of a bullet through the air, as though it had struck some hard substance. He jumped to his feet, feeling sure that an Indian had shot at him. Just then Mahoney shouted: "The kid has shot himself." Vic quickly ran to the wagon. Jumping up onto the wheel, he found the kid sitting up against the side of the wagon box, stone dead. Vic placed his hand over the kid's heart, but it had ceased to beat, and his lips were already purple.

Mahoney said that the kid had swiped a cartridge from Vic's belt and had put it into the gun. On the quiet, while fooling with the gun, which lay on a partly filled sack of oats, he said, "Arthur, see me kill a buffalo." When he pulled the gun toward him, the hammer caught in the sack, and the gun exploded. Powder burned him from the wrist to the neck. The bullet struck the neck bone, killing him instantly.

They rolled Jim up in the bedding and continued the skinning. At nine o'clock that night, the hides were all off and the men very tired. They took the kid from the bedclothes and rolled up in his place. Next morning the kid was placed in the bottom of the wagon box and the hides folded and placed about him to make a space for the body. Being thoroughly dry, the balance of the hides were laid over him and piled high. The broncos were hitched, and the funeral cortege started for Hardscrabble.

Mahoney sat high on the load of hides, while Vic rode his horse. When within six miles of town, a sirocco came up and blew some hides off onto the horses. The horses dashed off at full speed, throwing Mahoney to the ground and scattering the hides to the four winds. A half-mile farther, the wagon overturned and the kid's body landed in a buffalo wallow. Vic pursued the frightened, fleeing broncos but was fully two hundred yards astern. When the wagon upset, the animals ran away with the front gearing. Realizing that a stern chase is a long one, he stopped. When Mahoney came up, they lifted Aglew's body onto the saddle, securely lashed it, and led the animal to town.

The weather being very hot, preparations were made to bury the kid the next afternoon. Toward sundown, a motley crowd of buffalo hunters and wolfers gathered around the last resting place of poor Jim Aglew. Mahoney preached the funeral sermon, and a more impressive service is seldom rendered. Men who had faced dangers for years and knew nothing of fear shed tears like women. Night was drawing on, and the coyotes and wolves were howling a requiem as the sods were laid over the remains of poor Jim. Large stones were placed on the grave to keep wild animals from molesting the remains. Word was sent to Butte, Montana, and his parents communicated with. They were well-nigh insane with grief over the tragic death of their wayward boy.[19]

The government beef herd was running short, so the commander at the post offered ten cents per pound for buffalo meat to feed the Indians. As spring arrived, the buffalo moved over to the Redwater. All that were left were a few straggling bulls, none nearer than thirty miles from the fort, but even then the buffalo hunters reaped a snug harvest when they would run across a bunch of old bulls.

One day when Vic was on the head of Hardscrabble Creek with a teamster named Newton, they espied a large bull that Vic quickly dispatched. Although the grass was six inches high in the open, there was still deep snow in the coulees. After skinning and cutting up the bull, which easily weighed two thousand pounds, Vic looked up the creek and spied a large silvertip bear on a snowbank nearly a half-mile away. Making a detour, they approached the place and saw the bear sitting beside its den. Both fired and the bear fell dead.

At the report of the guns, a two-year-old bear emerged from the hole and ran about fifty steps, when a shot through its body turned his thoughts toward mother and home. He whirled at full speed, ran to the den, and dived in. Vic quickly gained the spot. On looking down the opening, he saw the bear coming up. He fired another shot into him, and the bear fell back loudly growling with pain and anger. The den was about two and one-half feet in diameter and ten feet deep. The last shot filled the den with smoke. As there was no draft, the smoke would not clear away, and one could not see more than two feet into the hole.

After fifteen minutes the bear quieted down. Newton tied a rope to Vic's waist and let him down to the bottom, where it opened into quite a spacious chamber. It was the bedroom of mother and son. It was a most reckless undertaking, as ten to one the bear would be alive, or there might be others in there. But long chances were of everyday occurrence in those days. Feeling about in the stygian darkness, Vic grabbed onto the bear's leg. As the bear gave one last convulsive shudder and loud human-like groan, Vic drew his knife and prepared to battle for his life, breathlessly awaiting the onslaught.

After waiting a couple of minutes and hearing no signs of further trouble, he felt again and found that bruin was dead. Tying the rope to the bear's neck, Vic climbed up the rope that Newton held taut. Soon they had his majesty out on the snowbank. The milk of human kindness flowing freely in Vic's heart, he gave the two bears and the buffalo to Newton, as he had a wife and kids enough to start a public school, while Vic had not at that period tackled the horrors of matrimony.[20] Newton turned the meat over to the fort for Sitting Bull's band and sold the bearskins to the officers at the fort, realizing about $275.

The Demise of George Grinnell

Before the railroads came to Montana, all freighting to the forts or trading posts was done with small stern-wheel steamers and from there to different places inland by bull train or government mule train. All along the Upper Missouri, woodyards fifty miles apart were established by frontiersmen who varied the monotony of chopping cordwood by hunting and wolfing. Hostile Indians were everywhere, and many a woodyard was found apparently deserted by the steamboat when they stopped for wood. Upon going to the cabin to ask the proprietor the price of his pine knots or cottonwood, they probably would see a few arms or legs nailed to the front of the cabin.

George Grinnell was one of the best known woodyard men and

all-around frontiersmen. Many an Indian he had shot, both in warfare, and, as he expressed it, to see them kick. Vic Smith and Grinnell had fought Indians and hunted big game together off and on for years. Indian warfare having ceased, Grinnell settled down to farming at the mouth of Dry Fork on the Big Missouri, eighty miles below Fort Buford. He had a fine ranch. One field of oats was five hundred acres. Having thrown aside the gun for the plowshare and settling down for life, a helpmate to him was a necessity and a luxury.

He accordingly laid siege to the heart and hand of Miss Anna Malnuri[21] of Fort Berthold, eighty miles below his ranch. There was some copper blood mingled with the silver, as she could trace her maternal ancestors back to the Piegan tribe. Her father, being an old French trader, objected to the marriage, but she became the wife of Grinnell in spite of parental opposition.

Vic had his teams haul his hides and furs into Glendive, where he received a good price for them. He took a month's vacation and went to Poplar Creek on the Big Missouri. Hitching up his team and sleigh, Vic started down the Yellowstone on his trip. The first night he camped with George Grinnell, sixty miles above the mouth. Grinnell was trading that winter with the Gros Ventre Indians under Chief Spotted Hawk, the whole tribe having come up from their agency to hunt buffalo.

It is a well-known fact that buffalo always face the storm, because their front parts are covered with a heavy growth of hair several inches long. Domestic cattle, on the other hand, always turn tail to the storm, because their hair is as short at one end as the other. For several days, the wind had blown from the northwest. Since buffalo always travel against the winds, they had all gone beyond the Redwater into Sioux territory, where the Gros Ventres dared not enter. The evening that Vic got to Grinnell's place, a feast was planned to propitiate the gods of the chase so that the buffalo might again cover the hills near their camp.

Grinnell's half-breed wife, a comely woman raised by the whites, told Vic and Grinnell to paint their faces, put on blankets and pull the folds of the blankets to cover their faces, leaving just space for the eyes, and walk in boldly. Shortly after dark, the bucks began to fill the council lodge (a tepee thirty-five feet across), and the boys also filed in unnoticed. Fact is, they resembled Indians with their faces artistically painted and wearing moccasins and leggings.

When all were seated, the chief called the lodge to order. (Squaws were not allowed to enter.) In a short speech, the chief told the gathering what they were called for and that their medicine should be strong enough to cover the hills with buffalo again. A long-handled pipe filled with plug cut and kinnikinnick was first pulled by the chief. Filling his mouth with the fragrant smoke, he upturned his old gold face, blew the smoke directly upward, and addressed himself to the Omnipotent in this way: "Oh, Great Mysterious One, we dance and sing before thee tonight. We ask you to make our Medicine triple strength so that the Sioux cannot steal our scalps; so that the buffalo will return; so that our lodges may be filled with peace and plenty; and so that our squaws and little ones fill their bellies with meat."

He then passed the pipe to a subordinate chief, who, after inhaling a handful of smoke, blew to the east and followed with a request in the same line to the great "Wacon." The next chief blew smoke to the west, the next one to the north, and the next to the south. Each one made a similar request until the pipe had gone the rounds. A feast had been prepared. Six dogs were sacrificed and stewed, hair and all (to make the medicine superlatively powerful), in a kettle large enough to scald a hog.

This lodge was built expressly for the occasion and would seat the crowd of about eighty able-bodied and hungry bucks. Each one had brought a dish and a spoon made from the horn of a buffalo, symbolic of what they were asking. The bunch was too large for all to eat out of the kettle, and that is why they all brought dishes. The spoon was only a figure of speech, as they all used their fingers to snatch out the hot slumgullion, and they drank the hot broth, hair and all, with a noise like that of a bathtub draining.

Grinnell saw that he and Vic were up against it, because if their identity was discovered they would be well-beaten, as the presence of a paleface in a medicine lodge would queer the whole proceedings. As their stomachs were strong in those days and nothing would upset them, they remembered the old adage "when in Rome do as the Romans do." They put dimmers on their lamps by closing their eyes and inhaled the dog and slumgullion copiously and actually relished the same.

After another smoke, more incantations were indulged in. Then four young bucks, in a state of nature except buffalo horns fastened on their heads, came bounding in on all fours, bellowing and pawing the ground and going through all the actions of young buffalo bulls. After the bucks had careened about the ninety-foot ring allotted them for about twenty minutes, four squaws of about eighteen years, dressed in their birthday suits with buffalo cow horns fastened to their heads, came in on all fours, and coyly tried to evade the familiarity of the bulls. Here we draw the curtain. But one thing is certain, the wind changed during the night, and the next day there were thousands of buffalo in sight. Nothing could make those Indians believe but what it was their "strong medicine" that brought back the buffalo.

After eighteen months of bliss, a child was born to the Grinnells, but George, who had always been exceedingly wild, had given birth to an uncontrollable appetite for booze. When in his cups,[22] he used the blacksnake[23] across the shoulders of his fair young bride almost daily. He kept a store, saloon, and post office and was also putting in a large irrigation dam about a half-mile from his house, on which he had about fifty men working.

One morning after a few rounds with the bottle, George proceeded to chastise his wife. She grabbed her babe and fled across the plowed field toward the men for protection from the husband who had promised to cherish, love, and protect her. He caught her inside two hundred steps and struck a stinging blow across the shoulders. We have read that the worm will turn at last; so the young wife, to save herself, mixed with George. Getting a hold of a long leather watch chain that George had about his neck, she gave it a few twists and turns, and both fell to the ground with George on top. She clung with a mortgage grip to the watch chain, until George's muscles relaxed. Then she crawled from underneath, picked up the child, and went over to the men to relate her tale of woe. They were surprised at the treatment George had ladled out to her. Realizing that the poor woman had plucked a "lemon in the garden of love," they marched over, intending to string him up, as there were several trees nearby where no one had been hanged; however, the open dull eyes proclaimed that hanging was unnecessary. The wife had "builded better than she knew." She had brought too much pressure to bear, and George's spirit had crossed the range to meet kindred spirits that he had sent on ahead years before with his trusty gun.

The weather was very warm. To prevent George from ripening too fast, one man threw the body on his shoulder and carried it to the house, where it was tenderly laid in state on the dining table. The young wife, on seeing the results of the morning's encounter, saddled her horse, a magnificent animal. Clasping her babe to her bosom, she mounted and never drew rein until she had covered seventy miles. There the horse faltered, staggered to one side of the road, and fell dead. She footed the remaining ten miles, arriving at the home of her parents at daylight with her babe.

Meanwhile, the crew went through the pockets of the deceased. Extracting the keys, they proceeded to give George the sendoff of his life, or rather death. Rows of bottles and candles surrounded the body. Whiskey was poured down his throat, at which the tipsy mourners swore they saw signs of returning life, but it was a waste of good liquor; thereafter, they confined the irrigating exercises to their own throats.

A triweekly stage plied between Bismarck and Buford. When the news got to the ear of Joe Leighton, the post trader, he sent his agent to the ranch with authority to close the saloon and to stop the orgies that had lasted three days. The agent was horrified upon entering the ranch and finding the body on the table covered with the tablecloth. One sober man was left in charge of the place, and a number of others went back to work again, saying they had enough.

Next morning the remains were loaded into the wagon. The driver and agent took their seats, while twelve boozy mourners in a lumber wagon brought up the rear and headed for Fort Buford. They made forty miles that day and camped for the night at the Big Muddy. The proprietor there was a lifetime friend of Grinnell's. He was so overcome with grief that he burst into tears and threw the bar wide open, saying, "Friends and fellow mourners, the freedom of the ranch is yours," an invitation they made no attempt to dodge. They gave the agent his choice to drink and be merry or be thrown into the river and drown. At last accounts, the agent was living yet.

After a three-day debauch at the Muddy ranch, the gang formed a funeral procession. With hats off, they marched to the river and threw the body of George into the wild, turbulent Big Missouri that seldom, if ever, gives up its dead. George had formed a matrimonial alliance some years previous with a pretty squaw by purchasing her for a Winchester rifle and a gallon of whiskey. When tired of her, he had divorced her with a club. The divorcée was an interested spectator. As the body splashed into the water, the woman said, "George, wash-ta-wa-nitche" (no good). Vic fell heir to the leather watch chain by right of freezing onto it.[24] He still wears it with a miniature skull that Cole Younger, the bandit, gave him when Vic visited the prisoners in the Minnesota penitentiary.[25]

After the funeral, Vic climbed into a bull boat and floated down the Big Missouri. That night he camped at Spaniards Point, where there were tents of several half-breeds. The matron of one family, a very comely woman who had a six-month-old child, laid him aside after he had lunched and picked out two young beaver from a box. Baring her breasts, she let them pull at the maternal fount until their little stomachs podded out like pollywogs. She had been nursing the animals for a month, and surely the sustenance agreed with them, as they were fat and sleek. Vic purchased them and presented them to an itinerant preacher that he saw going down the river. Though considered harmless, one little beaver bit the dominie. Blood poisoning supervened, and he lost one arm and was laid up nearly a year.

At this point of timber some years before, Vic was following the trail of an enormous cinnamon bear in the thick underbrush. To avoid the overhanging brush, Vic kept in a stooping posture while following the bear trail. The bear tracks led straight ahead in the fresh snow, but cunning old bruin had gone ahead and then backtracked and lay alongside the trail behind a large cottonwood log. As Vic was passing the log, peering intently ahead of him through the thick brush, the bear rose from behind the log and lunged at Smith. Vic, very naturally, jabbed the gun at the bear in self-defense, and by the luckiest chance it entered the wide-open mouth of the bear and discharged, killing him instantly.

Camping with the half-breeds was a character known as "Catfish Joe." Ten years earlier, Joe was working at a camp near Winnipeg. One day while grinding his ax, he asked the man who was turning the stone to let him smoke his pipe. The man replied that he would not give the pipe to Joe until he had finished his own smoke. Thereupon, Joe bowled the man over with the ax, cut off his head, and placed it on the grindstone. Then he took the coveted pipe and fled. While working on a river steamer as a deckhand, he was arrested at Buford and sent to Yankton, Dakota, for trial. That clever criminal lawyer Bartlett Tripp defended him, and Joe received a one year's sentence in the pen.

At this same Spaniards Point of timber in '73, there was a woodyard where the mountain steamers stopped to take on fuel. Two of the woodhawks had a fierce fight one day, in which "Dutch Pete" whipped his antagonist Aleck Brown. Pete then walked off a few steps, sat on a log, and lit his pipe. Brown, smarting under his defeat by a

Dutchman, went into the cabin, picked up his rifle, and shot poor "Dutchy" through the body. When the victim rolled off the log and tried to rise, Brown ran over to him and held him down until Pete's struggles and gasps grew fainter and fainter. In fifteen minutes Pete was dead.

Brown and his comrades hastily buried him, but during the excitement they forgot the wealth that was buried with him. They unearthed the body and relieved it of fifteen dollars and an old silver watch that his father had presented to him when Pete left the old country. All agreed to say that the killing was done by Indians. A year afterward, one of the men got drunk and told the truth about the affair. Brown was arrested, tried, found guilty, and sentenced to one year in the pen. Laws were as inadequate in those days as they are now.

Resurrection of the Virgin

The next fall, Vic boarded a steamboat at Scott's woodyard and went upriver. He was traveling only for pleasure. After passing Poplar Creek Agency, he changed his mind and contemplated going ashore and walking back a few miles, when on rounding a point the steamer swung in full view of a camp of about seventy lodges of Assiniboine Sioux. When the steamer was a mile below the camp, she slowly surged against the current, and the people had ample time to view the camp.

The camp was having a war dance and trying out warriors. (At seventeen years of age, Indians are tested as warriors.) A long pole like a well sweep was in position, and a young Indian was suspended from the end of the sweep about fifteen feet above the ground. Flesh of each breast was pinched together and a knife thrust through. A stick was thrust through the incision, and a rawhide thong of buffalo skin was fastened to it. Then the flesh of each side of the backbone was subjected to the same operation. Thongs were fastened to the end of the sweep, and the embryo warrior swung between the happy hunting grounds and earth, dancing in midair, endeavoring to tear the flesh out with his weight. If the young Indian faints or calls a halt on account of the torture, his standing thereafter is similar to a squaw. He has to wear a dress and cut and carry wood, something a self-respecting Indian will never do.

When within a quarter-mile of the camp, Vic spied a fleet of bull boats drawn up in the willows. He then told the captain Dave Marler to run out the foot plank, so he could jump ashore. As the willows were high, he was unobserved by the Indians. Getting into a bull boat, Vic paddled downriver, hugging the bank closely, and then struck out into the current. The atmosphere was sultry, and the sky gave every appearance of an electric storm. It was fifteen miles back down to the agency, and the average speed of a bull boat is only two miles an hour with a good paddle and plenty of muscle.

At midnight, Vic found himself within two miles of the agency. The storm came, accompanied by terrific peals of thunder and brilliant flashes of lightning. On rounding a bend in the river, his craft was struck by a tidal wave five feet high and was swamped. As luck would have it, Vic foundered over a sandbar, where the water was only four feet deep. He felt his way on the sandbar to shore and could see the fires in the lodges on the hill. Stumbling along in inky darkness, Vic finally reached the tepees.

He walked into the first tepee he came to. The fire was out except for some coals of cottonwood. Vic pushed the coals together, heaped some wood, and soon had a good fire. The lodge was unoccupied, except for a corpse that was lying on the ground wrapped in a buffalo robe and agency blankets and wound with a plaited lariat. An old kettle and a couple of old packsaddles completed the furnishings of the morgue.

After about an hour, a squaw of about forty snows came into the lodge. Vic asked her for enough bedding to sleep on, as he was partly dry now and very sleepy. He handed the squaw a dollar and told her to dig deep for bedding. She apologized in the Sioux language by saying, "Mea-nee-nie, wak-pon-a-chie" (I am very poor). She went out among her "rich relatives" and soon returned with half of a buffalo bullhide and a piece of parfleche (flint hide with the hair removed), saying it was all she could rustle.

As the earth was far softer than what she had brought for Vic to sleep on, he demurred a trifle. In the generosity of her heart, she offered to remove the blankets and robes from the corpse, who she said was her daughter, eighteen summers old, who had died that day of smallpox, but Vic declined. Vic was so sleepy by this time that he lay down on the earth floor of the lodge with a packsaddle for a pillow and was asleep in less than a minute.

The threatening storm had been on for a while. When the irrigation gates of heaven were thrown open, the storm lasted about two hours. About two in the morning, Vic woke with a start, chilled to the bone. A frost was settling down, and the sky had cleared. The fire had burned low, leaving just a heap of coals. Vic lay shivering for a moment in his damp clothing. By the fitful glow that the embers gave, he could dimly see the form of the dead girl slowly rise to a sitting posture. He did not rise himself, although his heart and hair did. He merely pushed the embers together and blew the coals vigorously. The harder he blew, the louder his heart palpitated. It seemed an age to him before the embers formed into a blaze. All this time, probably not more than a minute and a half, the apparition was rising slowly and moving toward him, trying to free itself from the folds of the shroud. At this critical stage, the embers broke into a bright flame, and the corpse was lying in the exact place that it occupied when Vic first entered the lodge.

Vic felt of his head and knew that it was all a hallucination (not his head, but the vision). He piled on the fuel, and, after his nerves had resumed their normal status, the mother of the dead girl came in again. Vic, who did not like the idea of the fire going out again, gave the squaw fifty cents to keep the campfire burning while he slept. His head again sought the downy packsaddle. Just when he was being launched into dreamland, the mother commenced the unearthly chant for the dead.

Vic, whose feelings were yet ruffled over the recent resurrection of the dead virgin, spoke unnecessarily harsh to the woman about the noise. She retaliated by leaving the side of the corpse. Quickly getting to Vic, she stood over him with a foot on either side of him. Drawing a long sheath knife, which all squaws carry for the dual purpose of protecting their virtue and for cutting up meat, she bent over and said, "You white dog, I will kill you."

Smith coughed up two bits, and the heartbroken mother hastily grabbed it and contracted to hide her grief in silence. At seven in the morning, Vic awoke. Taking a parting glance at the dead girl, he went over to the trader's for breakfast. While strolling about the village that day, he watched the burial of the girl, which took place at noon. First four holes were dug. Then posts were erected. A scaffold was built, and the body was placed thereon ready for the tom-tom of the great "Wacon" to waft her spirit to the happy hunting grounds of the departed Sioux.

The following October [1883], Vic pitched his buffalo camp on the headwaters of the Cannonball River, about thirty miles south of the Montana line. About ten miles from him was the camp of Bill Grover, a pioneer of the Black Hills. At one time in the Black Hills, Grover's check would be honored for $100,000. The people in the Black Hills had such unbounded confidence and trust in his integrity and honor that they named a city after him.[26] Unfortunate mining speculations had reduced Grover to the buffalo camp, and he was doing his share in wiping out the buffalo. He was a good hunter and a dead shot. Near Radersburg, Montana, some years later when wrongful charges were brought against him, and in defending the reputation of his wife and daughter, he killed a couple of deputy sheriffs and paid the extreme penalty at Helena, Montana, by walking the plank, as it were.[27]

Twenty miles from Vic's camp, on the main road from the Black Hills to Sully Springs, lived a closed-fisted old fellow named Maddox. The boys dubbed him "old generosity," because he was so stingy that if he owned Lake Erie he would not have given a duck a drink. He had a buxom wife twenty years his junior. Old Maddox hunted buffalo part of the time, and his wife kept a well-proportioned, good-looking fellow about the place during her wizen-faced husband's absence. Maddox always raised a row when, on his return from camp, he found the face of "Smiling Joe," but the majority ruled. Joe stayed, and Maddox kept out on the range after buffalo, at the urgent request of his muscular spouse.

One evening after dark in November, Smith and a man named Mahoney[28] rode up to the tent of this fellow Maddox and asked whether they could get some supper. Being answered in the affirmative, they hobbled their horses, turned them out to graze, came into the tent, and sat down. Maddox was cooking supper when his partner stepped inside and renewed a quarrel that had been going on for some time.

Maddox picked up his buffalo gun and shot Trapley through the heart. The moment Maddox fired, he said, "What do you think of that?" Trapley replied, "I think I am dead," and dropped lifeless across Smith's feet. Mahoney and Smith laid the corpse out in proper form while Maddox finished cooking supper, the most unconcerned of all. He remarked that he took greater pleasure in killing Trapley than he did in killing a buffalo. The boys remained overnight and buried poor Trapley the next morning. Maddox, unknown to Smith, induced Mahoney a few days afterward to go to Bismarck, the capital. Between them, they produced a clean bill of self-defense, and the cold-blooded Maddox was acquitted.

The first of January, Vic sold his hides: 860 prime cow robes, 200 bulls, and 90 large buffalo wolves, all killed in two and one-half months, to Gifford Brothers of Sully Springs, North Dakota, for $3,280. Then he boarded a train for Bismarck to cash his check. Vic remained two days and started back. The train stopped at Mandan for twenty minutes, where Vic ran across a Mr. Mitchell, whose father Major [Thomas] Mitchell was formerly an Indian agent at Fort Peck. Mitchell was pleased to see him, and they went into Pete Brannigan's saloon to get a cigar.

In '78, Brannigan was under a sentence of death for wantonly murdering Ned Massingale, a scout of General Miles. Brannigan escaped from the prison at Bismarck and was discovered near Moorhead and was pursued on the prairie by the sheriff of Moorhead in a terrible blizzard. The sheriff perished in the storm, and the next heard of, Pete was at Grand Forks. George Peoples, the Bismarck sheriff, went there, got the drop on him, and brought him back. Brannigan was given another trial and was acquitted on new evidence manufactured to suit the case.

Brannigan's wife, a notorious character, was tending bar, and Massingale was drinking at the place. Brannigan, jealous of his wife's "immorals," came in and shot Massingale. The "newly discovered evidence" was that Massingale had "insulted Mrs. Brannigan," and on that testimony this tinhorn murderer was declared not guilty by twelve men, good and true.

To return to Vic and Mitchell at the saloon, Brannigan knew Vic by sight, although they had never spoken. He insisted Vic and Mitchell take an eggnog with him, as it was the holidays. Brannigan had doped the eggnog. As the train was on the point of starting, Vic insisted on going, despite the entreaties of Brannigan and the blandishments of his wife to remain. The dope had not time to act, and Vic walked aboard the train and shook hands with Mitchell. As the bell rang, Vic sank back in his seat and fell sound asleep. Near Sully Springs the conductor awoke him, and Vic was greatly pleased to find his bankroll safe in his buffalo overcoat pocket.

PART V

BIDING TIME IN THE BADLANDS

Hunting with Theodore Roosevelt

In September 1883, Theodore Roosevelt came West for his health and dropped off at Medora, a hamlet at the crossing of the Little Missouri River in North Dakota. Medora was named after the wife of the Marquis de Morès, a French nobleman who was erecting a large cold storage plant at that place.[1] When Roosevelt came to the badlands, the country still contained a few thousand buffalo, but their nemesis in the shape of the hide hunter was still on their trail. Within a year, their spoor was no more except for a few stragglers, which W. D. Hornaday of the Smithsonian Institution killed and mounted for the government. Mr. Hornaday procured about a dozen head, which are now the most magnificent mounted group of buffalo in the world and can be seen at the Smithsonian.

Elk were very numerous in the badlands, also mountain sheep, black-tail and white-tail deer, and bear. Antelope by the thousands wintered in the badlands breaks for shelter, and all in all it was a paradise for game. Burning veins of coal were all over the hills, and the country was covered with petrified wood. Stumps perfectly petrified seven or eight feet in diameter were seen everywhere, as were plenty of coyote, wolf, and bear heads turned to stone, which had probably lain for thousands of years. It was to this section that

Theodore Roosevelt came.

Roosevelt looked the country over, and, with a discerning eye, he saw a magnificent opportunity to make a fortune in the cattle business. He located a thousand acres as a nucleus, set surveyors to work, and hired a dozen men to put up a log house and corrals. Being a humane man, he also ordered large sheds to be built in case of a severe winter so that the cattle could find shelter. He left A. W. Merrifield (who afterward was U.S. Marshal of Montana), a man in every respect, honorable, and square, to oversee the work.[2]

Roosevelt devoted the fall to hunting and rambling over the country. He was a perfect shot and seldom missed anything he drew bead on. There was something about the man, coupled with the report that gained credence everywhere that he was the champion lightweight pugilist at Harvard, that commanded respect. While as a general thing the cowboy crowds a man from the East when he will stand it, all were deferential to "Our Teddy" and fairly respectful in their behavior to each other when in his vicinity.

He killed all kinds of game that fall, except Indians, and no doubt would have bagged a few if the opportunity had presented itself.[3] One day Roosevelt strayed over to the buffalo camp of Vic Smith on the Cannonball. Vic, the champion shot of Montana, held no "aige" over Roosevelt when it came to handling a rifle. In those days, although he was just everyday Teddy Roosevelt, he was the same honorable, gentlemanly, progressive fellow, admired and respected by all with whom he came in contact.

While talking with Vic, Roosevelt happened to look up and observe about thirty buffalo on a bench about a mile away. He proposed that they should go and see what could be done with them. After a lunch of choice buffalo hump, good sourdough bread, coffee, and airtights,[4] they saddled their broncos and skirted the knolls until they were within two hundred yards of the game.

In those days, Roosevelt was as strong in his belief that game should be protected, as he was afterward. Before they reached the herd, he informed Vic that he would kill but one, as it grieved him to see the way the noble bison were being exterminated. In his opinion, their finish was in sight. His belief was vindicated by the fact that before the following Christmas day, of the millions of buffalo that had roamed America, not one hundred were living outside of an enclosure.

When within about two hundred yards of the buffalo, Roosevelt, whose nerves were strung up to the highest pitch, let out a yell. Slapping his horse, which was an exceptionally good one, he took great pleasure in riding alongside the game and quirting them or occasionally slapping them with his sombrero. Vic, who never had been in the company of a man before who was opposed to wholesale slaughter of game, could not help but admire the man, and entered into the spirit of the chase without firing a shot.

When the game commenced to tire, the strenuous Teddy picked out a handsome buffalo bull about five years old. Running alongside, Roosevelt shot at the bull's neck, intending to break the vertebrae and cause no needless pain to the animal. The bullet went through the animal's neck, just grazing the bone, but only knocking the huge monarch of the plains down. Roosevelt and Vic checked up while the herd ran on.

Roosevelt dismounted. Drawing his sheath knife, he drove it into the chest of the huge animal so that it might bleed well. He wished to save the head for a specimen. If it bled freely, the scalp would preserve better, as the neck skin on a bull is an inch or more thick. The driving of the knife to the hilt brought the bull to his feet in an instant, the bullet only creasing him. With a roar and a dash, away went the buffalo, as Roosevelt sprang aside and gave his majesty the right-of-way. Roosevelt quickly vaulted into the saddle. With Vic keeping pace on his bronco, they soon ran alongside the bull, who commenced to falter, the knife having touched a vital spot. Vic would have shot and killed the animal, but Roosevelt forbade him saying, "This is my funeral."

Here the adventurous and enthusiastic spirit again manifested itself. Teddy was in the seventh heaven as he slapped the mad animal with his hat. For nearly a half-mile, the maddened animal ran, the blood from the knife wound streaming at every jump. It was plain to see that the finish was not far away. Shortly, the bull began to flag and then came to a halt. His legs spread wide apart, and blood poured from his wound and nostrils, but he still looked the courageous and dangerous monarch as his eye rested on Roosevelt and his mount, twenty-five paces away. Straining every muscle to regain his feet, the noble animal pitched forward on his knees, struggled to regain his footing, and then went down for the count.[5]

Roosevelt always addressed Smith as "Old Vic," although there was only three years difference in their ages, and both were young men at that time.[6] Roosevelt says of Vic in his *Hunting Trips of a Ranchman:* "Old Vic, a former scout and Indian fighter, is concededly the best hunter in the West. I have seen him do most skillful work with a gun. He will cut off the head of a chicken or a grouse at ninety or a hundred yards with ease. A dead shot on running game, he can knock over deer when they are so far away that I should not dream of shooting. Men firmly believe that he never misses. Yet I have seen him make miss shots at game when his 'Medicine' was bad. He was cradled in the midst of wild life and has handled a rifle and used it against both brute and human foes almost since infancy."[7]

Old Chief Sitting Bull

The following October [1883] found Vic in relentless pursuit of the last of the noble bison. It was estimated that there were about ten thousand buffalo left out of the many millions that were on the plains only a few years previous, and there were not less than two hundred white hunters in pursuit of them. This last remnant was located on the Cannonball River, North Dakota. The last of October, when the robes were prime, old Sitting Bull, chief of the Sioux, moved up from the Standing Rock Agency with his camp of one thousand warriors, squaws, and papooses for a final buffalo hunt.

In the winter of '82, old Chief Sitting Bull came back from Canada saying he was tired of living in a country whose chief was a squaw. Queen Victoria was on the throne when he fled after the Custer fight and surrendered to the U.S. government. He and his tribe remained at Fort Buford until spring and were removed to Standing Rock Agency.[8]

Runners from the Platte to Canada had informed the wily old chief that this herd was the last of the bison, and he wished to be in at the finish and also to secure what robes he could. Sitting Bull's camp pitched their lodges near where old Maddox murdered the young buffalo hunter. The first day's run netted the camp over a thousand robes, and when the first of the year arrived the buffalo were a thing of the past. At every railroad station from Dickinson west were thousands of hides stacked up awaiting shipment.[9]

Then commenced the gathering of bones and horns, which proved fairly remunerative. So great had been the slaughter of these animals that the bone gathering industry gave employment to an army of men. Old bones were used as fertilizer. Choice fresh bones were used in the refining of sugar. Frequently time and the elements had decayed the fastenings from the bodies of Indians dead of war or disease that were laid in trees. These bodies had tumbled to the ground and were gathered up and sold with those of the lordly bison.

———

"Ta-tonka-utonka-me-a-lo" (I am the great Sitting Bull),[10] said the old chief as he greeted Vic Smith and his three companions in 1875 at the crossing of Milk River, a few days after killing four woodchoppers about thirty miles from there on the Missouri River. As the boys were eating their lunch, seventy-five Indians appeared on the bank above them. There was no chance to escape, so the boys reached for their guns, intending to take as many Sioux along with them to the next world as possible, as they were certain that their time had come to quit breathing.

The Indians wore nothing but breechcloths and paint. They were the pick of the tribe and were headed for a camp of Crows who were on their way to Poplar Creek, of which the old chief had inside information. As the Sioux filed past, not one deigned to speak, but all looked plum sarcastic until old "Sit" himself, who came last, made the aforementioned remark as he slapped his fat paunch.

The white men said "how," and not another word was spoken as the warriors moved on. It was certainly a close call. When hostile Indians are on a certain object, they will not attack anyone except on the return trip, and to those traits in their character, the men felt truly thankful. The Sioux missed the Crows, but they killed Joe Lambert, a well-educated Indian, and his half-breed wife and four children. If they would have encountered the boys on the return trip, their scalps would have adorned the belts of the Indians.

———

Indians get their names in the following manner. When a boy turns sixteen, he dresses in a breechcloth and goes into the hills without a gun, bow and arrows, food or bedding for five days and nights. During his absence, any bird or beast he sees that takes his fancy he names after himself. Chief Sitting Bull told Vic he took his name after a large buffalo bull that he saw that had fallen over a cliff and had broken both of his [rear] legs and could only sit up on his haunches.[11]

Old "Sit" passed in his checks on Grand River, North Dakota, December 16, 1890.[12] He first saw the light of day on Willow Creek, Dakota, in 1838.[13] He was killed during the great ghost dancing craze, in which he figured as special representative of the great supreme being "Wacon" sent to wipe the paleface from the earth and restore it to the Sioux as it was before the white man desecrated it with his presence. The day the arrest occurred at the agency, three Indian police and three ghost dancers were killed, as the Indians resented the arrest and put up a stubborn scrap. During the melee, Sitting Bull received a bullet amidships that put him down and out for the count.[14]

A Trip Underground

In October 1883, while looking for some stray broncos that had sought seclusion among a small bunch of buffalo, Howard Eaton, the well-known cattleman of the Little Missouri River in North Dakota,[15] and Vic Smith discovered the horses fraternizing with a light cream-colored buffalo, a rara avis[16] among bison. No such thing as a pure white buffalo has ever been killed, but at rare intervals a cream-colored one has been found. Possession of such a robe is considered among the aborigines as "strong medicine," and one that money cannot purchase from them.

Eaton, a splendid shot and rope twirler of no mean ability, roped the cream-colored freak, which had about two rings on its horns; but the powerful beast snapped the lariat when Eaton's horse settled on its haunches to hold it and ran with its comrades. If Eaton could not capture the animal alive, he knew he could commandeer the skin; so he quickly overhauled the fleeing quarry and dropped it with a shot from his big revolver. A buffalo, like nearly all wild game, is tenacious of life, and this one proved no exception.

At the first prick of the knife in its leg, preparatory to skinning, the buffalo staggered to its feet and wobbled about. Eaton sprang on the animal's back in a spirit of reckless sport. In lieu of a saddle, Eaton clinched his spurs beneath the bison's stomach. The animal crow-hopped[17] about for a minute or so, until it got its bearings; then it gave an exhibition of pitching and stiff-legged bucking that no bronco ever exceeded. In blind fear and fury, the bull started on a three-minute clip for the bluffs, with Eaton hanging on for dear life.

Greatly to Eaton's relief, the animal, after a 200-yard spurt, stepped into a badger hole and threw Eaton into a bed of prickly pear. His separation from the buffalo's back was a relief, but not the landing in the bed of prickly pear. Vic spent an hour extracting the prickly spines with a pair of tweezers. The cacti removed, Eaton was himself again. In a couple of hours they found the lost broncos. Shortly afterward, an Indian shot the cream-colored buffalo. The honda[18] end of the lariat was still about its neck, which in the Indian's belief weakened the strength of its medicine, as he thought in its infancy the buffalo had been a pampered pet fondled by white squaws and papooses of the hated paleface.

That winter[19] Howard Eaton, a graduate from Pittsburgh University, who, with his brothers, had a large cattle ranch a few miles from Medora in the heart of the badlands, went with Vic after some mountain sheep. Howard, a whole-souled, generous fellow, and one of the best companions imaginable, wanted to capture a pair of mountain sheep for the Pittsburgh Zoological Park. About fifteen miles from their camp, they saw a dozen mountain sheep feeding on some high bluffs. As both were familiar with the country and knew about where the sheep would run, Howard stationed himself on a flat across which the sheep would have to go, while Vic went to head them that way.

On seeing Vic right behind them, the sheep took the direction intended for them, passing within fifty yards of Howard, cached behind a small knoll. Eaton dashed after them on his favorite cow horse, as they came abreast of him. After a quarter-mile run, Eaton swung his lariat. As the sheep were banded together, he succeeded in roping two at one throw. At that critical moment, his horse stepped into a badger hole and fell, rolling completely over Howard and injuring his ankle, which bothered him for years. Eaton hung onto the lariat until the frightened rams dragged him about seventy-five feet. Seeing it was impossible to hold two large mountain sheep with a crippled ankle, he let go. Besides losing the sheep, he lost his lariat. His horse would come to him when called, and soon Howard was in the saddle. Seeing nothing of Vic, Eaton concluded there was no place like home.

The badlands of the Little Missouri are full of coal seams from one to ten feet thick; some have been afire for thousands of years. When a mine is burned out, the earth is hollow and very dangerous to travel over. While Vic was approaching the mountain sheep, his horse's hind feet sank through the earth, then his body, and lastly his forelegs and head. It happened so quickly that Vic did not realize where he was until he struck bottom twenty-five feet down.

The place he had landed in was cone-shaped and about fifteen feet wide on the ground floor. His horse, a gentle one, had fallen on Vic's leg, pinning him to the ground. The hole through the skylight was only the size of the girth of the horse, and the rider had what is called a driving fit in going through. When Vic's eyes got used to the semidarkness, he looked around and discovered that the horse's tail was hanging in a well about five feet wide. Vic picked up a couple of small stones that had been dragged down when he fell and threw them into the bottomless well. He could hear the rocks bound from side to side of the well. He judged from the length of time they were going down and the sounds getting fainter and fainter that it was several miles to the bottom.

Vic caressed the horse and held the rein gently in his left hand so that the animal could not rise, for if he attempted, chances were he would fall back into the well and drag Vic with him as his foot was yet in the stirrup. When Vic dug the sand from under his leg with his knife, the weight of the horse would force the leg down into the excavation. The pain was severe as the circulation stopped. About 11 P.M., Vic got his leg out. Hopping in the inky darkness to the head of the horse, he took the horse by the bridle, clucked him up, and turned him around so that he would not back into the hole. Then Vic lay down on the saddle blanket and was soon in slumberland.

It was about ten o'clock the next day before circulation was restored. After a violent rubbing of his leg, the circulation came back with a rush. Vic then placed the horse under the skylight. Mounting the horse, Vic tied his lariat to the middle of his rifle and pitched it through the skylight, which was a broken V-shape. Then drawing in the slack, it set fairly across the small end of the opening. Overhanding to the surface, Vic grabbed onto a solid sagebrush and drew himself out into the sunshine again, which seemed brighter and more heavenly since his forced imprisonment overnight than it ever did before. He walked to Medora and found Eaton with a badly wrenched foot under the doctor's care. Vic got a fresh mount. Then with Tom Carruthers, a cowboy, and editor A. T. Packard, he went back to the place where he had lodged the night previous. With pick and shovel they tunneled in, and in three hours they had the horse out where the grass grew.

"Flopping Bill" and the Stranglers

In the spring of 1884, a half-breed stole two of Vic's horses and headed for Sun River. Vic searched for seven days before he located the animals and then found them in the possession of a cattleman. As Vic was well-acquainted with the cowman, he let Vic have the horses with the remark that some day he would get the "breed."

Among the Hegira of the Arkansas and Missouri output in the early days was an acquaintance of Vic's (Smith says acquaintance, not friend), a fellow known as "Flopping Bill." Bill Quantrill was his name,[20] and he was sired by a brother of the notorious guerrilla of that name. He always boasted of his relationship with his uncle.[21] Bill was no coward, but he was a big overgrown brute, a horse-thief, a cowboy, and a squaw man. He related with gusto the deeds of rapine and murder committed by the guerrillas at the close of the rebellion, as told to him by his father.

In '84 Reece Anderson, a wealthy cattleman,[22] hired Bill to exterminate an alleged band of horse-thieves. Bill gathered thirty cowboys and horse-thieves. With Anderson, they ravaged the country from the headwaters of the Musselshell River in Montana, to the capital of North Dakota. Through pure cussedness they killed, shot, and hanged any and all small parties they came across. That summer "Flopping Bill" Quantrill, with his gang of stranglers, hanged and shot eighty-three persons. Among the first and probably the only guilty one was

Louie Lusierre, the man who stole Vic's horses. As far as it could be determined, among the eighty-seven [eighty-three?] men whom they killed, not more than a half-dozen had ever committed a crime as heinous as petty larceny.[23]

At Poplar Creek, Montana, seven men came down the Missouri in a Mackinaw and remained overnight at the post. The "Stranglers" put in an appearance. As the head man of the Mackinaw party and Bill were enemies, Quantrill saw an opportunity to wreak vengeance on him. Bill got one of the "Stranglers" appointed deputy sheriff by the cattle association before starting, so everything would be done under the guise of the law. Quantrill demanded the men be turned over to him. The party of men in turn told Captain Rhode, post commander, they were miners and prospectors from the Bears Paw range and had harmed no one and would be lynched by the "Stranglers" as soon as a tree was reached. Notwithstanding their pleadings for protection, the weak-kneed Captain allowed the "Stranglers" to take the men and hang them five miles from the post at the first convenient cottonwood tree.

Below Fort Buford the "Stranglers" met Evan Bronson, son of Lieutenant [Nelson] Bronson of the fort. They hanged him a half-mile from the trail and confiscated his horse and saddle, as they did all the belongings of their victims.[24]

Above Strawberry Island, the "Stranglers" met Jack Williamson and Bill Close riding in a wagon. They were men of unblemished character; yet they were shot dead while on the wagon seat and their horses appropriated.

Near the mouth of the Musselshell lived a recluse of probably sixty years of age named Downs. He was a perfect gentleman and well-educated. Downs had a well-stocked library of choice books and a neat cabin. To get from the turmoil of business and breathe the pure mountain air for his declining years, Downs had chosen this spot. One forenoon, while Downs was enjoying his paper that he got from a passing steamer, "Flopping Bill" with a dozen ruffians came up and accused him of being in league with the "mythical" horse-thieves. The old gentleman was so astonished at the accusation that he could not speak. Finally, he merely denied it thinking it was a joke of a boozy gang of cowboys. Bill soon disabused his mind of that notion by ordering one of the gang to "noose" him. A rope was thrown over Downs's head, and his hands were tied behind him. He was then led to a shade tree in front of his house, and the free end of the rope was thrown over a limb. Asked if he had anything to say, Downs replied that to his knowledge he had never wittingly injured a person in his life and was perfectly innocent of anything that the cowboys now charged him with. It is futile to say more. The burly chief of murderers gave the word of command, and another innocent victim was added to Bill's long list of crimes.[25]

Reece Anderson, Bill's second in command[26] of the "Stranglers," died on the Musselshell. The rest of the gang fled the country through fear of their deeds, and Bill was gored to death by a steer in the stockyards at Kansas City, Missouri.[27] While the "Stranglers" were pursuing their work, Vic was at Medora, North Dakota, with the Marquis de Morès. Smith immediately sent word to Bill Quantrill that for that cold-blooded murder,[28] he would kill him on sight, unless Bill was the quickest on the draw. Though living in the same state, they never chanced to meet, and Bill's death ended the feud.[29]

Medora Days

In 1881, the Marquis de Morès, a French nobleman,[30] settled at the crossing of the Little Missouri, where the Northern Pacific Railroad crosses. He called the place Medora after his handsome wife, a daughter of New York banker [Louis] Hoffman.[31] The hamlet was six miles below Theodore Roosevelt's cattle ranch.[32] Roosevelt and many other notables enjoyed the hospitality dispensed at the Marquis's house.[33] De Morès erected buildings for a great packinghouse to rival the Armours.[34] He said that he sank a million dollars into the venture. The sinews of war, as it were, were furnished by his father-in-law.

On the appearance of the Marquis in the badlands, the cowboy element sought to put him out of circulation, considering him a mollycoddle and a tenderfoot. One day when the Marquis was a mile from town, three of the "bad cowboys" lay behind the tie piles alongside the track to ambush him. De Morès, both honorable and brave, returned the fire. He shot Riley Luffsey dead, shot the belt off "Wannegan," and shot a scalp lock from the head of "Cherokee."[35] When they were running away from him, de Morès caused them to stop and then turned them over to the sheriff. The Marquis had a hearing and was acquitted.[36] He gave the rifle with which he did the killing to Vic. De Morès had a silver scroll plate put into the cheek of the stock and engraved: "From Marquis de Morès to Vic Smith," and presented it to Vic, a relic he still retains.[37] Thereafter, de Morès commanded their respect, and before he left the country the cowboys were thoroughly convinced he was the proper dope.

The Marquis hired Vic at a salary of $150 per month for two years to accompany him or his wife or his friends on hunting trips. The position was a sinecure, as the Marquis was too busy to do but very little hunting. However, the Madam was frequently escorted by Vic about the badlands, where there was an abundance of deer, antelope, and mountain sheep.

At Medora, six miles below the ranch of Theodore Roosevelt, was the home of A. T. Packard, editor of the *Bad Lands Cow Boy*. He had an interest with Bob Roberts in a couple of large silvertip bears that they kept chained to a post. The bears weighed about eight hundred pounds apiece. When the 4th of July arrived, the cowboys, who were very patriotic and thirsty, untied one of the bears. Letting the bear drag a short chain, they compelled a "Gentleman from Africa" named Rastus to mount the animal with a broom for a flag. The cowboys, on their broncos, herded the bear and the man about the place for three hours, until they were both exhausted. It was a miracle that the bear did not eat or kill the man, as the bear was quite savage at most times, and no one had been on his back before that day.

At the time of the New Orleans Exposition, Vic was engaged by Alec McKenzie, mayor of Bismarck, to kill specimens of the different animals of North Dakota, to be mounted and taken there on exhibition. Vic succeeded in getting a group of each kind of animal in less than six weeks. He received a thousand-dollar check and a free pass to and from New Orleans for his work. Vic got as far as Chicago and dismounted from the cars to see his aged parents. After two weeks of sightseeing, his dreams of the exposition, together with his finances, were shattered. He negotiated a loan of fifty dollars from a "Sodomite," who took a mortgage on his life for the same, and started west again.[38]

Vic landed in St. Paul next morning with just enough money for a shave and breakfast. At the Planters Hotel, where he went for breakfast, he met the Marquis de Morès and borrowed fifty dollars from him. De Morès introduced him to Vice President Oakes of the Northern Pacific Railroad, and they all went to the theater that evening. After staying three days, Vic borrowed one hundred dollars more from the Marquis, and Mr. Oakes gave him a pass. That evening, Smith shook the dust of St. Paul from his feet and started for the badlands of the Little Missouri.[39]

After Vic returned to Dickinson, North Dakota, he found that Indians had stolen some horses he had left with Jap Hults and had run them over on the Owl River. Hults and Smith got two saddle horses and two packhorses and struck out after the Indians. Now that the buffalo were gone and the killing of whites was a risky business, the Indians turned their attention to stealing stock from the settlers.

It was sixty miles to the Owl River. On the second day, from a high bluff, with a field glass, the camp of the Indian horse-thieves was made visible. There were twenty lodges. The boys approached the camp within about three miles. They turned their horses out and awaited nightfall, as the country was too open to do business without being observed. About dusk, Vic and Jap saddled and started, as did a terrific storm.

After traveling about two miles, it got so dark it was impossible to discern each other when their horses were side by side. Balls of phosphorescent electricity as large as a man's fist were perched on the horses' ears. Each man could see the fireballs on his own horse but strangely could not see them on the animal of the other rider. This natural incandescent light threw a dim glow that did not extend more than six inches from the ears of the horses, something similar to the phosphorescent fishes of the sea. Though the night was pitch black, their unerring instinct brought them within two hundred yards of the lodges.

When within about thirty yards of the stream, Vic's horse broke through the surface on what was known as a soapstone flat[40] and went down so just his head was visible. At some previous time, the water had run into a badger hole and had cut a tunnel underground to the banks of the stream and had left a roof on top, about a foot thick. Vic, using a hatchet, and Jap, a butcher knife, they dug around the horse until the saddle could be removed. Upon removing the saddle, they put it on the packhorse and threw the pack away.

By this time, the storm had quit and the clouds were breaking away. They mounted their animals, but when they were about fifty yards away, the horse in the hole, seeing it was to be abandoned, nickered most humanely, as much as to say, "Why do you leave me for the Indians?" Vic's heart was touched, and he said he would stay with the horse. Jap said he would assist him. With a hatchet and a knife they broke down the roof of the tunnel until they got to the bank of the river, freeing the animal at daybreak. The boys had no time to go to the herd and get away with their own horses. Only for the above accident, they would have played even.

Hults was of a belligerent disposition, always making war medicine. Two years later in the streets of Dickinson, he was shot dead in a duel by Frank Chase. It seems that Chase had spoken lightly of a young woman known as the "buffalo cow," and hence the shooting.

The previous summer, Vic's foresight, being in fairly good condition, foresaw the finish of the bison, and he caught and sold seventy buffalo calves at fifty dollars per head. He kept six head, knowing that someday their increase would put him on easy street when they would be worth one thousand dollars apiece. Being a "lead pipe cinch" on a horse race, he sidestepped his good resolution and sold the calves to Howard Eaton, who now owns a fine game ranch in Wyoming. Suffice to say, Vic's "winnings" sunk him deep in the hole.

Though the buffalo were gone, Vic still retained his buffalo running horse, which could run just fast enough to keep him broke. The day after the horse race, Vic started for Killdeer Mountain, forty miles from Dickinson, where game was very plentiful. When ten miles out, he saw a large bull elk with fine large antlers. As the country was nearly level, he ran his horse alongside the elk. Just as he raised his gun to fire, his horse stepped into a badger hole, stumbled, and fell flat to the ground. As the horse struck Mother Earth, the rifle discharged. The bullet hit the horse between the ears and came out his nostril, killing the horse as quickly as if he had been electrocuted. He had fallen on Vic's leg, and for two hours Vic lay there until a Gros Ventre Indian chanced along. Hitching his lariat to the dead horse's leg, the Indian turned the animal over and released Vic. Vic gave the Indian a dollar to let him ride to camp, as his leg was too lame for walking. It was a small cayuse that the Indian had; yet the lazy cuss climbed behind Vic and made the poor pony carry double in spite of Vic's protests.[41]

Near Dickinson was a young hunter named Billy Huggins, who, on his native heath of Texas, was a cowboy. He had fallen in love with a young woman whose father had a ranch three miles from Smith's place. The course of true love seemed to have the right-of-way for a while, but the wheel of affection required more lubricating on her part to suit her ardent lover, and, once when her love thermometer was down to zero, she passed him the frozen heart.

Huggins dropped into Vic's windbreak on a Saturday and remained overnight. He ladled out his tale of grief and said he would go to her home the next day to try to effect a reconciliation, as he could not live without her. Vic accompanied him the next day within a mile of the house and left him to go into the city. It seems that Billy was prepared for any contingency, as he had made his will, which was found in his pocket after his death. After a few minutes of conversation with the young lady, he asked her to reverse her decision. She refused to be more than a sister. Billy walked out the door, sat on the stoop, drew his revolver, and shot himself dead. The will in his pocket gave her all his property.[42]

Bear Hunting with Madam de Morès

The Marquis and his wife were a handsome couple. She was superbly built and had a peach and cream complexion. Madam de Morès was also a splendid shot and a fine rider. In September 1885,[43] the Madam planned a bear hunt in Wyoming. She had Vic gather seven men as cooks, camp rustlers, and teamsters. Before starting on the trip, the Madam, who had a practical idea of how a campaign of that kind should be managed, had the wagons corralled and the tents pitched on her spacious lawn for her inspection. Turning to Vic one day, she inquired if anything was wanting. Vic informed her that another length of stovepipe was required.

Addressing her half-breed coachman, she said, "Sweet, proceed immediately to the warehouse and procure the third division of this sectional tube." Sweet's jaw fell open in astonishment. He fairly gasped until Vic elucidated by telling him that a length of pipe was needed, and Sweet procured the article. The Madam often used words of four and five syllables that ran seven and eight to the pound.

Next day the Madam, her maid, the men, the horses, the wagons, and the camp equipage were loaded onto the train. Two days later they unpacked at Coulson, near where Billings, Montana, now stands.

That night they camped near the grave of Billy Preston, Vic's chum of long ago, who was shot and killed over a measly cayuse by Dan Leahy in 1885.[44] Leahy committed suicide before the mob could reach him.

The following morning, the outfit pulled out for the Greybull River in Wyoming. Vic knew where there was plenty of bear, and that was what the Madam's red blood craved. "Liver-Eating Johnson" was to join the party at the crossing of the Sundance but failed to materialize, as he was down with the mountain fever. The Madam killed two fine antelope on the road up. On Stinking Water, they were obliged to ferry the wagons on a raft and swim the horses.

Next day they camped on Meeteetse Creek, a tributary of the Greybull. Fishing was the order of the day, and the next morning the Madam told Vic that she, Vic, and the cook would go alone into the mountains, leaving the rest of the party on the creek. The trio made camp that night at the head of the creek, where the Madam and Vic caught a fine mess of trout for supper.

When ready to return to camp, the Madam looked up and spied three cinnamon bear. Vic handed his rifle to the huntress, but before she could get action the three bear scampered into the brush. The next day, they discovered four bears turning over boulders in search of worms and bugs. They were all grizzlies. Cautiously approaching within two hundred yards of the beasts, they tied the horses and approached within seventy-five steps of the bruins. The Marquise took the first shot and missed. Then Vic fired and killed the old mamma bear. When the rest stopped, the Madam shot and killed two and wounded the third. Vic followed the wounded bear down the mountain and killed it. Madam de Morès felt in high spirits over her day's work.

When they arrived near camp, they saw a large cinnamon bear lying in the trail near camp. Before they could get a shot at him, the bear jumped into the brush and ran up the creek. Putting spurs to their horses, they gave chase. When within range, the Madam fired and wounded it. The enraged brute whirled around and ran down the ravine toward them. The Madam's horse broke loose again and ran for camp, but the intrepid woman did not move an inch. A moment more and the Madam fired, and the great brute rolled over and over, falling dead at her feet. Five skins were the trophies of the day, and she justly felt proud over the results of the day's sport.

On the next day, she concluded to hunt sheep "just for a change," she said. There is no easy work about this. Hunting bear is a pastime next to climbing precipitous mountains and jumping over rocks and chasms after the nimble-footed mountain sheep. Yet the Madam was equal to the occasion, and after several hours' chase up dark gorges and over projecting rocks, she bagged two fine bighorns. They took them to camp, adding their meat to the larder and their pelts and horns to the other prizes won by the Madam.

The next day, Vic was taken with mountain fever, which came pretty near getting away with him, but the careful nursing of the Madam brought him around the tenth day. In the meantime, the Madam had killed a fine cow elk, which the cook packed into camp. On the morning after Vic got on his feet, the Madam, in looking over the country with her field glasses, spied two bears upon the mountainside about a mile and a half distant. She wanted those bears, and although Vic was so weak he had to be helped into his saddle they soon were after them.

Since the wind was blowing a hurricane, they had to make a long detour to get leeward of them, on the opposite side of the mountain. Madam de Morès led the way, and they soon had their horses tied to boulders by picket ropes. Then they crept over the hill and soon found themselves within fifty steps of the feeding bears. The Madam fired twice, but the wind swayed her rifle and she missed. As the bears ran, Vic fired, putting a bullet in the back of the larger one, which dropped him instantly; the bear, however, dragged itself to the bottom of the mountain, where it hid in a cleft or cave in the rocks.

They followed up on the other bear and in their search had passed its cover. The bear came growling out of its hiding place and rushed past within a few feet of the Madam, dashing over a precipice at least one hundred feet high. The force of the bear's fall was broken by the top of a cedar tree, through which he crashed. When the bear struck the earth below in a pool of water and mud, he soon got to his feet and took to the willows lining the stream at the foot of the precipice. Mrs. de Morès said she must have that bear; so they took an elk trail leading around the precipice to reach the willows. They got there all right, but there was dangerous sport ahead.

It wouldn't do to go into the thick willows after it. The wounded bear was desperate and might prove an ugly customer to handle. Vic threw some rocks into the tangled undergrowth, and presently the bear came out within twenty feet of them, open-mouthed, making directly for the Madam. Here the daring courage of the woman was put to the test. If she faltered, she was gone. When the bear came out, Vic was stooping down after another stone and was unable to aid her, but she needed no help.

Without a tremor of a muscle, or quiver of a nerve, she raised her Winchester and fired. Bruin fell dead with a bullet in its brain. They then returned to the wounded bear they had left at the foot of the mountain beyond, which the Madam killed with a single shot. Then they went to camp. That evening the men brought in the skins of the dead animals. This ended the bear hunt. The next day they broke camp and started homeward after a four-week hunt. During that time, seven bear, several elk, two sheep, antelope, deer, and plenty of grouse, etc., fell before the Madam's deadly aim.

The following winter,[45] Vic again visited Chicago, and some parties at a gallery seeing his wonderful skill with a rifle advised him to give exhibitions on the stage with his gun. He traveled over all the large cities for six months. His traveling partner had nerve and supreme confidence in Vic's ability. From the parquet[46] viewers could see Vic clip a peanut from his partner's head with a 32-caliber rifle, a peanut from each ear, and one from his nose. At such dangerous shooting, the female portion of the audience would duck their heads until the crack of the gun and draw a sigh of relief when on looking up no gore could be seen spattered on the walls.[47]

In May, Vic gave his last exhibition at St. Paul and boarded the train for the Yellowstone. At Bismarck, the Marquis de Morès got on board and was heartily glad to shake hands with Vic, congratulating him on the reputation he had sustained in the cities, as the champion shot of the West.[48]

At St. Paul, Vic packed his sombrero and bought a derby. As he and the Marquis alighted from the train at Medora, they were met by a crowd of cowboys who drew their six-shooters and riddled Vic's hat with bullets, admonishing him at the same time that if he were ever guilty of a like offense that he, and not the hat, would pay the penalty, as no derby or plug hat was ever known to live if the wearer of the same showed himself on the platform at Medora.[49]

Victor "Vic" Grant Smith, about nineteen years old, in St. Louis.

COURTESY OF JIM METCALFE.

Vic Smith wearing cowboy attire, June 1883.
Smith is depicted in similar garb in the painting of Roosevelt
and Smith hunting buffalo (facing page).

This 25$^1/_2$- by-34-inch monochrome oil painting (circa 1890) titled *Theodore
Roosevelt and His Hunting Guide, Vic G. Smith,* is housed in the Theodore
Roosevelt National Memorial Park in Medora, North Dakota.
The artist is unknown. Roosevelt reputedly gave Smith this painting
in exchange for a painted moose horn. Upon Smith's death, Dr. F. C. Grover
in Duluth, Minnesota, acquired the painting as payment for his services.
Dr. Grover's son Eugene donated the painting to the park in 1959.

COURTESY OF THEODORE ROOSEVELT NATIONAL MEMORIAL PARK, MEDORA, NORTH DAKOTA.

Vic Smith with "Liver-Eating Johnson" in 1890. Both were scouts during the Sioux-Cheyenne Campaign in the 1870s.

Vic Smith, fifty, poses in hunting attire for a newspaper article
in the December 16, 1900, *Anaconda Standard.* Despite his age,
he still appears "as supple as a panther."

Vic Smith stands next to an elk-antlered chair near Anaconda, Montana.
The photo was probably taken circa 1892-1909 at his ranch.

COURTESY OF JIM METCALFE.

Richard Anderson took this professional photograph of Vic Smith in
Minneapolis, Minnesota, circa 1912-1925. Thomas H. Irvine donated the
photograph to the Montana Historical Society in 1957.

Elizabeth Robinson Smith, Vic Smith's mother, in 1881.

Rae Smith, Vic's younger brother, in 1892. Rae was sometimes called "Bill." As teenagers, Rae and Vic took a raft over Little Falls in Minnesota.

COURTESY OF JIM METCALFE.

Frank M. Smith in 1886. He may have been another of Vic's brothers, possibly DeMorny.

COURTESY OF JIM METCALFE.

The Sharps rifle was the favorite weapon of buffalo hunters on the ranges of eastern Montana and western North Dakota. The great northern buffalo herd numbered in the millions in the 1870s. By the end of 1883, buffalo hunters had reduced it to a band of a few struggling animals. Along with Sitting Bull, Smith was present at the last slaughter.

Author and editor Joseph Henry Taylor, one of Smith's trapping partners,
wrote several books about his own adventures on the western frontier.
The two men met sometime in the 1870s in North Dakota,
where they shot and trapped beaver for several seasons. Taylor related
the tragic story of the woman Smith abandoned.

COURTESY OF THE NORTH DAKOTA STATE HISTORICAL SOCIETY, BISMARCK.

While living in Medora, North Dakota, in the 1880s, the Marquis and
Marquise de Morès hired Vic Smith as their private hunting guide.

Howard Eaton, noted cattleman in North Dakota and later in Wyoming,
roped and captured wild animals with Vic Smith on several occasions.

COURTESY OF THE NORTH DAKOTA STATE HISTORICAL SOCIETY, BISMARCK.

During the Sioux-Cheyenne Campaign of 1876-1877, Colonel Nelson
Miles hired Luther S. "Yellowstone" Kelly as his chief of scouts. Kelly
chose Vic Smith as backup protection as he traveled through the
Indian territory searching for Sitting Bull and his band.

One of the more outspoken Vigilantes, John "X" Beidler promoted his own brand of law and order in the raw mining camps in southwestern Montana in the 1860s. Afterward, he spent time with Vic Smith and other frontiersmen on the eastern ranges of Montana.

A typical wolfer's cabin in the Missouri Breaks. When not killing buffalo, some frontiersmen shot and poisoned wolves for money. Using dead buffalo for bait, the wolfers would lace buffalo with poison and later collect the wolf carcasses. Some of these hastily built cabins had escape tunnels in case the men were attacked by Indians.

PART VI

ADVENTURES OF AN AGING FRONTIERSMAN

Odd Neighbors

Vic journeyed on to Big Timber [Montana] on the upper Yellowstone, where three days afterward the Marquis joined him for a bear hunt.[1] The Briggs and Ellis cattle ranch lent them several pack and saddle animals, and the next day they camped near Jack Nye's quartz mine and borrowed Jack's bear dog. In six days, the Marquis had shot three large bears. Then he returned home. Shortly afterward, de Morès went to France, where he fought a duel and killed a man.

In April 1896, the Marquis de Morès started for Algeria from Marseilles to join the Mahdi and was foully murdered. As his other chimerical and impractical schemes, he started with but one European and a handful of Arabs to help the Mahdi conquer the whole Bahrel Ghazel country for France and to check Cecil Rhodes's conception of British dominion extending from Cairo to the cape. On May 9, at the oasis of Gabès, he hired forty camels and their drivers, and the expedition started. His guides proved treacherous. Knowing the Marquis had money plenty, they attacked him with their rifles on June 8. However, they did not count on the fight that an American-Frenchman could put up; the Marquis killed eight natives and wounded four more. Seven of the assassins were afterward garroted for the crime.[2]

After the bear hunt with de Morès, Vic drifted upstream to Livingston, Montana, where he ran across Dick Rock, who was head buffalo skinner for him some years prior. Rock was located on Trail Creek, sixteen miles from town. Smith and Rock unearthed a large coal mine, which they sold to Colonel [George] Anderson, proprietor of the *Bozeman Courier*. The boys got $160 for it, and today it is worth over a million dollars. It was ever thus, the discoverer of a mine rarely reaping the benefit.[3]

Smith and Rock went into partnership guiding parties after big game in the mountains where there was plenty of bear, deer, elk, moose, etc. Vic left Dick at Trail Creek and went to Wyoming to look up the best section for taking out hunting parties the next fall. He went up through Yellowstone Park, out through Sundance, and onto Bridger Creek. The weather turned very warm. From morning until ten o'clock at night, mounted on his saddle horse and leading two packhorses, Vic had traveled up Bridger Creek through a sandy sagebrush country without a drop of water.

At that season of the year, for a long distance, the creek sinks, or as a native said, "It's upside down." It was a half-moon, but a trifle cloudy. While traveling along about 10 P.M., longing to find water for himself, dog, and horses, Vic spied the glint of water at the bottom of the creek. Instinct told the horses and dog of its presence, and they all rushed frantically down the bank to quench their thirst. In spite of Vic's shouts, the dog jumped into the puddle of water that was covered with a heavy yellow scum.

Vic found a convenient tree, tied the horses, and drove the dog out of the puddle, which was about two feet in surface measurement. He threw off the packs and took a camp kettle and a coffeepot and filled them with the elixir. In the semidarkness he could not see how clean the water was. He then scooped the hole clean and enlarged it with a shovel. After it filled, there was sufficient water for the horses.

Being hungry, Vic built a fire of sagebrush, made coffee, and cooked a pone[4] of bread in the frying pan. He left the "greaser"[5] in the skillet when he put in the dodger.[6] The fire died down by the time he sat on a packsaddle to dine. By the feeble light of the pale moon, he ate by the sense of feeling as much as he did by seeing. Smith relished the meal, but the *pièce de résistance* was when he got to the "greaser" that was cooked with the dodger. Vic bit the "greaser" in two with a relish in the twilight and reserved the balance for breakfast.

Vic made his shakedown but first killed a large rattlesnake that had engaged the dog's attention close to where he made his bed. About 9 A.M., Vic woke and started on his morning injection of slapjacks. Seeing something floating in the coffeepot, he examined it and found a half-dozen cooked frogs about one inch long, which he had dipped up the evening previous. On turning over the dodger of bread, he discovered the tidbit that he had so relished the evening before was a fried frog about two inches that he had bitten square in two.

Next day Vic arrived on the Stinking Water[7] and camped with Curley Rodgers for a week. A German lived about a mile from there and was annoyed greatly by bears and mountain lions stealing his pigs. The old man had put out poison several times, but it would disappear, and no wild animals were killed. One day he was putting out some strychnine in lumps of tallow for the pests. His son-in-law looked on and declared he would bet his father-in-law he could eat one of those baits and run a mile before it killed him.

His father-in-law covered the ten dollars. Curley was chosen as stakeholder and referee. The son-in-law swallowed the bait, poison and all, and started for the line fence a half-mile away. He rounded the turn and came back on the homestretch in fine shape, but when within two hundred yards of the goal, a strychnine microbe nailed him. He fell, doubled up, and screamed with pain. He was quickly carried to his father-in-law's house. The old German, being out of stomach pumps just then, requisitioned a huge syringe used on animals that were attacked with stomachache or bloating. Soon the stomach was relieved of its dangerous contents. The old man claimed the stakes, but young Dutch disagreed, as he was back to the house now and was not dead and had eaten the bait. Curley decided a draw and handed back the stakes to each man.

The old man had three nephews ranging from fourteen to seventeen years old who came down to take care of the ranch for a few days while he and his "frow" went to the city. The second evening the youngsters played cards. When one lost, he was obliged to take two pills. By midnight, they had used up two boxes of Beechams purgative pills. Vic happened to go over the next morning about nine o'clock and found the boys doubled up in exquisite agony from the effects of the pills. Each one was crying agonizingly for Ma, if only she were home. Vic handed out some local treatment and soothed their fears and sufferings, and that evening their uncle returned from the village.

One day Curley and Vic went up Pinos Creek, where there were plenty of fine brook trout. They soon caught all they wanted. Vic started for camp, taking the fishing poles with him, while Curley stopped behind to clean the fish. The cabin had a fireplace. During their absence, the fire had gone out, and a large mountain lion had jumped onto the dirt roof. Scenting some fresh meat inside, the lion entered by way of the fireplace.

Smith opened the door, stepped in, and closed the door behind him. His eyes did not see the lion in the dark corner where the meat hung. The lion sprang past Vic for the fireplace and was scrambling up the flue when Vic caught sight of its tail hanging down the opening. Vic grabbed the tail with both hands, knowing full well that the game would be gone before he could get his gun in the corner of the windbreak. He had a firm grip on the tail and hollered loudly for Curley, who quickly responded and came on a run. Seeing an angry lion on the roof, he ran into the cabin, but he could hardly refrain from laughing as he saw Vic being jerked up and down the chimney as the lion surged about in his frantic efforts to escape. Curley got his gun, stepped outside, and killed the lion.

One day their old German neighbor was breaking calves to nurse on a rubber nipple to wean them. He would first use his fingers for a few times dipped in a bucket of milk. The calves would crowd around him and suck his fingers even after the milk was all gone. One evening while walking from the barn to the house with a bucket of milk poised on his head, his fingers wet with milk, he felt what he supposed was a calf sucking his fingers. When the calf would not let go, he put the bucket down with the other hand. Looking for the calf, he found a large bull snake about nine feet in length and four inches through, clinging to his fingers. Although they are a perfectly harmless snake, it gave the old German a shock that he did not relish, especially when the snake wrapped its slimy folds about him while trying to disengage himself.

At one period, the parents of this old Teuton lived in a Dutch colony in New Mexico. His father was greatly annoyed at times by the Mexicans stealing his chickens, etc. One day his father, who was quite nearsighted, saw three Mexicans carrying away one of his favorite porkers that they had slaughtered. His dad grabbed the rifle, cut them off, and killed two of them. He then returned to the house and seemed to regret but one thing: that one man escaped. He said if he had his glasses on he would have got him also.

Years later, Curley Rodgers was a guide for Mr. Claflin, the dry goods merchant and millionaire of New York, and his wife, on the head of Tom Miner Creek, which flows into the Yellowstone below Yankee Jim's Canyon. One day Curley and Mrs. Claflin were on a high crag after mountain sheep. He was about fifty yards in advance, when a lightning bolt struck him, and he was hurled from the cliff down a sheer descent of five hundred feet. Mrs. Claflin was so shocked that she was unable to return and probably would have perished, but her friends were watching them approach the sheep from the camp and immediately rushed to the rescue. Curley's body was recovered and buried, but the accident had such a depressing effect on the party that the hunt was declared off, and they returned to New York.[8]

After Vic returned to Trail Creek, Rock and he went east of Yellowstone Park and wintered on Hell Roaring Creek, two miles from the Park line. They had great success that fall and winter, taking out parties after big game. Bears were plentiful, and there was no end to elk, sheep, deer, etc. One day, a dozen Bannock Indians (the squaws all riding gent fashion), with their families on their way to visit the Crows at Custer Agency, passed Vic's camp. Judging from the number of dogs and papooses, they seemed fairly opulent.

About an hour afterward, a toboggan drawn by a large dog with a papoose wrapped up in blankets on the sled returned. It was a chilly day, so the dog was tied up and the papoose brought into the cabin to warm up until the mother returned for it, as it would be beneath the dignity of a coffee-cooling[9] siwash to trudge back after a measly papoose. The baby soon thawed out, and contrary to the usual custom of Indian babies it commenced to cry. A bacon rind was given to the papoose, then a sugar titty,[10] but still it exercised its lungs in a frenzy.

Vic rushed out and brought in the large Newfoundland dog of the female persuasion that belonged to Rock, the two little puppies following. After the dog was muzzled and thrown down on the dirt floor, the two puppies and the young aborigine scrambled for the fullest teats. The boys dubbed the kid Romulus. In about an hour, the mother returned to claim the maverick. As the boys did not have the youngster branded, they cheerfully parted with it.

At Christmastime, the trout would not bite. Rock, who was well-versed in the use of giant powder, went to the river at a large eddy and threw a charge of giant powder with a time fuse into the pool, expecting to get enough fish for a Christmas dinner. A favorite dog went along and watched Rock throw the dynamite weighted with a stone. The dog, being used to retrieving sticks thrown into the water, swam out in spite of Rock's frantic calls and received the concussion when directly over the charge. Of course, the dog was killed, but no fish were secured.

That night Jack Baronette, chief of scouts in Yellowstone Park, camped at Vic's windbreak. Jack, who was well-educated, clever, and an old-time Indian fighter, related with droll humor how two years before Jim Toole had been married to a buxom, handsome ranch girl.

Before the marriage, Toole, notoriously shiftless, had secured a position for the bride as cook at a sawmill fifteen miles down the Yellowstone on Mill Creek.

The day after the nuptials, as Baronette was driving along in a box-seated buggy, he overhauled Toole and the young bride trudging along, hand in hand, on the road toward the sawmill. She was carrying her shoes and stockings in one hand, as she did not know when she would get another pair. With an economical mind, she walked barefoot, while Toole carried a seamless sack containing their worldly possessions. Baronette, who saw a chance to play a joke on Toole, told the perspiring bride to jump in and ride. The weather was very warm. Greatly pleased with the opportunity, she hopped in, but Jack refused to let Jim in, saying that the buggy would accommodate only the bride and the sack. Jack was driving a fine span of roadsters, which he clucked up at a five-minute gait. It was about twelve miles farther to the mill, and Jack never slackened speed.

Frequently, the bride would look back and wave her handkerchief at her husband, who was bravely keeping up his gait, while dripping with perspiration and covered with dust. When within two miles of the journey's end, the bride looked back and saw Jim's tongue hanging out, lolling from side to side, with drool hanging from the corners of his mouth. She wiped away a tear and said to Baronette, "Gawd, there is great leather in Jim." There was, as Jim was only three hundred yards behind the buggy, and up-to-date they have thirteen children.

Twenty miles farther up was Cooke City: a mining camp, a store, two saloons, a post office, and about sixty inhabitants with unlimited expectations. A young fellow named Jones living there was married to a splendid young woman, and they possessed a ten-month-old baby. Jones was a very shiftless fellow and in fact a living example of "nothing doing." He seldom had a dollar. For a cradle, he used a cracker box with rough rockers nailed on. The baby fell sick, and after a few weeks of suffering its spirit took flight. Vic was at Cooke City that day and was not at all surprised when Jones knocked off the rockers and used the cracker box for a coffin. Snow had been falling steadily for about ten days and was about seven feet deep. Everyone who followed the cracker box to the little mountain graveyard that day was obliged to do so on snowshoes.

Elk Ranching

The following spring, Smith and Rock went to Henrys Lake, Idaho, on the west side of Yellowstone Park. There they took up a handsome location for a game ranch.[11] Game was plentiful. Vic kept busy guiding Eastern parties after big game, while Rock and a couple of hired men built good log houses and corrals and fenced in 140 acres with a 10-foot high fence that was game-proof. Game never got over it, but Vic frequently saw elk, in their endeavors to jump over the fence, land with their forefeet on top and fall back again.

Vic and his partner Rock broke several teams of elk and hauled logs for firewood with them, but as a draft animal they never could be considered a brilliant success. One cow moose was broken to harness and cart and was a clever roadster and very docile.[12] Rock and Smith remained in partnership for five years. In that time, they caught and shipped to Eastern parks over five hundred full-grown elk, deer, moose, and antelope, etc.[13] Vic was the first man who got next to the scheme of catching big game by running them down on snowshoes.[14]

Elk were worth $85, F.O.B., moose $200, deer $30, mountain sheep $150, and bears, of which they always had quite a number, were worth from $20 to $50. They sold 157 elk to the late multimillionaire Austin Corbin for his game preserve in New Hampshire. Not long after purchasing elk and other animals from Smith, he was driving over his great game preserve in his carriage when a wild elk of the late consignment ran toward his team. The team took fright and ran away, and Mr. Corbin and the driver were dashed to death.[15]

A mile below Vic's game ranch lived a white man named John

Smith, dubbed "Captain John," and his Piute wife "Pocahontas."[16] She was a full-blooded Piute Indian, a daughter of old Piute Chief Winnemucca of Nevada,[17] who long since has been gathered to his fathers. "Pocahontas" had a fair education and was a good moral wife and a credit to many whites. One midwinter day when the snow was at least five feet on the level, Vic mounted his skis and headed for the big springs several miles below the lake, where he knew some bull moose were wintering.

He passed within a half-mile of "Captain John's" house, when a shout caused him to turn. On going into the house, Vic found "Captain John" quite sick with pneumonia. Vic did the chores, split the wood, went back home to get some medicine, and sent his hired man to remain overnight with the sick man. The third day, "Captain John" died and was buried about two hundred yards from the house, alongside the trail where General Howard followed wily Chief Joseph of the Nez Perce and his tribe in 1877.[18]

"Pocahontas" was the chief mourner, and her honest and sincere grief was pitiful to see. Her grief was so great that she begged to be shot and cremated then and there on the grave of her husband so that she might join him in the world beyond. The Indian stoicism of her race was broken for once. Poor "Pocahontas," who "seen God and heard Him in the wind," gave way to grief similar to her more civilized and enlightened sisters. It was the custom of her people ages ago for the wife of a warrior to sacrifice herself at the grave of her buck.

She had a sister, Miss Sarah Winnemucca, a very bright woman, educated in the East, who came to visit the following season. Miss Sarah, who was about thirty-five years old, had scouted for General Howard during the Bannock and Nez Perce wars. Sarah did good service and got great credit from her commanding officers. She wrote and published a book, *Life Among the Piutes,* and traveled over the states giving lectures, selling her book, and devoting the proceeds to the betterment of the Piutes. Sarah died at Henrys Lake and was buried beside "Captain John."[19] She was a noble example of her race.

"Pocahontas" passed on to the happy hunting grounds in October 1920.[20]

Fishing for trout through the ice in the winter at the lake was a lucrative business. The fish were salmon trout, and the catch was something enormous for a season. Taking three hundred to five hundred fish daily by one person with hook and line was frequently done. One day when the fish would not bite, Vic thought he might snag them, as plenty of fish could be seen at the mouth of the creek through the ice. He took a three-foot length of steel wire and bent the end into a hook with a three-inch curve. Then he built a shade over the hole in the ice with some blankets to exclude the bright sun and caught 1,327 in one day. At present, fishing for market, especially game fish, is prohibited in nearly every state.

One day Vic saddled his horse. Leading a pack animal, he started for the east fork of the Madison about fifteen miles. Halfway there he remembered he forgot to bring salt to season bear meat with, as that was what he was after, having seen the track of a large one the day before. Fortunately, at the crossing of a small stream, he saw a Mormon with a span of burros attached to a light wagon. The man was unhitching and preparing to camp overnight, when Vic rode up and asked, "Can I get a handful of salt?"

The Mormon, who was quite deaf, replied, "Camp here, why certainly. I'll be glad of company for the night," and he kept on unhitching the burros.

Vic, catching his eye again, shouted, "Can I get a little salt?" Again the man extended the invitation to dismount and camp. Vic then slid off from the cayuse, walked up close to the man's ear, and shouted "salt."

The man answered, "A little louder, please, I am a trifle hard of hearing."

Again Vic yelled "salt" at the top of his voice.

The man said, "Pshaw, there must be something wrong with your vocal machinery." He walked over to the wagon and dug out an ear trumpet from a box that was partly filled with potatoes. He put the horn to his ear, but in the mouth of it was firmly wedged a large potato that had been jolted in solid by the rattle of the wagon. Taking in the humor of the situation at a glance, Vic grasped the horn with both hands, and yelled "salt" until he was nearly hoarse.

The Mormon then took down the horn and gazed in blank astonishment at Vic, who burst out laughing and turned the horn so that the man could look in the large end. Without a word or even a smile, the Mormon calmly dug out the spud, put the horn to his ear, and said, "What did you want?" Vic made known his request, when the Mormon said, "Salt. Well why didn't you say so?"

Vic went on and before dark he had killed the bear, a very large cinnamon. Next day Vic took two doctors from Alabama on a hunting trip for big game, about twenty miles from his ranch. They shot elk, deer, sheep, and antelope in plenty. One evening, one doctor shot a large bull elk that ran into a lodgepole thicket before it fell. Years before a storm had blown down the trees, and they were criss-cornered in all directions, and the lodgepoles had grown up since the hurricane.

Smith saw the tracks of a large cinnamon bear near where the elk fell and rightly conjectured that bruin would be on hand after the hunters left. Next morning Smith and one of the doctors repaired to the windfall and walked along a fallen tree that was fully ten feet above ground, lying across other logs. Approaching carefully, they saw the bear, a monster, rise up on his hind legs not more than twenty feet distant. When a rifle ball struck the bear fairly in the center of the breast, contrary to custom, he ran away, when he might as well have grabbed the hunter, as the recoil from the gun caused him to lose his balance and fall from the log to the ground. The men then took up the trail, followed it by the blood for two hundred yards, and found the bear dead. On skinning and opening the body, they found the heart torn to pieces by the 40-82 bullet, exploding the theory of those who think that any animal shot fairly in the center of the heart will never run twenty feet.

The following day, the other doctor shot a mountain sheep through the heart, which ran nearly a hundred yards before dropping. At the end of three weeks, the party was obliged to go back to Alabama. On their return to the lake, they stopped for dinner at Marble's ranch.[21] Marble's son had just come in from the cliffs, where he had been after mountain sheep, and he related his story of "good judgment" but poor luck.

He said while following a couple of large rams, he came onto them about one hundred yards away. They stood side by side, with a tree of about ten inches in diameter between them. He said he soliloquized thus, "Now, Marble, you know if you shoot at one of them sheep, you will miss it at that distance, but if you shoot at the tree between them, you misses the tree and hits one or the other of the animals; so I drew down old 'meat in the pot' for the center of the tree, and bang, I'll be blankety blanked if I didn't strike that tree square in the center, and away flew the sheep." He apologized for aiming at the tree by saying, as a general thing his "line shots" were a little to one side.

The next winter was a severe one in Centennial Valley, Montana, and nearly all the stock perished. Vic camped most of that winter with Jack Lynch, who had a large cattle ranch and was a nephew of mining millionaire Marcus Daly.[22] Jack was a jovial honorable fellow and in those days always ready for a drinking bout or a scrap. The consequence was that every spring Daly would get a tale of woe from Jack about the loss of stock, terrible winter, etc., with a request that Marcus dig deep to help him on his feet again; otherwise, he would have to hold up a train. Daly was always generous to Jack and invariably sent him the necessary to start the cattle business again. The leg-pulling business prospered for a few seasons, until Daly got wise. Then Jack left the ranch and rode away with his worldly possessions tied up in a nose bag fastened behind the saddle.

One day Vic and Jack came home after dark. On lighting the lamp, they saw a large skunk on the bed that had crawled in through the cat hole in the door. Vic started to light the lantern, intending to follow slowly toward the skunk, which could then be induced to go out through the cat hole into the cold world. But Jack, who had been wrestling with a quart bottle, unnoticed by Vic, seized a poker and dealt a death blow to the animal. The stinkpots of the Chinese were as the balm of a thousand flowers compared to the aroma that filled the room. Smith and Lynch took refuge in the stable for the night. As the bedding was thoroughly impregnated with the fumes, they could not use them and had to play freeze out through the night.

Jack had a bulldog that weighed about sixty-five pounds and was very savage. Vic and Jack were away one day, and on their return they found an Indian agency blanket covered with blood at the door. The dog seemed more than unusually vicious that day and jumped onto Jack and sank his teeth into his shoulder. Jack pulled his gun and shot the dog dead. Jack's dog had dragged the blanket over the snow from the hills. Taking the backtrack of the trail about two miles into the hills, the men found an Indian terribly lacerated in a thicket that the dog had attacked. They agreed that mum should be the word, and the affair was never mentioned until a year ago.

One of the most intelligent and polished men in the valley was a Virginian named "Wood Tick" Jones. He was well-off in cattle and horses and had a fine ranch. One day Vic went to see "Wood Tick," but he was absent in the hills. About dusk, "Wood Tick's" son looked out and saw their large and hungry foxhound coming over a knoll. He rushed in with the intelligence that "Dad is coming, for I see the dawg."

The young man proceeded to cook supper, as the feminine portion of the ranch had gone to a quilting. He was in the act of putting a very large slice of meat into the frying pan, when the foxhound rushed in, grabbed the meat from the boy's hand, and had it halfway down his throat in a flash. "Son" kicked the "dawg" in the slats and pulled vigorously on the steak. While the "dawg" opened his mouth to yelp, he lost his grip on the meat. The canine was assisted outside by the young man's boot, and the meat was dropped into the skillet to fry with no apologies. Just then Mrs. Jones returned from the quilting and saw the conflict over the meat and said it gave her "nervous prostitution to witness such doins."

Vic and Rock ran the game ranch at Henrys Lake until 1890, when Vic sold out to Rock. Rock took care of the ranch, breaking horses, etc., while Vic killed the game, took out hunting parties, and acted as guide.[23] They made good money. Rock took unto himself a wife of Teutonic breeding, and Vic went to the Big Hole country. Among other animals on "Yellowstone Vic's" game ranch at the lake were a half-dozen buffalo. One very large and savage bull known as Sampson corralled Rock and gored him so frightfully that he lived about only fifteen minutes.[24]

Rock's widow quickly threw his memory and her "weeds" in the discard and married again before the hair had slipped on poor Dick. The widow roped for a fresh victim and succeeded in throwing her riata of fascination over the head of Jack Fish,[25] a cowboy. She dragged him to the matrimonial hitching post and procured a marriage permit, while the sky pilot[26] applied the branding iron, as it were, and fastened the unfortunate couple with a diamond hitch, and they lived happily ever after.[27]

Predator Control in the Big Hole

Vic continued to catch large game for shipment several years afterward. When not doing that, he hunted bear, wolves, and other large game, or guided parties in search of big game, at which he always was successful. In the Big Hole country, the bears were numerous, and the cattlemen induced Vic to come there and clean them up, as the animals killed hundreds of head of stock every season.

For many years, there was a bounty of $3 to $5 on coyotes and from $5 to $25 on coyotes and wolves paid by the state stock association. Vic had a hybrid wolf and a hybrid coyote that were very tame and intelligent that he taught to act as decoys. He would mount his bronco, sally out to the rolling hills and buttes, and dismount. With a powerful field glass, Vic would scan the surrounding country. Soon espying a stray coyote or wolf, Vic would point out the game to his hybrids. If too far for their vision, they would take the direction. After Vic rubbed a few drops of a certain decoction on them, the hybrids would go. On finding the game, they would fraternize with it. Invariably, the animal would return with the hybrid to Vic, who, concealed, would kill the game when within range. He got his hybrids by digging them out of dens when they were young pups, the mother having made the acquaintance of some shepherd dog.

There were some very large bear in the Big Hole country. One huge grizzly that he killed weighed 1,300 pounds and had decimated the herds for nearly ten years. The bear was well-known to the ranchmen, and many a round they had with him. Although he always won out, he frequently had to carry away a few ounces of lead. After Vic shot him and removed the hide, he found thirteen bullets encysted in the hide on the opposite side from their entrance. The bear had been trapped sometime, as all the toes were gone from one hind foot. He was named old "Moccasin Foot," and the cattlemen offered $150 reward for his death. Vic killed him the second day after striking his trail. In addition to the hides and meat, the cattlemen paid Vic $10 bounty on any bear, large or small, that he killed. Consequently, the bear have not bothered the stockmen for several years, as he wiped out most of them.

Once as Vic hiked through a forest in Idaho, with his packhorse following, he climbed atop a six-foot fallen tree trunk to get a better view of where he was headed. As he looked down, Vic saw a bear that he had just roused from its bed. He looked down at the bear, and the bear looked up at him. Vic's gun was on his packhorse, and the only weapon he had was a hunting knife. Vic slid down the tree to get his gun. Meanwhile, the bear reared up on its haunches, placed its forefeet on the tree trunk, and began to growl. At the sight of the bear, the horse took fright and fled, with Vic running after it. Vic ran for about one hundred yards and looked back at the bear, which remained at the log because it could not climb it. Vic caught up with his horse several hours later.[28]

Once in '87 while in Wyoming, Vic had a thrilling experience with mountain lions that he does not wish to repeat. Near Big Medicine Hot Springs on the upper Stinking Water, now a famous health resort, Vic shot a large bull elk and went to camp to get his packhorses. On his return, he saw signs of two mountain lions that had been feeding on the freshly killed elk. They sneaked away upon hearing him approach. He cut off the hindquarters and head of the game and securely loaded them on the packhorse. Mounting his saddle animal, with the pack animal following, he started back to camp. Hearing a racket, Vic looked back just in time to see the pack animal go down, with a large mountain lion clinging to its head.

Vic threw up his gun and put a ball through the lion, but he was too late to save the life of the pack animal, as its neck was already broken. A moment afterward, before he could reload his rifle, the other lion bounded from the side of the trail and pursued Vic. Smith gave his horse the spur, but the lion landed on the horse just behind the saddle with its forepaws. With one blow, the lion raked the clothes from Vic's back and badly lacerated the hips of the horse. The horse kicked furiously, landing a hoof in the lion's solar plexus, which caused it to relinquish its hold and land in the middle of the trail.

The horse, thoroughly frantic by this time, kept bucking and pitching so that Vic could hardly retain his seat. It was in an open glade that the encounter occurred. Vic, wanting to kill the lion but unable to shoot from the panic-stricken horse, took a chance on being crippled by springing off the bucking animal. As a result, he badly bruised his leg. He gained his footing just in time to see the lion, which had gathered wind and courage, making thirty-foot bounds after the horse. Vic put two bullets through the lion before he had gone fifty feet.

When Vic was thirty years old,[29] he married Miss Eugenia Dengler,[30] a comely girl of Montana stock.[31] It was no puppy love this time. It was the full-grown dog.[32] She was at home on a pitching cayuse and had engaged in several riding contests in which she invariably took first prize. An expert with the gun, she had handled a rifle from childhood and had killed plenty of small game. After they were married, Eugenia would often accompany Vic every summer just for health and pleasure, far back up in the mountains, where big game and fish were plentiful. There they would pitch camp. They did no killing, as it was closed season, except now and then Vic would bring a haunch of venison into camp. Sometimes Eugenia would remain with Vic in the fall on a hunt, and then she was as eager for the chase and was nearly as successful as Vic. In the open season she frequently killed elk and deer, and no less than five bear have fallen to her rifle.

As a general rule, the north side of the main range of the Rocky Mountains is nearly perpendicular for a distance of several hundred feet, all cliffs, crags, and deep seams. One day, Eugenia spied a large white buffalo wolf, about three hundred yards above camp, following the trail of a bunch of white goats that had passed half an hour before. Dressed in shirtwaist[33] and knickerbockers in order not to impede the free movement of her limbs, Eugenia snatched her rifle and climbed within a hundred yards of the wolf and gave him a fatal shot. In his death struggle, he rolled over the cliff as she got within a few steps of him. To her dismay, she saw her quarry pitch from crag to crag, until it had landed in the valley hundreds of feet below, with the chance that the skin would be ruined.

She signaled to Vic, who climbed to the comb of the Rockies. She pointed to about where the body of the wolf was when she last saw it rolling down an incline to the shore of a small body of water. It was impossible for anyone to climb down the face of the cliff. Vic made a detour of about four miles, crawling down a mountain sheep trail and back around under the cliff to where the dead wolf lay by the small lake.

Vic could plainly see Eugenia on the comb of the range, silhouetted against the sky. While from Eugenia's high position, Vic appeared to her about the size of a woodchuck. Vic peeled the bark from the wolf and found enough of it left for a memento. As the face of the cliff did not look so hideous from the ground looking upward, Vic thought he would save the long detour by climbing straight up. Tying the wolf pelt across his shoulders, he started to ascend the almost perpendicular face of the cliff. He had not proceeded far when he found it necessary to remove his shoes to enable him to secure a foothold onto the smooth rocks. It was a most foolhardy and hazardous undertaking, and not again in a thousand times could it be done. Slowly and laboriously picking his way upward, Vic found that the greatest caution would have to be exercised if he ever reached the top. It was so near perpendicular that Eugenia, on the comb of the Rockies, awaiting his coming, neither could see nor hear him climbing painfully upward, until over three hours had elapsed. He frequently found himself clinging to jutting rocks. Twice during the climb, when relying on a small rock for a hold it gave way, and Vic found himself balanced between the sky and certain death below.

Daylight faded into darkness, and like the boy on the burning deck Eugenia held to her vigil, waiting with a sinking heart Vic's coming. At no time did Vic dare look down, as that would ensure certain death. It was utterly impossible to go back, as the first move to retrace his steps would send him bounding from crag to crag, a shapeless mass to the bottom. Nothing but an iron nerve such as a steeplejack's could save him. Several times he thought it was all off with him, but either the Lord pulled with him, or the devil cares for his own. He never knew which, and finally he found himself about thirty feet from the top. His further progress was barred by a perpendicular wall, or rather the top was farther out in space than where Vic rested on a small six-foot-square surface. He shouted, and for the first time in several hours Eugenia knew that Vic was in the land of the living. He told her he could climb no further and to go to camp to get a fifty-foot picket rope.

Scrambling down to camp, falling over boulders and logs, and once tripping and falling prostrate alongside a large porcupine that struck viciously with his quill-armed tail, Eugenia finally got to camp. She was bruised and bleeding, but thankful to her maker that Vic was alive and that she could aid in his rescue. With the rope, she clambered back to the comb of the range. Driving a stake in the cleft of the rocks, she fastened the rope to it and tossed the other end over the cliff to Vic, who lost no time in ascending hand over hand to the top, but there he stuck, as he could not get over the edge. Bringing up the slack of the rope, he fashioned a stirrup and rested for a minute. Then putting fear into Eugenia's heart by telling her that if he could not get up at the next effort he would have to hang there and die, Vic exerted all his strength, and she got him by the collar. Thoroughly frightened at the certain death he said was his unless she did her best, it gave her superhuman strength, and in a few moments they were in each other's arms—a great relief after flirting with the undertaker for over three mortal hours.

Two months later, W. S. Turner, a captain on the federal side through the rebellion, hired Vic and his outfit to guide him on a hunting trip in the Big Hole country. As cook and horse wrangler, he took along Ben Osborne, the best trapper in Montana. On the head of Wise River, they got elk and deer. Then they trekked to the main range of the Rockies, forty miles west, in search of mountain goats and grizzlies. They followed an old surveyor's trail that was nearly obliterated, having been made thirty years previous. They camped in an ideal spot, where the spoor of game was abundant. At that time, the limit on goats was eight.

The next day, they found fifteen goats lying on a small plateau among the cliffs, and the men reared their packs skyward. Approaching the goats cautiously, the Captain shot four fine billy goats. A large one struggled to the edge of a cliff. As it was disappearing, Vic, who had not fired a shot yet, put a bullet through it. The goat toppled from the cliff, falling at least one hundred feet. Its body bounded from crag to crag, until it landed in the basin nearly a half-mile below, beside a beautiful mountain lake on the lower side of which was a heavy growth of fir and mountain tamarack. After skinning the goats, they packed the hides and heads down to camp. Since it was impossible to get to the goat down below, unless by a long detour, they left it until the next day.

On horseback next morning, they followed the old surveyor's trail and went through the pass and around to the lake where the dead goat had rolled. Before they got to the spot, Vic saw fresh signs of an enormous grizzly bear. Leaving their horses, they approached carefully and found that the bear had dragged the goat away. Following the trail carefully for about a quarter-mile, they found bruin covering up the goat carcass with leaves and grass, intending to come back and finish it for supper.

The Captain was an excellent shot but carried only a common .44 Winchester. His first shot struck the bear in the shoulder. With a deep growl of anger, the bear lunged toward him. It was not until Turner fired seven shots into its huge body did the bear drop. When but fifteen feet away, the last shot struck him in the eye. Osborne, hearing the shooting, soon came up with the horses, peeled the hide from the carcass, and all hands returned to their wickiup. The next day, the Captain shot four more billy goats. As the limit was killed and Captain Turner had enough, they all returned to camp and next day trekked for home.[34]

More Bear Tales

In June 1896,[35] Vic, with his "Rib," hitched up a span of half-broken broncos and made moccasin tracks in and around Yellowstone Park. The second night, they camped at Virginia City, Montana, which in 1862 had the richest placer gold diggings in the world. There in '62 and '63, the miners rose in righteous wrath and hanged [Henry] Plummer, the sheriff, and about three score[36] road agents who had robbed and murdered many people. Plummer was the leader of the road agents while pretending to be a law-abiding sheriff. An unfinished log building stands there yet on the ridgepole of which they hanged five agents at once.

When gold was discovered at Alder Gulch, Montana, desperadoes crowded in and terrorized the country. Murder and robbery occurred almost daily, until the patience of the populace was exhausted. A vigilance committee formed, and a few dozen of the tough element were strung up, and the rest were compelled to leave the country.

J. X. Beidler was chosen as chief of the vigilantes,[37] and well and thoroughly he did his work. He was a fearless man, an expert with a revolver, generous to a fault, a genial companion, but implacable to the enemies of the law. Beidler served the territory as deputy marshal for many years and also after Montana became a state.[38] He was a great friend of Vic Smith's in later years.

Beidler related his experience in pursuit of a lost cabin mine that was interesting. Every state has a legend of a lost cabin where an old miner came to some camp with a packhorse loaded down with gold nuggets. He took sick with mountain fever or delirium tremens, and on his deathbed drew a rough sketch of the locality, the richness of which would make the wealth of Midas look like thirty cents.

Beidler said an old prospector produced a map and made him believe that his knowledge of the location was the only genuine one, and all others were base imitations. On the strength of the dope that was thus ladled out, Beidler stood good for four packhorses, two saddle horses, and provisions for a trip to the mythical lost cabin. The location of the cabin was around the headwaters of the Clearwater, the roughest country in Montana.

Ten gallons of old bourbon were included in the outfit, to ward off the effects of any chance snakebites. They left Bozeman, Montana, in April. Every evening and morning during their wanderings for six months, "Old Enthusiastic," as "X" dubbed him, would smooth off a three-foot space in the sand. With his forefinger, he would map out the trail. As the sign of snakes grew more plentiful and the sign for the lost cabin more remote, they took longer and more copious drafts from the demijohn. At the expiration of six months, the bottled inspiration and all hopes of finding the cabin were gone. In sorrow and thirst, they returned from their journey. The only thing accomplished on the trip was the loss of "Enthusiastic's" finger, worn off up to the middle joint by his persistent map drawing in the sand.

Vic and Beidler traveled together on many hazardous trips between '75 and '85, but the good Lord always pulled with them. "X" always expressed a desire to be buried at the "big tepee," as he called it, when he quit this earth, and his monument can be seen where he wanted, at Helena, Montana.[39]

A few nights after their stay in Virginia City, Vic and Eugenia camped at Yankee Jim's on the Yellowstone River. It was a tollgate. There Vic related to his "Rib" how a few years prior he came to the locked gate and in a spirit of hilarity refused to pay Jim the toll.[40] Vic jumped into the river with his horse. Meanwhile, Jim, who was pretty drunk, staggered into the cabin and returned with his Winchester. He emptied the whole magazine of sixteen shots at Vic, who was swimming alongside his horse, making for the opposite shore. Fortunately for Vic, Jim was too drunk to shoot straight.

Next evening they camped at Old Faithful, the geyser that gets seasick every hour and gives up the contents of its stomach. Every evening the wild bear come from the timber and devour the slops from the hotel kitchen. They counted thirty-two bears that evening, some of them large grizzlies that would make a Fairbanks[41] register 1,200 or 1,300 pounds.

At the thumb of the lake was a large canvas lunch house, about fifty by sixty feet, presided over by a man named Silvers and his "Rib." The lady in question was a trifle abundant and would register 250 pounds in the shade. While Vic and Silvers were fishing on the lakeshore and the two "ribs" were confiding their little womanly secrets to each other, a large silvertip bear, followed by a cub, entered without even the formality of knocking, or with "by your leave." No one had firearms, as they are not allowed in the Park except to the soldiers. Vic's "Rib" jumped through a window, while the bear followed Mrs. Silvers to the kitchen, where the lady spied a sliding kitchen window, at which she essayed to escape. Sliding back the window, she got halfway out and stuck. Her avoirdupois was too ponderous, and she could not make the grade. The bear made one swipe at her garb, and lo she appeared like Godiva separated from her garments. Then she easily slipped through the small sliding window, only to be met by a small squad of soldiers, one of whom lent her his coat.

Smith and his wife camped on the Madison River the next night. A large bear came into the tent about midnight and walked away with a ten-pound sack of sugar and a ham. Much to their relief, he did not insist on taking them along.[42]

One day on the head of Fish Trap Creek,[43] as Vic led his horse under a cliff, along a narrow rock ledge, with the bridle rein over his arm, he passed a natural cave. The next moment, an enormous silvertip bear jumped out and struck the horse a violent blow, hurling him over the cliff. Since the bridle rein was over Vic's arm, he was jerked off balance and went over the cliff also, while his rifle went sailing down the mountain. Luckily for Vic, the first drop was only about twenty-five feet. He landed on steep sliderock, which carried him along for about fifty feet, until he grasped a large boulder and checked his fall. Casting his eyes upward, Vic saw the bear complacently sitting, watching the horse that was bounding from crag to crag until it landed fully two thousand feet below. Every bone in its body was crushed.

Vic lay quiet for about fifteen minutes until the bear, not noticing any signs of life in the neighborhood, decamped. After an hour of tedious work, Vic found his gun with the stock broken off and the sights gone. With a badly bruised leg, Vic experienced great difficulty returning to camp, where he mounted his packhorse and struck for home.[44]

A few years before, Vic was on the head of Salmon River in Idaho with Tom James, deputy sheriff then. Tom was a nephew of Jesse James, the outlaw. They were after a horse-thief who had stolen James's horses, and whom James captured a month later after shooting him. Tom was without fear either with a gun or in a fistfight, he being a muscular fellow and extremely active and a bull's-eye shot with rifle or six-shooter.

A slight snow had fallen, and they discovered tracks of four bears that had evidently holed up for the winter. They trailed them to the cliffs, where they had entered their winter den. The bears had gone into a long tunnel of solid rock. About sixty feet below where they had entered, there was an opening from above. By shading their eyes, the boys could see pine boughs that the bears had used to fill the lower end of the tunnel. To get down to the boughs, Vic had to squeeze through the jagged rocks for about twelve feet. Tom remained above with Vic's rifle, while Vic carried a small revolver downstairs with him. The intentions were to make a fire of fat pine, then crawl out, fill the hole with dry limbs, and smoke out the plantigrades.

When Vic reached the bottom, he began pulling out some boughs to make a place for the fire. The bears set up a heavy growling and sniffing. Then the largest one commenced to tear away the thin partition of boughs blocking the space between them and Vic. As the bear tore away the obstruction with his powerful claws and pushed his head through, Vic, not more than four feet distant, shot him between the eyes, killing him instantly. Finding the hole blocked by the dead one, the other bears went out at the entrance and were killed by Tom with a shot apiece.

They proved to be all grizzlies, probably one family. After skinning the bears Tom shot, they went in with torches of fat pine to the dead one. Finding the natural tunnel too small to skin the bear, they removed the entrails and fastened a rope about its neck. After an hour of hard labor, they succeeded in dragging the bear to the entrance. Tom, who had studied for an M.D. shortly afterward, went into practice and hung his shingle at Kalispell, Montana. About the only use he has for a gun now is to make his patients disgorge.

Up-to-date, Vic has a record to his credit of 211 bear[45] and 57 mountain lions that have fallen before his rifle, besides thousands of buffalo. He killed over 5,000 buffalo in one season on the Redwater, thirty-five miles north of Glendive. Deer, elk, and antelope also fell before him in proportion. Joseph H. Taylor, in his book *Kaleidoscopic Lives,* says that Vic killed 10,000 buffalo in two seasons. Times have changed, and Vic at present is a strong game protectionist, regretting the slaughter of his early days.

APPENDIX

OTHER STORIES

Following are verbatim excerpts from various frontier newspapers and magazines that featured stories by or about Vic Smith. They appear as originally printed, with typographical errors and misspellings intact. These articles demonstrate Smith's popularity and add information to the original manuscript. The Bad Lands Cow Boy *often wrote about Smith, but only a few of those accounts have been reproduced here.*

March 2, 1882, Glendive Times, *p. 1:*

Communicated. Hardscrabble, M.T., Feb. 11th.

Circumstances over which we had no control compelled us to take a trip down the Yellowstone and up the Missouri. Leaving the poverty stricken settlement of Hardscrabble on the 11th, we arrived at Tom Cushing's ranch, on the Missouri, at dark. Tom has been government scout and guide for the last thirteen years, been wounded several times, and suffers yet from a wound received in an Indian fight several years ago, but he has thrown aside his gun for the more peaceful impliments of agriculture. His buildings cost him fifteen hundred dollars he has one hundred and sixty acres under the plow, several teams and has settled down at a go-as-you-please gait of an old granger. Crossed the river next morning at daybreak and ate breakfast at the Ft. Buford Hotel, presided over by Mrs. and Miss Ayott, two ladies who are educated and highly accomplished. Here we were joined by Mr. Ayott, a United States Marshal and the terror of all evil doers. There we exchanged our wagon for a buggy and having secured the services of Mr. Bronson as Jehu. We set out at daybreak for the Big Muddy Ranches, arriving in due season, we were hospitably entertained by Mr. and Mrs. Allen, pulled out and reached Ed. Lamberts Ranch at dark. Here Ed. and his amiable spouse have settled intending to remain until their checks are called for. We were provided with a comfortable bed, and daybreak next morning found us traveling at the rate of ten miles an hour; reached Jack Culbertson's store, stored and lunched. His place of business is five miles below Poplar Creek Agency. He carries the belt as a violinist and is one of the old school. Our intentions were to stop at Poplar Creek, but our team became unmanageable and Mr. Bronson was unable to check them until we were about ten miles beyond the agency. It was ration day and on the road we met Mr. and Mrs. Coon and all the little Coons bound for the Fort to draw their rations. Three o'clock found us at Wolf Point, our destination. We ran afoul of our old friend Tom Camel that we had not seen for years. He still runs the store and is the veritable individual that compelled the beaver to climb a tree on the open prairie. While there we made the acquaintance of Mr. Hederberg, United States Commissioner, a gentleman in every respect and the right man in the right place. Fearing that time might hang heavily on his hands, the government has imposed several duties upon him, he deals law and justice (a rare thing), he is post pharmacist and surgeon. Fearing the seductive smiles of the dusky maidens would exercise a demoralizing influence over him he is compelled to wile away the evenings teaching the half civilized dog-eaters to read, write and cypher. Though not acquainted with our language they have learned several hymns that they sing very good. While there Sumers arrived from ten miles above Ft. Peck, reporting that buffalo in vast numbers were crossing the river going north, and that the Assinaboine camp of Indians were slaughtering them, it being near the end of the robe season.

I here made the acquaintance of a person who was present at the death of Mike Welch, it will be remembered that Welch was killed early last fall at Bill Norris' ranch, a short distance above old Ft. Peck. This gentleman's statement, which I think is an unbiased one is as follows concerning the tragic affair. Mike Welch, who was considered the best hunter and the best shot on the Missouri, came with Pasty Doyle to Norris' store. After a few drinks of fighting whiskey, Mike became boisterons and abusive, shaking his fist under Doyle's nose and insisting on fighting. Welch being a powerful man Doyle refused to fight. When bed time arrived Mike who was still wrangling, started for his blankets, whether it was with the intention of going to sleep or getting his gun which was under his bedding is not known. Doyle fearing the latter surmise correct picked up a gun and shot Mike, the bullet striking him in the right breast killing him instantly. The shooting was hardly justifiable, but the circumstances were extenuating. Doyle expressed regret at the deed shook hands with the corpse, mounted his broncho and left.

The Indian farm at Wolf Point, under the supervision of Mr. Hedelberg is in a flourishing condition, they have three hundred acres under the plow and raise first class crops of potatoes, onions and other vegetables, also corn and oats. Considerable ground will be broke this spring, and as the game grows scarcer strict attention will be paid by these nomads to agriculture.

On our return trip we remained at Poplar Creek over night, square meals at Jim McDonald's for fifty cents a head is where we hung out. Mr. Shaw loaned us robes enough to make a comfortable shakedown in his store. He evidently mistrusted us, for on awakening at intervals during the night, an augur eyed clerk with a double barreled shot gun for a bed fellow and a lamp burning (presumably to take aim by) lay on the counter with one eye open, and it is hardly necessary to state that we remained quiet. Everything about the agency is looming up; it is a little over a year since we made a flying trip there; We hardly had time to take in the surroundings, when circumstances and the wrath of the agent compelled us to take a hasty departure, since then however barracks have been erected for U.S. troops, a telegraph station connected with Buford, three rival trading stored, a good school house, an agency church, wire fences (in good condition) and other improvements. The competition of the thre trading stores is looked upon with satisfaction, by the people that are compelled to buy provisions there. Coffee is only forty cents per pound, bacon thirty five, sugar thenty five, flour $12 per hundred pounds and everything in proportion and at these ruinous prices it is impossible for the traders to keep long above water, but if necessary they can follow the style of the Miles City bank officials, but judging from our intercourse with them they are individuals of a different stamp, what you buy from them you pay well for and what they purchase of you they pay the top price cash down and no grumbling. Arrived in due season at Buford. Before closing allow me to state for the benefit of the public, that anyone wishing to secure the services of a first class driver and guide, I hearby recommend Mr. Bronson, he never failed to make a dead center on a rock, stump or tree with the buggy, and as to washouts and chuckholes, it was utterly impossiable for him to notice them until the buggy was upset or the occupants thrown out. An accident insurance agency at Ft. Buford would be a paying institution if this individual is allowed to run at large any length of time.

May 18, 1882, Glendive Times, *p. 1:*

Vic Smith has been heard from. He is still on the east side of the Little Missouri, in the neighborhood of the Grand river. He says tell all the boys I'm getting there in good shape and will astonish some of the natives yet. He asks if the buffalo have come into the settlement yet.

June 29, 1882, Glendive Times Supplement, *p. 1:*

HARDSCRABBLE, M.T. June 25th

After an absence of four months I again arrive at Seymore creek only to find that some old fossil with a diseased brain had changed the name to Hen creek. This same individual evidently fancies that I wrote a quarter section for your paper, entitled "Hardscrabble or what." This poor crank is laboring under a delusion. The name Hardscrabble must touch him and several more in a tender place. I think it quite appropriate, when a woman living all alone in the neighborhood, has the window and door kicked in, two masked men, with revolvers makes her throw up her hands and robs her of a few dollars, as occurred here last winter. But as buffalo did not come into the settlement and deliver themselves up last winter, "old timer" and everybody else were obliged to eke out an existance by fair means or foul. "Old timer" sayes he takes the responsibility, but as he or his friends forgets to sign their name, we fail to see where the responsible part comes in. He also dates his letter Ft. Buford, when in reality he and his shack is but a short distance from the ballance of the shacks here on the creek. Changing the name to Hen creek damaged the prospects for us to either sell or give away our land, but if our crops pan out rich, and the buffalo range around our buildings this fall we will (if the weather is not too severe) be able to pull through the winter. I droped into J. O'Brien's ranch and he was sitting with his face in his hands, presenting altogether a dejected appearance, muttering to himself hard times, jawbone, hope the buffalo will come in etc., growing desperate he jumped up, swallowed a glass of water, remarking that times was hard and beer cost money. A stranger came in and "set em up" then tendered a five dollar william for pay. John looked twice to assure himself that it was not counterfeit, and remarked (sotto voce) that if the stranger could only be induced to squander the ballance of the william that it would help him out wonderfully, as he had not taken in a bill of such dimensions for a month. That is only one instance, but it goes to show that times are awful flush here, no hard-scrabbling to make a living here, oh no, its a mistake.

Stopped at J.L. Burns' ranch over night, and like the balance of the pumpkin rollers I had met, he dragged me out to his potato patch and compelled me, sore against my will to acknowledge that his "craps" was just a "leetle" ahead of those at hardscrabble. He informed me that his cottonwood sprouts had been eaten off by the crows. As a granger myself, and knowing a thing or two about horticulture, I investigated the matter and found that J. L, having entrusted the planting to his young hopefuls, they, for pure cussedness had put them in upside down. He had in four acres of corn. After it was about eight inches high he rolled the ground and corn with a thousand pound roller, to keep the cows from trampling down the corn. Then we visited the potato patch and dug potatos for supper. They were about the size of hens eggs. I was obliged to he again and say that they were ahead of our burg. After visiting the balance of his garden and oat fields, and thoroughly conversing the prospects (which by the way is very poor compared to Hardscrabble) the conversation turned on stock raising. John was enthuastic on that subject, his hobby in fact, he spoke of his fine haired thorough-breads running stock etc. He warmed up to the subject so strongly that fearing the consequences that a refusal would entale, I followed him without a murmer to his stables, when "ye Gods," John's blooded stock, that he prided himself on, was the commonest of the buzzard-heads, spavined and wind-galls all over them. I pitied John, and in soothing tones directed his attention to the cattle herd that was coming in. He entered fiercely on this theme, and grasping by the tail, which he claimed was a through berd short horoned bull. He gave me its pedigree, and the price of the animal was eleven hundred dollars. Poor John, the animal was a mooly, and worth about forty dollars.

The editor of the Glendive "slasher" got away from here just in time and the probabilities are if he ever shows his ugly face here again, the coroners services will be required, if he can't afford to donate the "slasher" free for a few years without insinuating that the "filthy" for the same would be acceptable, we will sit down on him and withdraw our patronage.

A fiendish attempt at outrage was made on the person of Mrs. Frank Murphy a few evenings since. As she was attending to her household duties, a tramp who was prying around the neighborhood, dressed in "walk pom a na" goods, and wearing a heavy growth of fiery red whiskers, bald headed and a large wart on his nose and flat feet, assaulted her, knocked her down and tore the most of her clothing from her body. She scratched his face and kicked him, all the time screaming at the top of her voice. After she had caught her second wind, and finding she would never surrender her virtue (that shows what stuff the people of Newland are made of) he desisted from further efforts and skined out over the buffs. The people of Newlandville are indignant and declare that it is about time horse thieves and rapists were cleaned out of the neighborhood. Mr. Murphy has blood in his eye, and if the perpetrator is caught, the coroners services will be required instead of a jury. Vic Smith.

July 20, 1882, Glendive Times, *p. 1:*

Communicated. Cantonment, July 14th.

Desiring to improve the domestic herd of cattle and give the beef a gamey flavor, by crossing them with buffalo, I enlisted Vic Smith into the scheme of taking teams and bringing in a few hundred calves from the main heard, up the Little Missouri. Throwing our eagle eye around us it lit onto, the very men we wanted, McGilligan, McGregor, from the sloap and "Kanudale Snort" from Sauk Center, Smith and myself, followed up the river to Eaton's cow camp, while the others took the main road for the Star Route stage crossing of the Little Missouri. Arriving in due time we secured ten cows from the ranche, to play wet nurse to the calves, which we intended to run down and rope. We found on reaching the river that it was bank full. Smith had a span of buzzard head mules that he claimed were daisies to swim. On reaching the middle of the stream the daisies settled down to the bottom of the stream like so much sediment, while bedding, cooking utensiles and our teamster Kanudale Snort, floated gracefully down stream. After superhuman efforts the mules, wagon and Snort were landed. The water was rolled out of the daisies with the aid of an elm club about four feet long. What few articles were saved were deposited on the grass to sun themselves. A heavy thunder storm came on which aided us somewhat in drying our plunder. We had about twenty five miles further to travel before we should find buffalo. Our teamster K.S. claimed that he knew a short trail through the badlands which would save about fifteen miles. Vic and myself pulled out at daybreak, leaving the team to follow on the "short cut." We traveled all day expecting every hill we assended to see the team. Night overtook us and yet no sign of the mob. Bright and early next morning we took the back trail in search of the crew. At noon we overhauled K.S. He had made a complete circle and was within a half mile of where he left the trail a day and a half before. We had some trouble convincing him that he had not saved that fifteen miles by following the short trail. After catering to the wants of the inner man, we resumed the trail and next day found the game we were in search of. Our horses being down at the heel somewhat, we concluded to bask in the spray of a drenching rain for a day or two that they might recruit. The "modus operandi" that we had mapped out was for two of us to surround the calves. To make assurance doubly sure we secured some half breed horses of G. Paddock at Cantonment; nags that he claimed were "burners" only touching the ground in high places. After giving them ample time to recruit their wasted strength, we surrounded the herd or rather attempted to. We approached to within fifty yards before the buffalo discovered us. They raised their tails and started followed by us and the 'burners.' In about three minutes the buffalo were a mere speck in the distance, while we, we were sad. In finding our way back to camp, we raised two small calves that had hid in the sage brush, and evidently the milk of human kindness (so to speak) had been witheld from early calfhood. We rounded them up in true cow boy style, put them in the ambulance, and having lost confidence in Paddock and his horses, we struck a bee line for home, wiser by experience by far than when we started. After hauling the calves two days they took sick which caused McGregor to remark that his opinion was, that the calf loved his maker, and would probably "climb the golden stair," which prophecy proved true before morning. That was the last straw: we thirsted for gore, and none but G. P.'s blood would do. Fortunately for him, on hearing of our arrival, he had pressing business on Fallon creek which would necessiate his absense for two or three weeks. Disapointed again we failed to interview him.

N.B.—The "daisies" and "burners" are for sale, cheap.

August 3, 1882, Glendive Times, *p. 1:*

"Notes on Newlon."

....If it will not be taxing your patience past indurance, I will relate a little conversation I overheard the other evening between an honest granger, of this place, and a tenderfoot, who by the way was acting the part of reporter and very inquisitive at that.

Tenderfoot.— Is this the house of the famous hunter and scout, Vic Smith I believe they call him.

Granger.— W-a-ll yes he has a comfortable house just over the creek for Mrs. Smith and he lays up for repairs at intervals of about three months. You see Vic is a rustler from way back, and don't wait for the buffalo to come in but makes a break for the main herd and rounds them up plenty.

Tenderfoot.— Vic acts as reporter for a change does he not?

Granger.— W-a-ll I don't like to pass opinion on any one, but I don't believe Vic would tell anything if it did not really happen unless—or, well— unless he was orful anxious to have it happen.

Tenderfoot.— You don't seem to understand me. I am not speaking of his manner of speaking: I mean does he not write for the paper.

Granger.— Oh, yes I see; write stories: well yes I should presume to remark. That is reportin, writen letters.

Tenderfoot.— He must be a college graduate.

Granger.—How?

Tenderfoot.— He is a college graduate is he not?

Granger.— W-a-ll ye-as I believe he did in an early day, when Gen. Miles first come to the country.

Tenderfoot.— You don't seem to understand. I mean he must have a good education to write for papers.

Granger.— Oh, well sartin, now I sa-va. Well I can't say, but you see Vic reads a great many useful and wise books, such as "Mark Twain's adventures in China," "Bobolink," "Ignorance athome,'"Helen's children" &c. and he has a wonderful remembery and I suppose this helps him on terrible.

Tenderfoot.— Is it realy a fact about the amount of game it is reported Vic kills and captures.

Granger.— W-a-ll stranger that is a question I should hate to decide, but I will give you a history of one of them, just as he related it to me. You see I kinder like to visit Vic when he is laying over for repairs and hear him relate his bold and darin adventures. You see he was in one time last winter with his five repairmen, to bush out his reloading outfits and temper his knives and gun barrels, and he happened to think of having a couple of hundred beaver traps over on the west fork of the Big Tunkle Head Creek that he had not visited for about four months, so he thought this would be a favorable opportunity, so his skinners all being out on the range he took his five repairmen and started, distance about 80 miles, intending to make the point in time for a round up the first day, but he had not got over half way when coming across a nice herd of young antelope, and remembering that he had a contract to fill for two dozen live antelope, he took this as his chance. As they was going a little out of his way, he told his men to follow up with the wagon and load them in and not let him get out of sight. As the band scattered a little and he was anxious to secure those of a certain age and sect, it took him some forty minutes to accomplish this catch, and worst of all when the men came up with the load of daisies they had heated the axeis, so it took an hour to cool them off so the wheels would roll. This delayed them so that they fell short 16 miles of their station. When Vic saw that it would be too late to make clean over, he directed Bill Guzeler, his foreman of repairs, to go into camp at the mouth of Owlseye Canyon and he would ride over to the head of Tunkle and take observations. Game was very scarce in this section at the time, but just as he was going down the slope, he looked to his right and saw a small band of about nine thousand buffalo, grazing in a small coulee. His first thought was to round them up and make a killing, but remembering he had only about 130 rounds, he concluded to kill a load of meat and return, so he laid out 87 of the choicest and upon counting his cartridges he found he had only 100 rounds left, and not allowing himself to get short in a case of this kind he concluded to retire. Upon returning to camp and finding everything in order, he concluded to have his repairmen skin up those few in the morning, while he looked after his traps, but as they did not seem anxious to do much out of their line, he concluded to do it himself, so picking up a sack of newly tempered knives, he struck out two hours before daylight, and just as the sun was making its appearance above the horizon, he had the last hide off, being by the watch, just one hour and sixty four minutes. He would have made the minutes just even with ease, but in going over before daylight, he took a short cut and fell into a washout 80 feet perpendicular, striking on some stones he dulled some of his knives.

Just here the conversation was interrupted by one of Vale Miner & Co's. coaches rolling up...

The opinion we formed of Vic was that he was a good whole souled, free hearted let them down plenty sort of a fellow, always had money to pay his bills and some left.... Signed Settler.

March 3, 1883, Glendive Times, *p. 4:*

FROM THE DAKOTA RANGE Sulley Springs, D.T., Feb. 21.

Wishing to catch a glimpse of the noble buffalo before they became a thing of the past, we applied to Al. Gifford for information. He referred us to Vic. Smith living on the Little Missouri. We were about to make a break in that direction with the intention of clearing up the balance of the herd. After sampeling the mixed drinks of Sulley, water and whiskey equal parts, we procured a five gallon keg of the liquid, and thus fortified sallied forth. That evening we camped at the cow ranch of Mr. Eaton, a retired merchant. There we received genuine western hospitality. The next day we made the acquaintance of Smith. He promised us a rare time and plenty of sport, and don't you fail to remember we got it. The thermometer ranged among the twenties. Before starting we broke the ice in the keg and sampled the contents. Our road lay over those famous Bad Lands to Maddox' ranch on the old road. Long before reaching there our ears and cheeks were frozen in good shape. Close by Mr. Auld of Dickinson, keeps a supply store for hunters and freighters. Mrs. Maddox, the hostess at the ranch, spreads the best layout in the shape of a good table between Sulley and the Black Hills. Following a dim trail we reached George Edgar's camp next night about 10 o'clock. We thawed out our fingers with snow that evening; the boys thinking that not more than a joint or two would come off. Our nose got another freeze and the next day was puffed up so much that our best friends would hardly know us. We had started with an insufficiency of bedding—only seven robes and ten pair of blankets; but by sleeping with our clothes on we managed to keep from perishing at night. Next night made the camp of Buckskin Buck who entertained us with tales of border strife, hair breadth escapes and contests with buffalo bulls until the air smelled of gore. It also smelled quite strongly of buffalo chips and bones, which is all the fuel between the streams. I forgot to remark that we joined parties with Edgar on horseback. Next day we proceeded ahead of the teams and on rounding a knoll a buffalo bull quite unexpectedly loomed up. We promptly opened fire and downed him in good shape. We skinned him and about that time one of those beautiful blizzards, of which I had heard so much and wished to see, broke upon us. At first it struck me as sublime, next it struck through my bones. We covered ourselves with the hide, and at no time during the day was the sun visible; when no longer finding our shelter tenable we faced the storm. It took us four hours to go two miles, crawling over the hills on our hands and knees, the wind being so strong we could not stand up on a raise. Death stared us in the face and it was then we promised reform—to ever abstain from the bottle and hunting buffalo in winter. At last we reached camp. Near the tent we stumbled over one of Edgar's mules frozen stiff. We were welcomed by our comrades who had all gone to bed as there was no wood to make a fire with. Alas for human weakness, we took a comforting nip from the bottle. Edgar seized an ax and demolished a wagon box. A comfortable fire and a good supper we turned in thankful we were alive. Shortly after turning in a stinging sensation caused us to rise and make an investigation which revealed to us that our toes were frozen. Next day we camped on Buffalo creek where wood was reparted in abundance and found it to be green willows hardly larger than a pipe stem. By this time the bark had peeled from our proboscis which made it exceedingly tender and we were obliged to wear a liver pad on it. The following day timber was sighted on the Cannon Ball also an Indian encampment. From the Cannon Ball to Sulley, about fifty miles, it took us five days, but don't you forget we had a bully time—not a stick of wood from there in Praise God from whom all blessing flow, Sulley was reached at last, where a warm meal at Robert's restaurant and a few tom and jerrys to warm the inner man we forgot the past until reminded by some one stepping on our toes, stumbling over our ears or or pushing against our nose. Our intention was to give Smith a rare old time which would send him to the hospital but he escaped. Mr. Gifford reports about forty horses and mules perished in the storm. An affecting meeting took place between Edgar and Mr. Davis, hyde buyer. He had received a telegram to the effect that Edgar had been frozen stiff. It was a hoax. As soon as able we will go the sunny Yellowstone where when the weather is cold we can at least have some shelter other than a green bull hide or a canvas tent. Where blizzards are unknown. Hunter.

March 20, 1884, Bad Lands Cow Boy, *p. 4:*

Johnny Goodall, Frank Smith and Rev. Silas Cheval are the latest contributors to our Bad Lands museum. The latter "held up" a passing freight and secured a good specimen of galena.

March 27, 1884, Bad Lands Cow Boy, *p. 4:*

Again has Frank Smith come to the front with valuable additions to our Bad Land curiosities. If we don't have a collection to be proud of it won't be the fault of the Smith brothers.

J. Slatcher, of Dickinson, is making a gun stock for Vick Smith which is the prettiest thing of the kind we have ever seen. It is made of English walnut, the veins showing out beautifully. It is worth a trip to Dickinson to see. Mr. Slatcher appreciates the value of The Cow Boy as an advertising medium and comes out in a good advertisement this week. We can personally recommend him as as a skillful and honest workman.

July 31, 1884, Bad Lands Cow Boy, *p. 4:*

Vic Smith suffered a peculiar mishap last Monday morning which might easily have terminated fatally. While out hunting, about nine miles northeast of here, he had just killed a deer when his attention was directed to a band of mountain sheep. Just as he started after these the ground gave way and horse and rider were tumbled into an underground wash-out twenty feet deep. Vic was pinned to the ground for several hours but at last succeeded in extricating himself and getting the horse on its feet. Tying his lariat around the barrel of his gun and standing on the horse's back he made a lucky throw and lodged the gun across the apex of the V-shaped hole at the top. A walk of nine miles brought him to Medora, where a party was made up that soon rescued the imprisoned horse.

December 4, 1884, Bad Lands Cow Boy, *p. 4:*

Count Rembielinski of Russia and Vic. Smith have been hunting down the river for about ten days, and during that time, the Count killed sixty-five deer and antelope. This is the best tenderfoot record to date. Vic says he is a dandy.

February 5, 1885, Bad Lands Cow Boy, *p. 4:*

We are in receipt of a letter from Vic. Smith, written from Chicago, in which he gives a vivid description of his travels so far. Happening into a shooting gallery in Milwaukee he "gave a specimen of western markmanship," and was immediately offered a salary of $40 per week. He says "Medora is good enough" for him, and will return. He had with him Bob Robert's buckskin suit and took first prize at a masquerade. As he stepped off the cars in Chicago, one man was engaging in the festive operation of shooting another. He did a good job, and as Vic says, "as clean as I ever saw it done in the west." Vic's father and brother are very sick, and this, coupled with bad reports of the New Orleans exposition he heard from friends, has decided him to give up his trip there. He intends returning about February 25.

July 2, 1885, Bad Lands Cow Boy, *p. 4:*

The meeting to get up a programme for the 4th. of July sports met according to call in the skating rink last Friday evening. J. C. Fisher was elected chairman and A. T. Packard stated that the object of the meeting was to informally discuss a programme of races and contests for the 4th. and moved that a committee of five be appointed to take charge of affairs. Bob. Roberts moved to amend by placing the name of the original mover at the head of the committee. The following committee was then elected: A. T. Packard, Bob. Roberts, E. Deffenbach, John Goodall and Vic Smith. It was decided to make the principal event a six hundred yards' cow-horse race, with prizes of $25, $15 and $10. This race is open to cow-horses only or to those that are not considered or known to be fast horses. Besides this race, there are on the programme a free-for-all three hundred yards' horse race, with prizes of $15 and $10, a slow mule race, a hundred yards' dash foot race, a fat men's race, a rifle contest and other races contests which will be arranged on the ground. The base-ball will be in the forenoon, the rifle contest at one o'clock. The other contests will follow. Entries in any of the contests can be made with any of the committee.

October 13, 1896, Anaconda Recorder, *p. 1:*

MIGHTY HUNTERS RETURN

Captain W.S. Turner returned last night from a four week's hunt in the Big Hole basin under the guidance of the famous hunter Vic Smith. The captain was highly pleased with his trip and says of all the hunters he ever been out with, and he had been with many, Mr. Smith is the best. He differs from most of the guides in the fact that he is anxious to have those who engage his services get the game and does not care about killing any himself. During the outing Captain Turner killed two elk, eight white mountain goats, one silver tip bear weighing 560 pounds, one martin, a wolf and a badger and fish and grouse without number. Mr. Smith killed a buck antelope and a deer. All the hides of the animals and two goats in their entirety can be seen at Mr. Smith's home up Sheep gulch, just a mile from town.

Killing the bear gave the captain the most sport. The day before he had climbed to the top of a high mountain peak in search of goats. He killed four of these animals, one of them falling off a ledge as it was shot and rolling and crashing down the mountain side a distance of 4,000 feet. Mr. Smith followed the goat up and dressed it, with the exception of taking the hide off. He returned next morning to perform that duty, and found that during the night a bear had been making a meal of goat meat. He tied the carcass to a tree, and that evening Captain Turner and himself lay in ambush about fifty yards from the dead animal. The bear did not disappoint them. He came back for his evening dinner, but when within a few yards of the goat he noticed that it has been moved. Bruin raised up on his hind legs to investigate matters, and just as he straightened up Captain Turner's Winchester rang out and sent a bullet through the animal's neck, but not killing it by any means.

Immediately after the captain shot, a little dog he had with him charged down upon the bear, but soon returned, closely followed by the bear. Captain Turner fired five shots into him while he was approaching, all of which took effect, but the animal had got within a few feet of the hunters before the captain succeeded in placing a well directed bullet through the brute's heart.

Mr. Smith, who is an old and experience hunter and one who has taken such famous people out on trips as the late Marquis De Mores, says that one of the goats killed by Captain Turner weighed 280 pounds and was the largest he had ever seen. They had six pack and saddle horses with them and took Ben Osborne along as cook, whom they say is a regular maitre d'hotel.

October 14, 1896, Anaconda Standard, *p. 2:*

ALL KINDS OF GAME

Captain Turner returned yesterday from a hunting expedition to the Big Hole country under the guidance of Vic Smith, the famous hunter and trapper. They were out four weeks, in which time Captain Turner killed a silver tip bear, eight goats, two elk, a marten, an antelope, a deer, a wolf and a badger. He not only killed them, but brought home the pelts to prove it and last evening took a wagon load of them to his home at Silver Lake.

Vic Smith is the famous scout who accompanied Generals Miles and Terry in their Indian wars and for some years was in the employ of Marquis de Mores during the latter's ill starred Montana ventures. One of the hunter's greatest treasures is the rifle which bears in the stock a silver plate inscribed "Marquis de Mores to Vic Smith."

Mr. Smith does not live in the hills as he used to do, but now has a comfortable home in a picturesque spot about one mile up the Sheep gulch canyon. He is married now and he seldom cares to wander from his own fireside. But during the game season he escorts parties to the hills and when he goes out there is always game to be found, because he knows where and how to find it.

December 7, 1896, Anaconda Recorder, *p. 4:*

Vic Smith, the mighty huntsman and mountaineer, returned yesterday from another hunt in the hills and, as usual, did not come home empty handed. He brought in a majestic elk head, a deer and a large mountain goat.

May 26, 1897, Anaconda Recorder, *p. 4:*

VIC SMITH KILLS TWO BEARS

Vic Smith, the famous hunter, returned last night from the Big Hole country with the carcasses of two bears—a cinnamon and a black bear. The cinnamon had tackled a heifer the day before Mr. Smith started after him. He found Bruin near a creek feasting on a bed of ants. One shot in the back of the head brought the bear into Mr. Smith's possession. The black bear he killed at the summit near McCune's store. There are a lot of horse carcasses there, the horses having perished during the winter in the deep snow. Bears had been getting their daily meal there, and Mr. Smith laid in waiting Monday afternoon and was not disappointed. While this particular black fellow was feeding on horse meat, Mr. Smith shot him. Today he was distributing fat and juicy bear meat among his friends. The two hides will net Mr. Smith about $50. Mr. Smith never fails to bring home a bear or two when he starts after them. Last year he killed four.

He reports that the unusually warm weather has driven off the snow from the mountains much earlier than usual and thinks the placer mining season, in consequence, will be very short.

July 1897, Recreation, *p. 44:*

WHERE THE BUFFALO WENT

Anaconda, Mont.

Editor Recreation: In 1876 I was Government scout under General Miles. Little did I think then that the immense herds of buffalo which were continually in sight, would so soon be swept off the earth.

In September of that year, "Yellowstone" Kelly, "Billy" Cross and I were sent by General Miles to locate the camp of the Ogallalah Sioux. We followed down the Yellowstone 50 miles, and about 10 o'clock that night, found where their camp had been during the day. The next morning we took a straight cut for Cedar creek, reaching it at dark, then travelled up stream 8 miles. Every half mile we ran into herds of buffalo. They were not wild, and at times it seemed certain they would run over us. It was a peculiar situation— hunting Indians and dodging buffalo.

We camped in a thicket that night. In the morning, Miles' command was seen about 8 miles away, exchanging shots, at long range, with the Indians. Cross and I were for lying low until night; but Kelly insisted on taking daylight for it. So, with almost a certainty of being shot, we started for the command.

The Indians had set fire to the prairie, and the smoke had shut off our view; but every time the wind lifted the screen, we got our bearings. Fortunately for us, the enemy had gone to the farther side of the command, leaving clear sailing for us. The Indians told Cross, afterward, they saw us, but through the smoke took us for Indians.

When within 250 yards of the troops, we saw them sitting on a sidehill, resting. As the air was still smoky, they also took us for Indians, and fired volley after volley at us. The bullets rattled about like hail. We found shelter in a convenient washout until a sergeant, with small detail, came down to the scalp the dead. The soldiers were certain they had seen a number of Indians fall from their horses; but it was only us, as we tumbled to the ground, looking for holes in which to cache ourselves.

From '76 to '82, on both sides of the Yellowstone, buffalo were slaughtered ruthlessly by whites and Indians. At every shipping point there were thousands of hides piled up. All that was saved of the animals were the hides and horns. The former averaged the hunter $2.50 each, while for the horns he got 1 cent a pound.

In those days, from any prominence, 10,000 buffalo might be seen "at one look." It was certainly a magnificent sight. The cattlemen wanted the buffalo exterminated, so the cattle could have the grass. As no one interfered, the white hunters slaughtered, indiscriminately, male, female and young.

One day, on the Redwater, 35 miles North of Glendive, I counted from a butte 18 hunters, all shooting into different herds of buffalo, with their Sharps rifles. Yet people wonder how the buffalo could have been so quickly exterminated.

In '83 there was practically but one herd left. That was between Moreau and Cannon Ball rivers, in North Dakota. There were about 10,000 animals in this herd. In September of that year, Sitting Bull, with his followers, went up the Cannon Ball, hunting. The 1st day they killed 1,100—an average of 1 buffalo to each Indian. White hunters would have killed 20 to 60 in the same time. By the middle of the following November the herd was completely wiped out. From that month, the American bison was practically a thing of the past. Vic Smith.

May 25, 1898, Anaconda Standard, *p. 4:*

VIC SMITH'S BEAR HUNTS

Vic Smith, the famous hunter, returned yesterday from a successful chase in the Big Hole country. Vic brought to town with him two great black bears. He killed the animals on the Big Hole river, a mile or two from Ethredge postoffice, on La Marsh creek. Those who have been in the Big Hole country will remember that when going southward, just before coming to the Anaconda road, there is a vast green slope that declines gently from the top of the hills to the valley of French creek. On this slope the inhabitants of the Big Hole region have watched for bears for any number of years, and they are seldom disappointed, for the green sward is a favorite spot for the animals, who make their homes in the high hills.

A day or two ago Smith was heading for home, when he chanced to cast his eyes upon the green slope. There was a monster of a bear there, and Smith thought he might as well bring him along as not. In reaching the place where the bear stood Smith had to cross a little coulee. As he climbed up the opposite bank he found himself not more than 30 feet from bruin. The bear looked at Smith in surprise and Smith looked at the bear. But Smith didn't look at the bear out of curiosity. He looked at the animal over the top of the shining barrel of a savage rifle, and when he thought he had looked long enough he touched a little spring at the bottom of the gun. The bear turned over on his back and began clawing the atmosphere. With each claw the vigor of the blows grew weaker. Smith stood watching the gear for a moment, and while he was engaged in this interesting occupation he heard the well-known snuffing of another bear close behind him. He turned about with lightning speed. The second bear did not seem to be aware of Smith's presence, as a slight rise of ground intervened between the hunter and the hunted. The second bear was evidently searching for the animal whom Smith's bullet had cut off in his prime.

Smith moved cautiously toward the second bear, congratulating himself on having had the opportunity of bagging two such fine specimens of bearhood without having to move out of his tracks. Smith is said to be about the best rifle shot in these parts, and he always has his range finder just above his right cheek bone. As soon as the range finder found its object the bear who had snuffed ceased snuffing and will never snuff more. Smith got a wagon from one the ranchers out there and brought his prizes to town.

Smith says that there are any number of bears in the hills along the Big Hole. Last week he killed a black bear and captured another alive. The one he caught is a yearling, but is of pretty respectable size and looks as if he might have made things lively if Smith's trap hadn't been a good one. Smith has also been camping on the trail of a big silver tip, but he is afraid that somebody else has got his game. About a week ago Smith got a quiet tip that there was a big silver tip at a certain spot in the hills, and the hunter organized himself into a strategic board and went after the silver tip. Smith set his trap and awaited results. The next morning he found that his trap had worked all right, but that the bear had been too much for the steel and had broken it in bits. Ever since that Smith has depended on his gun. Some days ago he found the silver tip's tracks and followed them. After he had walked about five miles he heard three or four shots in rapid succession in a clump of timber, some distance away, into which the tracks led. He thinks that some other huntsman has got his silver tip, for there have been no signs of him since.

Smith states that the roads leading into the Big Hole are in much better condition than they usually are at this time of the year. The rains have made them soft and muddy in the lower country, but there is not much difficulty in getting over them. He says that the snow in the mountains is about all gone, only the peaks being still covered. There is no snow on the Mill creek pass, and this is rather surprising, for it is generally well along in June before the snow disappears from that pass. Smith reports that there are many herds of deer in the Big Hole country, in the region below French gulch, and that they come down into the hay fields without fear. No one molests the deer, and they make themselves perfectly at home. The deer herds winter down about Dewey's Flat, but in the summer they make their feeding grounds in the hills about Ralston. There are also elk and goats in the hills in considerable numbers. The goats, of course, remain among the crags of the high peaks far back from the traveled roads and seldom come down to the lower ground.

May 1899, Recreation, *pp. 365-366:*

ROPING BUFFALO CALVES BY VIC. SMITH

In the spring of '79 I had a contract with an Eastern firm to furnish them 50 buffalo calves. I was to bring them to the banks of the Yellowstone river and put them aboard a steamer to be forwarded to their destination.

I secured the services of Frank Muzzy, and with 5 teams, 4 good Buffalo horses, and a cook we were soon on our way to the Redwater, a stream 40 miles North of the Yellowstone. At the breaks of the Redwater we saw herds of buffalo up and down the river as far as our eyes could reach.

We pitched camp at the edge of an ash grove near a fine spring, 300 yards from the stream. After supper I saddled a horse and approached a small bunch of buffalo about a mile from camp. Selecting a fat yearling heifer I downed her, and cutting off the hump and choice pieces, loaded my horse and returned to camp. That evening 5 Sioux Indians dropped in and materially assisted us in eating the heifer. The next morning we left the cook in camp to watch the horses. Muzzy and I, with lariat and straps, were soon among a bunch of about 20 cows and calves. We were mounted on fleet buffalo runners, and it was short work to rope a calf apiece. Snubbing the ropes we jumped from our horses, and after tying the feet of the calves, left them lying on the ground, and again sought the bunch. We soon came up with them and caught 2 more, but the mother of Muzzy's calf turned on him and forced him several times to drop his rope. When I had my baby buffalo tied I turned my attention to the old cow and soon had her scampering after the herd. We caught 7 calves that forenoon; then took a team, brought them to camp and staked them out. They were old enough to eat grass and live on that until we got back to the Yellowstone, where we could give them a mixture of milk, water, and bran.

By noon of the fifth day, I had within 2 of the number of calves wanted. After dinner we started for a herd about 4 miles away. They were lying on the side of a hill, near the summit. Muzzy remained in the valley while I rode around the herd, which we estimated at about 600 head. I found they lay in a V shape on the face of the slope. It had not rained for 3 weeks, and the ground was dry as powder, yet the whole country was cut up by small, deep washouts. I rode at a fair pace in between the wings of the herd. The old bulls were so surprised at my impudence that they stood amazed until I had passed them and was almost into the main bunch. Suddenly all the animals started down the slope. The wings of the herd closed about me, as the dust was so thick the buffaloes did not notice me. At full speed I went with them, their shaggy bodies rubbing against my legs. I could reach out and touch a buffalo on either side. Though they were stumbling and falling in badger holes and washouts all around me, yet my horse never stumbled; had he fallen I would have been trampled to death. It was the most exciting race I ever took part in. I do not say I was afraid, but I don't wish to repeat the run. On reaching the valley, where the grass was quite high and there was no dust, the herd gradually drew away from me. Before we parted company I roped a calf, and Muzzy caught another. Next day we pulled for the Yellowstone river.

My wagons carried racks similar to those in which sheep are hauled, and gave ample room for the calves to move about. Morning and evening we cut juicy blue grass and boiled it in large camp kettles. When sufficiently cooled we poured the juice into the troughs in the racks; the calves would eagerly drink it, and it apparently satisfied their wants. Only one out of the 50 calves died before we reached the ranch.

I put the animals in a well fenced pasture of about 15 acres. Eight good cows were milked night and morning for the benefit of the calves. The milk was mixed with boiled grass juice and poured into log troughs. Besides, there was a fine growth of grass in the pasture.

Three miles below my ranch was a camp of Gros-ventre Indians. They looked with disapproval of my scheme of fencing in "their buffalo," as they called them. The Indian still claims everything that might still have been his had Columbus never sailed the sea.

All the steamboats had gone up stream a week before, and I was impatiently awaiting their return that I might ship my calves. The sixth morning after I put my captives in the pasture I arose to find my fence torn away by the ignoble redman and my herd of calves had vanished along with my visions of wealth. Muzzy and I saddled our plugs and scoured the country all day. The Indians had driven the calves out of our reach; or rather they had killed about a dozen of them and driven the rest toward the Redwater. On our return we picked up 2 of the youngest calves, strapped them on our saddles and brought them in. One died, the other I sold to the trader at Ft. Buford. That wound up my first speculation in catching buffalo.

July 27, 1899, Anaconda Standard, *p. 5:*

IN THE NATIONAL PARK

Anybody who has it in mind to make the Yellowstone park trip this summer, and is undecided between that tour and some other, would not be on the fence very long if he could hear what Vic Smith has to say about his trip through the park. Vic Smith is the famous bear hunter of the west side, and has more of bruin's scalps at his belt than an ordinary mathematician can count. Mr. Smith spends at least seven-eighths of his time in the mountains and along the streams of Montana, and he knows every fishin' hole and every draw where game is wont to congregate. He is an enthusiast about outdoor life, and his wife in none the less so.

Vic knows of lots and lots of places where game is as plentiful as cracks in Missouri river bottom land, and where fishes fight with each other to get the first whack at the fly. But of all the hunting grounds that have come within the observation of Mr. Smith, none, says he, can hold a candle to the park and its immediate vicinity.

"By George," said Mr. Smith yesterday. "I've seen lots of game in my time, but I never run across anything like the herds of game in the park. I saw one herd of elk that must have numbered more than 200, and bears and deer and all the rest of them were as numerous as anybody could wish to see. I tell you it was a mighty fine thing for sore eyes to see all those animals grazing peacefully and paying no attention to us whatever.

"We had a very fine trip indeed. We left Anaconda just a month ago, with four horses and two wagons. We went by way of Virginia City and Alder gulch, where we took in all the sights and scenes made famous by the association of Montana's earliest pioneers. We saw every tree upon whose branches were hanged the notorious characters who came within the corrective measures of the vigilantes, and I never believed that so many men could have been hanged in so short a time and in so limited an area. From Virginia we went on to the park with one team, stopping whenever we felt so inclined, and generally taking things easy. Once in the park we avoided the traveled roads and kept off the routine journey path. We went this way or that as we pleased, and pitched camp when we pleased. We saw it all, and a good deal more than most people see, I imagine. Altogether, it was the grandest outing I ever had and Mrs. Smith enjoyed it fully as much as I did."

Vic tells a pretty good story on himself—an experience he had with a bear. One night, while they were asleep in the tent, Mrs. Smith was aroused by hearing a noise outside, where the camp stove and provision boxes were. She concluded at once that a bear had found his way to the dainties in the stores. She awakened her husband and told him about it. Vic don't mind a little thing like a bear. He has been in close quarters with so many of them that their bluffs are commonplaces. So Vic thought he would just get up and frighten him off.

"I poked my head out through a narrow opening in the tent," said Vic, "and just as I did so one of the biggest silver tips I ever saw raised up on his haunches not more than four feet from his nose. The bear gave just one grunt, but that was enough for me. I tell you. I never was so scared in my life. By George, but it just set my heart a-thumping like a trip hammer."

November 17, 1900, Anaconda Standard, *p. 4:*

A YOUNG BEAR HUNTER

Vic Smith, who has been hunting bear and other big game alone for these many years, now has an assistant. While this new hunter is not yet quite old enough to shoulder Vic's gun, and has not yet acquired Vic's unerring aim, it will not be long ere he shall have attained both strength and keenness of sight. The companion who is to accompany Vic in his chase after the elusive mountain goat henceforth is nothing more nor less than a bouncing baby boy, who was born to Mrs. Smith yesterday at the family residence in Upper Main street. Both Mrs. Smith and the child are reported as doing well, and while no direct intelligence has come from the father, it is safe to say that he is the happiest man in Montana. Doubtless he will be satisfied to give the bear a rest for a few days now in order to fully enjoy this new happiness which has come to him. There is no man in the entire state who deserves good luck more than does genial, good natured Vic Smith, and his friends rejoice with him at this time when his cup of joy is filled to the brim.

December 16, 1900, Anaconda Standard, *p. 7:*

VIC SMITH SAW STIRRING TIMES IN THE EARLY DAYS

The hardships, sufferings and privations that are included in 30 years of the life of a frontiersman, hunter and Indian fighter might reasonably be expected to leave their mark on any man, but there is one man who seems to have entirely escaped the wearing influences of this strenuous life and who to-day shows not a sign of the thrilling and exciting events in which he has participated during more than a quarter of a century. All these years of stirring work, of exposure to wind and weather, of days and days without rest or food have not left the slightest suspicion of stoop in his arrow-straight form, nor halt in his firm tread. His eye is as keen as ever it was and his hand holds the rifle with a grip as steady as it did 20 years ago. True, there are a few wrinkles beginning to show in his tanned and weather-beaten face, and now and then a suggestion of a gray hair shows among the black. But these are not the effects left by years of adventure, they are the things that are the portion of every man when he passes the mid-way post in life's journey.

The man of whom these things are written is Vic Smith, a name that will recall to the minds of many pioneers of Eastern Montana memories of the stirring days of the '70s and early '80s. Mr. Smith at this time gives his attention to a prosperous ranch in the vicinity of French gulch, 20 or 25 miles from Anaconda, beyond the Continental divide. He claims Anaconda as his home, however, and here his family reside in a comfortable cottage just south of the court house. Recently Mr. Smith's home has been blessed with a son, in whom the father has centered the affections of his big heart.

While his ranch claims some of his time, Mr. Smith still, in great measure, follows the life which has been his for so many years. There are no Indians to wage war upon now, it is true, and the government no longer requires the services of scouts and game-providers, but these facts have made little difference in Mr. Smith's mode of life. There are still bears to be killed and Smith kills them; there are still deer and moose to follow and Smith follows them; quail and pheasant still afford delicious food and Smith's larder, in season, is filled with them; the sport of chasing antelope on the prairies of

Eastern Montana 20 years ago has given way to the sport of chasing the Rocky mountain goat among the crags. Conditions are somewhat changed, but Smith's spirit of the hunt is as keen as ever and scarcely a week passes without bringing added laurels to this man of the alert eye and unfaltering aim.

During the summer and fall months Mr. Smith devotes nearly all of his time to escorting hunting and fishing parties who seek diversion in this region. As a guide he has attained an enviable reputation, which is by no means local, and which is in a sense national. In New York city and elsewhere one will hear Vic Smith spoken of in terms of high compliment by men whom he has piloted through the wilds of this western country. Europeans of distinction, too, have traveled under his guidance. Each succeeding season brings with it an increased demand for his services, and each eastern sportsman whom he takes under escort is sure to recommend him to others. And it is not strange that this is so, for Smith is an invaluable guide. He knows where the game is most abundant, the spots where this or that specie is most wont to congregate, where the biggest and gamiest trout are to be had; he knows how to pitch a camp and where to pitch it; he knows how to cook and to cook well; he knows how to handle horses; how to mend a broken wagon, how to find water when apparently there is none; he knows how to follow a blind trail and he always knows where he's at. His long experience, his unerring judgment, his clear understanding of the affairs of the chase, all these combine to make him an ideal guide, to say nothing of his own genial personality and his faculty to keep everybody good-natured and in a happy mood. It is no wonder, therefore, that Vic Smith is in demand as a guide for hunting parties and that his services command compensation accordingly.

The elements which go to make up Vic Smith's character form a combination which is seldom met with in a man whose life has been devoted to rough and adventurous pursuits such as his has been. Old trappers, hunters and scouts are, as a rule, contaminated with the vices that seem to form a part of the life which they have lived. They are often heavy drinkers, always inveterate users of tobacco, generally their morals are lax and their line of demarkation between right and wrong is usually of the zig-zag kind. Very often they are given to vain glorious boasting of the deeds they have done, and they do not hesitate to throw in a spicy mixture of lies when by so doing they are enabled to accomplish a bit of self-aggrandizement. The direct opposite of this is true in regard to Smith. Liquor is practically foreign to his taste; tobacco he never uses; his ideas of right and wrong are clear-cut, and his moral character is best attested by the esteem and respect in which he is held by his fellow citizens. His modesty is of such a deep-rooted kind that it is a task like that of pulling a tooth to get him to talk about himself or about the incidents wherein he has figured. When he does talk he so carefully eliminates his own personality from the story that the tales loses its spice and resolves itself into a commonplace narrative. Smith has a distinct aversion to heroics of any kind, and when one brings the conversation around to a point within hailing distance of his days on the plains, Smith draws forth his watch and says it's time to go home.

Physically, Smith is not remarkable. In stature he is but little above the medium standard. His frame is not bulky, but it is well knit. His muscles do not form knots like those of an athlete, but they are hard as steel and flexible as rubber. His shoulders are broad and his chest is deep, indicating both strength and endurance. He walks with the step of a man whom experience has taught that missteps are fatal and who knows the value of a cautious tread. His face is bronzed by the weather and is adorned by a black moustache, which overhangs a mouth whose curves show firmness and determination, yet withal gentleness and an entire absence of cruelty. His eyes are sharp and keen and must be possessed of great powers of penetration and range of vision. His dress is modest and usually of black. When hunting he wears leggings which are made for warmth and comfort and with the aim of affording ease of movement. A light colored hat and a handkerchief tied carelessly about the neck complete an equipment of clothing wherein there is an absolute lack of attempt at the spectacular. A rifle that has had years of trial and that has ever proved true is his steadfast companion.

Vic Smith's first experience as a frontiersman was when, as a mere boy, he carried a mail route from Fort Totten, on Devil's lake, in North Dakota, to Fort Abercrombie, on the Red River of the north. His trips were made by dog teams, and in the entire journey of 140 miles there was but one habitation, that of a settler who, during the next season, was murdered by the Indians. Smith discontinued his occupation as a government mail carrier in 1872, and for the next year he engaged in hunting and trapping. He joined a party of half-breeds and hunted with them for a considerable length of time. In 1873 Smith found himself at Bismarck, which at that time consisted of a few log cabins, some tents and a very tough population. In 1875 he started from Bismarck for the Black Hills in company with two other men. On the Cannon Ball river the Sioux Indians stole the saddle and pack horses, and at night they killed one of the men. Smith escaped, however, and returned to Bismarck. The next year, 1876, Smith began his service as a government scout. He did duty under Generals Terry and Miles and remained with them until the Indian wars were over. During this time Smith, as perhaps did every other scout, had many thrilling experiences and more than once was encompassed by circumstances where death seemed sure. His own bravery and cool and calculating judgment, however, saved him and he always escaped. Upon these matters Smith is reticent to the point of exasperation.

Smith takes a pardonable pride in telling how, in the early days, he was hunted for months and months by Indian police, government officers and sheriffs' officers, who had a warrant for his arrest, but whom, in a spirit of fun, he took a pleasure in eluding. This incident being humorous, Smith is willing to talk about it. In 1881 two young men named Boyd and Knapp ran an eating house at Poplar Creek on a Sioux reservation. They asked Smith to bring them some whiskey. He knew that the federal government was severe in its punishment for this offense, but to accommodate his friends he took the risk and carried to them the liquor. Some of the Indian police learned of the transaction, and while he was in the place eight of them appeared bearing a warrant for his arrest. Realizing his position Smith hastily slipped on a big fur overcoat and sprang through a window just as the moment when the Indian police entered. Outside he found a cordon of Indians drawn about the place, but through strategy and diplomacy he passed through the line. As soon as it was known that the man whom they were looking for had escaped them, the Indian police began a vigorous search and were assisted by the government officers. For three days Smith lay hidden in a graveyard, with nothing to eat but rosebuds. At midnight of the third day, when the search had relaxed somewhat, Smith came forth from his hiding place in the thicket, cut down two "good Indians"—dead ones—secured from the corpses blankets and the lariats with which they were tied, and made his way to the hills, where he caught an Indian pony and made his escape. The warrant, however, was in pursuit of him, and years afterward he was arrested at Miles City. When taken before the United States commissioner at Fort Buford he was promptly acquitted.

There are many incidents of this kind in the life of Smith. Some of them are exceedingly interesting and all are entertaining and amusing.

Smith was one the frontier when game of all kinds was there in abundance. He tells in a simple yet pathetic way the story of how the last big herd of buffalo in the Northwest was practically exterminated.

"In the days when I first took to following the life of the frontiersman," says he, "there was game in plenty. Buffalo roamed the plains in vast herds. I could not calculate their numbers—no man could. I remember when, on the Missouri river, steamboats had to lay by for days to allow a herd of buffalo to cross. Elk, deer and antelope were equally plentiful, and the only regret I have of the life which I have led is that I thoughtlessly slaughtered many hundreds of these animals when I could have easily refrained from doing so.

I wish now that my aim hadn't been so good. But the end of the big buffalo herds was a short time in coming. In 1883 the vast herds had disappeared until there was but one congregation that was worthy of the dignity of the term "herd." That group contained about 10,000 head and they had gathered on the Cannon Ball and Moreau rivers in what is now North Dakota.

"The Indians seemed to come to a knowledge that the mightiest game on earth was being speedily exterminated, and they apparently concluded to take the last whack at it. In the fall of 1883 Sitting Bull with 2,000 of his people came up the river after the game. The first day's run netted them more than 2,000 head, and by Christmas day the Indians, aided materially, I am ashamed to admit, by the whites, had virtually exterminated the last of the big herds of buffalo in the Northwest."

June 2, 1901, Anaconda Standard, *p. 4:*

BEARS RAID THE RANGES

Vic Smith, the mighty hunter, is in the city from his Big Hole ranch with a load of skins. Three bears and five coyotes have fallen before his rifle recently and these are the animals that furnished him with the pelts he brought in.

One of the bears was a monster in life. He was one of those huge creatures that Seaton Thompson likes to draw and write about, but that most people like to keep away from. For his thieving propensities this bear was executed.

In recent weeks the bears have been living on fresh meat at the expense of Walker & Bielenberg and other Big Hole cattle owners. It became the practice of the bears to run off a few head of cattle every few days and have a feast after the manner of the Sioux in the old days. They killed a dozen or more head in this way.

Now cattle are in demand and are high. Walker & Bielenberg have been bringing all the cattle they could spare to Anaconda for shipment to the coast and to Alaska. It began to look down in the Big Hole as if the coast people and the gold hunters in Alaska would have to go hungry if the bears were to continue their thieving operations much longer.

Then Vic Smith was called in. He girded on his hunting knife and cartridge belt and taking his rifle in hand he struck out to do business with the bears. The latter had no idea such a man as Vic Smith was about. Then suddenly the big chief bear of the whole bunch, the boss cattle thief of the lot, was caught almost in the act of taking cattle that did not belong to him. He was tried and executed on the spot. Two other bears, not so large, also were slain by the great hunter. This broke up the bear family and it is believed the cattle will be safe for some time to come.

October 21, 1901, Anaconda Standard, *p. 2:*

VIC SMITH'S NARROW ESCAPE FROM DEATH

Vic Smith, the noted hunter and trapper, on Friday evening narrowly escaped a tragic death. At about 4 o'clock Mr. Smith attempted to take the hobbles from a horse in a field of his ranch on Seymour creek, a few miles from the road that skirts the Big Hole river, about 35 miles from Anaconda. The horse was restless and refused to stand still while the owner removed the restraining straps. He continually went around in a circle, so that Mr. Smith was sometimes in front of him and at other times behind him. After an hour or so of this sort of thing Mr. Smith and the horse neared the bank of the stream.

When Mr. Smith made another effort to reach the animal's forefeet the horse suddenly swung about and kicked Mr. Smith in the jaw. The force of the blow threw Mr. Smith into the stream and rendered him unconscious.

How long he lay in the water Mr. Smith does not know, but when he regained his senses it was quite dark. His body was completely covered with water and his face was half covered. Fortunately his mouth and nose remained above the surface and to that fact is due his salvation.

As soon as possible, but with great difficulty, Mr. Smith made his way to his home. All the while the wound bled with great profusion and within an hour the injured man found himself so weak that he was barely able to stand. He realized that the flow of blood must be stopped at all hazards. He went in search of his horses and by a lucky chance found them near by. He drove to the ranch of Mr. Deno, a distance of about five miles. Several times during the journey his strength failed him and it was with the utmost difficulty that he maintained his seat. When he arrived at the Deno ranch he as so weak from loss of blood that he was obliged to crawl on his hands and knees from the road to the house. The inmates of the house were soon aroused by his feeble cries for help. Mr. Smith was taken inside and the flow of blood was checked.

Mr. Smith remained all night and until the following day at the Deno ranch and then proceeded to Anaconda, where his injuries were attended to. It was found that he had sustained a fracture of the jawbone besides a deep cut in the lower part of his face. He is now much improved and expects to return to the country within a few days.

Mr. Smith counts himself lucky in two particulars—that the horse's foot did not land squarely on his forehead and that he was not drowned before he regained consciousness.

Mrs. Smith and the family have been in Anaconda for some weeks, and there was no one at the Smith ranch when the accident occurred.

April 13, 1902, Anaconda Standard, *p. 19:*

DICK ROCK, THE TRAPPER, AND HIS ODD CAREER

One of the old time associates of the late Dick Rock has prepared for the Sunday Standard the following sketch of the famous frontiersman's life:

Charles W. Rock, better known as Dick Rock, who was gored to death by a tame bison recently, was born in Vermont 49 years ago. His parents and relatives now live near Glendive, Mont. In the fall of 1880 he was hired by Vic Smith, the veteran bear hunter, to skin buffalo north of Glendive on the Redwater. Those were the days when all men were game hogs—at least buffalo hunters were. Indians and buffalo had no rights which the hunters were bound to respect. Most old timers are ashamed to 'fess up to the killings they made then. Rock skinned buffalo three years for Smith. He then went to Livingston, where he discovered a coal mine, which he sold to the late George Anderson for a snug sum.

In the fall of 1885 the famous Marquis de Mores came to Big Timber and joined Vic Smith, who had acquired the reputation of being the champion rifle shot and boss hunter of Montana, on a bear hunt. They killed four bears, all large silver tips, in one week. On their return to Big Timber Smith again met Rock and they renewed their old friendship and looked about for a location for a game ranch.

They drifted to Henry's lake, Idaho, where Rock met his death at the hands, or rather horns, of his pet buffalo. There they established their game ranch, which for years bore the name the Smithrocksian.

Smith was the first person to scheme the catching of elk by chasing them on skis. In the five years that the two men were partners they caught and sold more than 300 elk alive. Smith was a big hearted, generous sort of man with his money, while Rock was rather saving and careful in regard to financial matters. At the end of five years Smith had what he started with, a cayuse and saddle and gun, while Rock, having saved his money, had $5,000 in bank. Smith always guided the hunting parties, while Rock, who was a powerful man and a first class worker, ran the ranch. Rock claimed that he never got tired, while Smith was always tired. Rock was perhaps the best and swiftest man on skis in Montana. At the end of five years Smith and Rock dissolved partnership, but not friendship, for their friendship was like that of Damon and Pythias.

Rock greatly disliked a reputation that was given him but to which he was not entitled. He frequently said he never was a scout for the government in any form, and did not know how the report that he was one started. His old time partner, Vic Smith, was scout for Terry, Custer and Miles at the same time that Jack Conley, sheriff of Deer Lodge county, was a packer and master of transportation.

Rock was a born animal trainer, and could hold any animal with his eye, but it seemed the pet buffalo which killed him was not entirely susceptible to Rock's mesmeric glance.

April 25, 1902, Anaconda Standard, *p. 4:*

IN THE BIG HOLE COUNTRY

"There is more snow in the Big Hole country than there has been for years," said Vic Smith, the trapper, guide and ranchman, who has just returned from a trip to the great cattle county. "In fact, an old placer miner who has operated in French gulch for more than 20 years told me that he had never seen so much snow in the region before. Fences cannot be seen and in many places where there has been drifting the snow lies 10 and 12 feet deep. I should say that there is an average of at least four feet. The deep snow begins at a point five miles this side of the summit of Mill creek pass and it continues into the Big Hole basin.

"The deep snow, however, does not interfere with traffic. The road has been kept open all winter by the passage of thousands of head of beef cattle, which have been coming out of the range country in great droves.

"The stock has stood the winter in excellent shape. I have heard talk that there were losses, but not a single cattleman with whom I talked spoke of losing a hoof. Last year was a good season for hay and the ranchmen put up large quantities of it, so that they have been able to feed whenever necessary. There is at this time no shortage of hay. In fact, there is a bountiful supply of it, and there is not the slightest danger of losses from lack of feed.

"Abundant as hay is, however, one finds much difficulty in buying it. Figures as high as $20 a ton, I hear, have been refused for hay. This is in decided contrast to conditions existing in former years, when hay could be had for $3 and $4 a ton. The principal reason for the advance in prices, I am told, is the fact that so many cattle are being moved. These drove are fed over night at various ranches and the owner of the ranch and the hay stacks has not been backward in taking advantage of the conditions. Fifteen cents a night per head is now the ruling price for over-night feeding, whereas formerly it was only 7 cents."

September 6, 1902, Anaconda Standard, *p. 5:*

BAD BEAR OF THE BIG HOLE

"Vic" Smith, Montana's famous scout, guide and hunter, had a thrilling experience and narrow escape from death while in the Big Hole country on Thursday. That the Anacondan is alive is simply the result of extreme good luck on the part of Mr. Smith. As it is he is nursing a bruised hand and a badly lacerated right leg, the natural consequence of a fall he had from a mountainous cliff directly caused by the sudden attack of a large silver tip bear while the hunter was on Goat's peak at the head of Fish Trap creek in the Big Hole county. One of the horses Mr. Smith had with him at the time of his mountainous trip was killed, and rolled fully half a mile down the mountain side before stopping. When its progress was stopped the animal was a battered, torn and disfigured mass, without a sound bone left in its body.

Mr. Smith left Anaconda on Thursday a week ago to hunt bear at Walker's ranch in the he Big Hole country. He had been offered a good reward in the event of his bringing down a silver tip bear which had been killing the stock in that vicinity. On Monday last, while on his way to the ranch, he visited the Fish Trap creek county and had killed some deer and mountain sheep. The day following the hunter took a saddle and pack horse and started to bring his game to camp. On the way he had occasion to pass over a rugged and rough mountain cliff. While here he noticed bear tracks. He secured his gun from the pack saddle and had gone only a few feet distant from a natural cave in the mountain side when his horse shied. The jerking of the animal on the bridle made Mr. Smith turn, and as he did so he saw a huge bear raised on his haunches in the act of striking the horse. The trapper jumped, but not soon enough to escape the fury of the bear. The beast struck the horse and sent bear hunter and animal down the mountain side. The horse cleared the hunter in his fall. Mr. Smith fell about 25 feet, but managed to secure a hold on a projecting rock and stopped his progress. The horse went over and over bounding, at times, according to the hunter, 50 feet in the air. He finally lay at the bottom of the ravine, half a mile away. Mr. Smith carefully got back to where his pack horse had remained standing, and after two hours' of hard work got down the mountain side. His saddle horse was dead with every bone in his body broken and the saddle was badly torn. The hunter returned to camp, and yesterday came back to Anaconda with friends.

September 7, 1902, Anaconda Standard, *p. 5:*

VIC SMITH'S THRILLING EXPERIENCE WITH A BEAR ON SUMMIT
OF THE ROCKIES

"The most satisfactory way, from a self-preservation point, to shoot a
bear is to first find a comfortable seat on a limb of a well developed tree,"
remarked "Vic" Smith yesterday when asked regarding the proper method
to purse when hunting Bruin. "I find that when the hunter is up a tree and
has sighted a good-sized bear all conditions prove more satisfactory for the
man behind the gun. Of course, the real clever hunter is not frightened to
death when he spots a bear, but the bears you are likely to encounter over in
the Big Hole country are big fellows and they have an unusual amount of
strength and vitality. Why, you can plug one of those fellows square in the
heart and he'll run fully 200 feet before dropping. I've known them to do
this even after their heart has been literally torn to pieces. When the hunter
is sure the bear will come his way soon he knows that if he remains on the
ground the brute will scent him a long distance away. If he is up a tree the
wind blows over Bruin's head and he gets no clew."

"Vic" Has Had Experience.

Montana's unique scout, Indian fighter and hunter knows whereof he
speaks, for he has hunted buffalo, bear and the other large game of the West
for many years. He climbed over the mountainous peaks of the Big Hole
range before a piece of ground was broken by the footprints of man or domestic
animal. He knows the cliffs, the ravines, the valleys and the gorges of the
mountains for 50 miles about this country like a book. "Vic" Smith is not a
hunter who likes to tell of his experiences or of the big game he has brought
down in his time. His manner when speaking of the many thrilling adventures
in which he has taken an active part is more the style of a modest country
school boy. He delights to hunt, but he doesn't consider that he has moved
the world in its position when his gun brings down a fine, antlered deer, a
mountain sheep or a savage silver-tip bear.

So it was yesterday, when relating to the Standard representative the
experience he had during last week in which Bruin got the drop on the hunter
and not only killed his horse, but brought about the fall from a cliff which
nearly cost Mr. Smith his life.

The Hunter's Own Story.

In relating the story Mr. Smith said: "I went out Thursday a week ago.
My purpose for making a trip into the mountains was to bring down a big

bear which had been killing off the cattle at the Walker ranch in the Big Hole country. A good reward had been offered for the brute's death, and I concluded to try my luck. On the 1st of the month I camped on Fish Trap creek, about 35 miles south from Anaconda, on the Big Hole river. On that day it occurred to me to go after game and I climbed to Goat's peak, some distance above timber line. That particular locality is not at all an inviting place, for it is infrequently visited by man and consequently the wild game abounds there. The point visited by me is the summit of the Rockies and affords considerable sport for the hunter. I managed to kill three mountain goats and two deer and returned to camp well pleased with my trip into the peaks. On the following morning I took saddle and pack animal and started again to the mountains, expecting to bring my game to camp. I had reached a high altitude and was walking leisurely along leading my saddle horse with the pack animal following when I noticed exceptionally large bear tracks on the ground ahead. Securing my rifle from the pack saddle I continued on my way. Shortly our path had led over the top of a rugged peak. The path was hardly four feet wide and continued to wind around the mountain top. On my left were innumerable natural caves here and there in the mountainous wall.

The Bear Appears.

"When I had proceeded some 50 feet along this treacherous pathway my saddle horse snorted and pulled hard on the rein fastened over my shoulder. I quickly turned my head and saw standing erect on his haunches, with outstretched paws, a big silver tip bear. The animal was in the act of striking the horse. I jumped, as did the saddle horse, while my pack animal turned and ran back. Bruin's paw struck the saddle, and as the horse winced the claws of the savage brute scratched along the seat of the saddle. The blow, however, was sufficient to knock the horse from his footing, and he tumbled over the ledge, pulling me with him. My gun went spinning down the mountain, and horse and man fell in a conglomerate mass some 25 feet below. The animal struck on my right leg and severely bruised it. Besides this injury my left hand and arm sustained bruises and cuts. I managed to secure a hold on a projecting rock, after I had gone some 50 feet further in sliding rock. The horse found itself unable to stop, and soon was bounding and bumping, like a boulder, down the steep incline. At times the horse shot into the air 50 or 75 feet, and then it would strike against a rock and go on further down, bumping and rolling. Strange to say, the animal could not straighten out, or it might have been saved considerable of the fall. When it went over the cliff it struck head first, and that's the way it continued down the mountain for fully half a mile.

The Bear Was There.

"I looked up as soon as I saw that there could be nothing done to save my horse, and there was the bear calmly looking over the ledge. I had neither gun nor knife, as both found their way from my grasp and tumbled to the depths below. Bruin looked savage enough to jump from the cliff after me, but soon he pulled his head back and was gone. I concluded to save the pack horse at any rate, and after no little difficulty got back to the path by a circuitous route. My horse was standing about 100 yards distant, and securing him I continued on to where I had left my sheep and deer the day before. The sight that met my eyes demonstrated why the bear had not made a greater effort to kill one of the horses or me. Both deer had been attacked by the brute, while one of the goats was partially eaten. Bruin had feasted on my game and was doubtless in his cave asleep when I passed along the path with the horses. Thanks to the deer and goats, I was save a fiercier struggle with the bear single-handed and unarmed.

"I managed to get back to camp by riding the pack animal, and later I was overtaken by Councilman Luxton and his party of friends. They kindly assisted me and made matters comfortable, and yesterday I returned to Anaconda."

The hunter had some badly bruised limbs as evidence of the rough and tumble experience. He said he had no intention of going back for the silver tip bear that has raised such havoc with him, but those who know him best say "Vic" will get that bear or the bear will get him before the winter sets in.

August 29, 1909, Anaconda Standard, *Part Two:*

When Roosevelt Hunted With Vic Smith

With mingled modesty and frankness Vic Smith, noted hunter, government scout and Indian fighter, speaks of his acquaintance with Theodore Roosevelt, formed more than a quarter of a century ago in the center of the rugged bad lands of Montana and Dakota. The friendship then formed has grown to admiration, and it has often occurred that the man who in recent years has been so prominent in the management of affairs of world interest has taken time at odd intervals to scribble a note to his friend of the plains—to the man who gave him his primary lessons in the science of hunting big game.

Naturally, while contemplating the spoils of his hunt in East Africa, Mr. Roosevelt's mind is sometimes carried back to his hunts for deer among the breaks of the Missouri, the chase after great buffalo herds along the Cannon Ball, and the more difficult, if less dangerous, expeditions after elk in the mountains; and then comes the desire to let his friend and hunting companion of years ago know about it all. Such men do not require to be told the full particulars of a hunt, just a line is enough to tell the story of a trip, and so Mr. Roosevelt, in his jungle tent with his rifle leaning against the improvised table ready for instant use, writes the brief note, commonplace enough to the average person, but to "Yellowstone Vic," the hunter, containing volumes of exciting detail.

Yellowstone Vic.

Vic Smith, or Yellowstone Vic, as he was called during his scouting days, has a quiet gentleness of manner and soft, low voice that contrasts singularly with the wild and dangerous life he led. It seems strange that this man, whose life history and actual experience duplicate the Leather Stocking tales of Fenimore Cooper, this hunter, trapper, scout, who for so many years placed sole dependence on his rifle for his livelihood, should now be one of the individuals who merely add to the total of a large industrial center like Anaconda.

Proof that Vic was a man of more than ordinary force is found in Mr. Roosevelt's book "Hunting Trips of a Ranchman," in which he says: "Old Vic, a former scout and Indian fighter, is conceded to be the best hunter in the West. I have seen him do most skillful work with the rifle. He can cut the head off of a chicken or a grouse at 90 or 100 yards; a dead shot at running game, he can knock over deer when they are so far away that I would not dream of shooting. Yet I have seen him make miss shots at game when his 'medicine was bad.' He was cradled in the midst of wild life and has handled a rifle and used it against both brute and human foes since childhood."

Game was Plentiful.

As told in practically the hunter's own words, it was in September, 1883, that Theodore Roosevelt came West for his health and dropped off at Medora, a hamlet at the crossing of the Little Missouri in North Dakota, named after the wife of Marquis de Mores. At that time there still remained in the country a few thousand buffalo and the future president enjoyed his first buffalo hunt in company with "Yellowstone Vic." In less than one year all were gone, sacrificed to the greed of hide hunters—all with the exception of a few stragglers which W. D. Hornaday of the Smithsonian Institution at Washington killed and mounted. Mr. Hornaday found about a dozen head on the north bank of the Yellowstone, which he slaughtered and mounted, and they may now be seen at the Smithsonian Institution.

Elk, mountain sheep, black tail and white tail deer were very numerous in the Bad Lands, and antelope by the thousand wintered in the river breaks. Coyotes, wolves and bear were as plentiful as dogs around a Crow camp. It was to this country that Roosevelt came for the purpose of engaging in the cattle business. He located and secured possession of 1,000 acres of land, constructed corrals, houses and cattle sheds, and, when the work he had planned was well under way he employed A. W. Merrifield, who is now United States marshal for the district of Montana, as foreman. Then Roosevelt devoted much of his time to hunting.

They Get Acquainted.

One day Mr. Roosevelt rode over to the buffalo camp of Yellowstone Vic, on the Cannon Ball, and there formed an acquaintance with the scout that has ripened into lasting friendship. Vic, who at the time was easily the best rifle shot in the country, says he had no advantage over Mr. Roosevelt. The two enjoyed many hunts together, but it was the first time out that the embryo ranchman secured the respect of the veteran hunter. While riding across the prairie Mr. Roosevelt was the first to see a small band of about 30 buffalo. The animals were on a bench about one mile distant, and the hunters carefully worked their way to within 20 yards of the animals before it was necessary to appear where they could be seen. While riding along Mr. Roosevelt informed Vic that he proposed to kill only one animal, as he was dead opposed to the extermination of this noble animal.

Roosevelt's First Buffalo.

When within 200 yards of the buffalo Mr. Roosevelt, whose nerves were strung to a high pitch, yelled and, slapping his horse with his cowboy hat, dashed into the herd. His horse was an exceptionally good one, and, instead of at once shooting, Roosevelt rode by the side of one of the animals and urged it forward by repeatedly slapping it with his hat. Vic, who had never been in company with a man who was opposed to wholesale slaughter, was filled with wonder and admiration and finally entered into the spirit of the chase without firing a shot.

When the game began to tire Mr. Roosevelt picked out a young bull and, riding by the side of the animal, fired a bullet into his neck, intending to break the bone. The bull fell and the hunters stopped. Roosevelt dismounted and, drawing his hunting knife, went to the animal and drove it to the hilt in its breast. Desiring to save the head for a specimen, he wanted the animal to bleed well and this was his reason for using the knife.

The bullet had only creased the bull and the knife only served to revive him. With a roar he jumped to his feet and dashed after the fleeing herd.

Roosevelt jumped to one side, giving his majesty right of way. The two hunters then remounted and were soon again alongside of the animal, now rapidly bleeding to death from he knife wound. Vic would have ended it all, but Mr. Roosevelt forbade him, saying "This is my funeral," and on they went across the plain. Soon the bull began to tire and he finally stopped, the blood pouring from the wound and from the nostrils. He still looked the courageous and dangerous monarch that he had been, and strained every muscle to remain on his feet, but finally he pitched forward on his knees and down, never to rise again.

The letter which photographed above is self-explanatory. It will be noticed that Mr. Roosevelt writes in the hunter's vernacular, using the singular instead of the plural when recounting the number of animals killed.

Readers of Bret Harte will recall that his California characters talk that way. Analogous to this westernism is the employment of the present tense of verbs when speaking of past events. Gamblers, even those who are educated, never say "I won," or "I lost," but always "I win," or "I lose."

ENDNOTES

INTRODUCTION

1. June 14, 1860, U.S. Census, Oshkosh City, Winnebago County, Wisconsin. Vic also may have had a brother named Frank. Several news briefs in the *Bad Lands Cow Boy* (1884-1886) allude that Vic and Frank Smith were brothers, and Jim Metcalfe, great-great-grandson of Frank M. Smith, has photos and old news clippings of Vic Smith among his family papers. However, to date, no official document showing a lineal relationship between Victor Grant Smith and Frank M. Smith has been located. It is possible that Frank was a nickname for DeMorny. Mr. Metcalfe has a postcard of the John J. Ryan Building in Omro, Wisconsin, noting that "Railey and Morney" were born there, and another postcard stating that "Frank and I were born there."

2. Smith uses Rae and Bill interchangeably in his manuscript. The 1860 U.S. Census for Oshkosh City, Winnebago County, Wisconsin, lists the name Ray, and the 1870 U.S. Census for Douglas County, Minnesota, lists Rae. No records listing Bill were found.

3. 1870 U.S. Census for Douglas County, Minnesota.

4. *Anaconda Standard*, December 16, 1900, "Vic Smith Saw Stirring Times in the Early Days."

5. Ibid. This story is also recounted in *The Rockies and N. W. Educator* (March 1892).

6. See Luther S. Kelly, *"Yellowstone Kelly": The Memoirs of Luther S. Kelly*. Milo M. Quaife, ed. (New Haven, Conn.: Yale University Press, 1926).

7. In 1935, Tom Ray interviewed Bill Cheney's niece Susie Harrington, who used to keep house for Cheney. According to Ray's notes, "Bill Cheney rode as protection for Vic Smith, who was a dispatch rider—and a band of Indians overtook them north of Glendive and a memorable ride for life took place." From Tom E. Ray files at Mon-Dak Heritage Center in Sidney, Montana. Also see Eva Marie Dawe et al., *Courage Enough: Mon-Dak Family Histories* (Richland County, Mont.: Bicentennial Edition, 1975) and Tom Ray, *Yellowstone Red* (Philadelphia: Dorrance & Co., 1948).

8. For more details on Smith's buffalo exploits, see Larry Barsness, *Heads, Hides, and Horns: The Compleat Buffalo Book* (Fort Worth: Texas Christian University Press, 1985); Mark H. Brown and W. R. Felton, *The Frontier Years: L. A. Huffman, Photographer of the Plains* (New York: Henry Holt & Co., 1955); Wayne Gard, *The Great Buffalo Hunt* (New York: Alfred A. Knopf, 1959); William T. Hornaday, "The Extermination of the American Bison with a Sketch of Its Discovery and Life History," Report of the National Museum. 1887. Reprint. (Seattle: Facsimile Reproduction, 1971); Frank G. Roe, *The North American Buffalo: A Critical Study of the Species in Its Wild State* (Toronto: University of Toronto Press, 1951); Erling Rolfsrud, *The Story of North Dakota* (Alexandria, Minn.: Lantern Books, 1963); and Zena Irma Trinka, *Out Where the West Begins—Being the Early and Romantic History of North Dakota* (St. Paul, Minn.: The Pioneer Co., 1920).

9. *Glendive Times*, April 20, 1882, "Is It Hardscrabble or What?"

10. *Glendive Times*, August 3, 1882, "Notes on Newlon" refers to a Mrs. Smith. In a letter to local historian Tom Ray, Lower Yellowstone Valley pioneer Leslie Lovering noted that Vic Smith and his wife lived on Fox Creek in 1882. See letter in the files of the Mon-Dak Heritage Center in Sidney, Montana.

11. 1880 U.S. Census for Dawson County, Montana Territory.

12. See Joseph Taylor's *Kaleidoscopic Lives: A Companion Book to Frontier and Indian Life* (Washburn, N.Dak.: Privately published, 1902).

13. See *Glendive Times Supplement*, June 8, 1882, and *Glendive Times*, July 27, 1882.

14. Handwritten notes from the Billings County Museum in Medora, reportedly taken from *Bad Lands Cow Boy*, June 2, 1883.

15. See this cited in the reprint of Harold E. Briggs, *Frontiers of the Northwest* (New York: D. Appleton-Century Co., 1950).

16. *Dickinson Press*, August 4, 1884.

17. See Taylor's *Kaleidoscopic Lives*.

18. See Hornaday's "The Extermination of the American Bison"; also *Anaconda Standard*, December 16, 1900, "Vic Smith Saw Stirring Times in the Early Days," and *Recreation* (July 1897), "Where the Buffalo Went."

19. *Anaconda Standard*, December 16, 1900.

20. *Bad Lands Cow Boy*, June 26, 1884.

21. See Lewis F. Crawford, *The Medora-Deadwood Stage Line* (Seattle: Shorey Book Store, 1964); Irma Klock, *All Roads Lead to Deadwood* (Lead, S.Dak.: North Plains Press, 1979); and Arnold Goplen, "The Career of Marquis de Mores in the Badlands of North Dakota," *State Historical Society of North Dakota Proceedings* 13 (January-April 1946). In "Medora-Black Hills Stage Line," Lewis F. Crawford wrote, "Bob Roberts and Vic. Smith helped in erecting the stage stations. The latter was one of the most renowned market-hunters in the region round about, conceded to be the best shot in this part of the country where every man was a good marksman. He acted as guide to the Marquis on some hunting trips and on several occasions hunted with Theodore Roosevelt when the latter held interests at the Maltese Cross and the

Elkhorn." In *Collections of the State Historical Society*, vol. 7, editor O. G. Libby. Grand Forks: State Historical Society of North Dakota, 1925.

22. *Bad Lands Cow Boy*, September 18, 1884.

23. Although documents showing a blood relationship between Vic and Frank Smith have not been found, these references in the *Bad Lands Cow Boy* allude that they were brothers: February 28, 1884; March 6, 1884; March 27, 1884; May 7, 1885; July 16, 1885; August 13, 1885; August 20, 1885; October 22, 1885.

24. *Bad Lands Cow Boy*, February 28, 1884.

25. *Bad Lands Cow Boy*, March 6, 1884.

26. *Bad Lands Cow Boy*, March 27, 1884.

27. *Bad Lands Cow Boy*, April 3, 1884.

28. *Bad Lands Cow Boy*, September 25, 1884.

29. *Bad Lands Cow Boy*, October 2, 1884, and October 16, 1884.

30. *Bad Lands Cow Boy*, October 30, 1884.

31. *Bad Lands Cow Boy*, November 20, 1884.

32. *Bad Lands Cow Boy*, December 25, 1884.

33. *Bad Lands Cow Boy*, December 4, 1884, and January 1, 1885.

34. *Bad Lands Cow Boy*, November 20, 1884.

35. See A. C. Huidekoper's *My Experience and Investment in the Bad Lands of Dakota and Some of the Men I Met There* (Baltimore: Wirth Bros., 1947) and Donald Dresden, *The Marquis de Morès, Emperor of the Bad Lands* (Norman: University of Oklahoma Press, 1970).

36. From the Lewis Crawford papers, A37 Book #23 p/9, North Dakota State Historical Library, Bismarck, North Dakota.

37. See Joseph Taylor, *Beavers, Their Ways, and Other Sketches* (Washburn, N.Dak.: Privately published, 1904).

38. *Bad Lands Cow Boy*, March 5, 1885.

39. *Bad Lands Cow Boy*, March 19, 1885.

40. *Bad Lands Cow Boy*, May 7, 1885.

41. This probably refers to the collapse of the cut bank where Smith was standing.

42. *Bad Lands Cow Boy*, May 7, 1885.

43. *Bad Lands Cow Boy*, January 1, 1885, and January 15, 1885.

44. *Bad Lands Cow Boy*, February 5, 1885.

45. *Bad Lands Cow Boy*, February 12, 1885.

46. *Bad Lands Cow Boy*, January 14, 1886.

47. *Bad Lands Cow Boy*, May 13, 1886.

48. See Trinka's *Medora, The Secret of the Badlands* (Lidgerwood, N.Dak.: First Award Books, 1960) and *"Teddy," The Saga of the Badlands* (Lidgerwood, N.Dak.: International Book Publishers, 1958).

49. From Caroline McGill files, #945. Mrs. Eda Benson, 5-1-39, in Merrill G. Burlingame Special Collections, Montana State University, Renne Library, Bozeman, Montana.

50. See Philip Ashton Rollins, *The Cowboy: An Unconventional History of Civilization on the Old-Time Cattle Range.* 1922. Reprint. (Albuquerque: University of New Mexico Press, 1979.)

51. *Bad Lands Cow Boy*, June 25, 1885.

52. *Bad Lands Cow Boy*, July 16, 1885.

53. *Bad Lands Cow Boy*, August 13, 1885.

54. Reprinted in *Bad Lands Cow Boy*, September 3, 1885.

55. *Bad Lands Cow Boy*, August 20, 1885.

56. *Bad Lands Cow Boy*, October 22, 1885.

57. *Judith Basin County Press*, 1925, "Death of 'Vic' Smith in Duluth Recalls Many Stories of His Life As a Hunter in Montana." In Montana News Association Inserts file, Montana Historical Society, Helena, Montana. The watch chain probably belonged to George Grinnell. In his autobiography, Smith mentions that he acquired a leather watch chain from Grinnell when he died and that Cole Younger gave him a miniature skull.

58. Letter dated April 16, 1913, from Vic Smith in Chicago to Theodore Roosevelt. In the Theodore Roosevelt Collection at the Houghton Library, Harvard University, Cambridge, Massachusetts.

59. Letter dated April 22, 1913, to Vic Smith in Chicago from Theodore Roosevelt. In the Theodore Roosevelt Collection at the Houghton Library, Harvard University, Cambridge, Massachusetts.

60. Letters from Eugene F. Grover to personnel at the Theodore Roosevelt National Memorial Park in Medora, North Dakota, July 29, 1958, July 18, 1959, and December 5, 1959. In the collections at Theodore Roosevelt National Memorial Park, Medora, North Dakota.

61. *Anaconda Standard*, August 29, 1909, "When Roosevelt Hunted With Vic Smith," Second Section; see Appendix to this volume. Letter dated May 12, 1913, from Vic Smith in Chicago to Theodore Roosevelt at Oyster Bay, Long Island. In the Theodore Roosevelt Collection at the Houghton Library, Harvard University, Cambridge, Massachusetts.

62. Letter dated October 27, 1905, to Vic Smith in Anaconda from William Loeb, on behalf of Theodore Roosevelt. In the Theodore Roosevelt Collection at the Houghton Library, Harvard University, Cambridge, Massachusetts. On the bottom of this letter, Smith wrote that this referred to their buffalo hunt.

63. See Theodore Roosevelt, *Hunting Trips of a Ranchman: Hunting Trips on the Prairie and in the Mountains,* Executive Edition (New York: P. F. Collier & Son, 1893). c.1885 by A.P. Putnam's Sons.

64. See Eva Marie Dawe et al., *Courage Enough: Mon-Dak Family Histories.*

65. See Charles Marble ("Buckskin Charley"), "Fifty Years in and Around Yellowstone Park," typescript 1932 at Merrill G. Burlingame Special Collections, Montana State University, Renne Library, Bozeman, Montana. Also see "Cowboys," Park County Biography—WPA files 34-0-1-27. Interview of Charles Marble by Elva Howard, in Merrill G. Burlingame Special Collections, Montana State University, Renne Library, Bozeman, Montana.

66. Marriage license for Vic Smith and Eugenia Dengler, dated July 27, 1892, Silver Bow County, Montana.

67. *Judith Basin County Press*, 1925. In Montana News Association Inserts file, Montana Historical Society, Helena, Montana.

68. In school records for 1906-1907 for the Anaconda school district; see also *Anaconda Standard*, November 17, 1900, "A Young Bear Hunter."

69. *Anaconda Standard*, November 17, 1900.

70. *New Northwest*, April 21, 1894, "A Famous Hunter," taken from Vic Smith folder in vertical file at Montana Historical Society. In 1894, Vic and Eugenia resided at the Allerdice ranch near Lima, Montana; see also Anaconda City Directories, 1902-1909.

71. *Judith Basin County Press*, 1925, "Death of 'Vic' Smith in Duluth Recalls Many Stories of His Life As a Hunter in Montana"; also Anaconda City Directories, 1902-1909. "Vic was a guard or a gunman for Marcus Daly or the Walker Brothers in 1891," from notes from Mrs. Eda Benson (9-8-39) in Caroline McGill Papers 1-148, Box 2, Merrill G. Burlingame Special Collections, Montana State University, Renne Library, Bozeman, Montana.

72. *Anaconda Standard*, December 16, 1900, "Vic Smith Saw Stirring Times in the Early Days."

73. *Ibid.*; also see Marian Geil, comp., *All Things Considered: A History of the Anaconda Methodist Church, Among Other Things* (Anaconda, Mont.: Jean Mills, 1984), especially section entitled "Recollections of the Rev. Euster," circa 1912.

74. *Judith Basin County Press*, 1925.

75. *Ibid.*

76. *Duluth Herald*, August 10, 1925, "Frontiersman Called by Death. Vic G. Smith, Friend of Roosevelt, Dies in Duluth."

77. See U.S. census records for 1900, 1910, 1920, as listed in Bibliography.

78. L. B. Hall funeral records in Grants Pass, Oregon; *Weekly Rogue River Courier*, March 28, 1913, "Rae Victor Smith."

79. Anaconda City Directories, 1902-1908.

80. The Anaconda City Directory for 1909 lists his address at 609 East Ninth Street, and the Great Register of Voters for Anaconda dated April 5, 1909, lists his address at 504 West Third.

81. 1900 Census of the United States, June 13, 1900, German Township, Silver Bow County, Montana.

82. 1900 Census of the United States, June 1900, Anaconda, Deer Lodge County, Montana.

83. *Anaconda Standard*, September 5, 1909, "About the City."

84. *Judith Basin County Press*, 1925.

85. See Geil's *All Things Considered*.

86. 1910 U.S. Census for Grants Pass, Josephine County, Oregon.

87. Letter from John Bradley at Holland House, New York, to Vic Smith at 511 Rogue River Avenue, Grants Pass, Oregon, March 31, 1910. In the Theodore Roosevelt Collection at Houghton Library, Harvard University, Cambridge, Massachusetts.

88. Letter from Vic Smith at Federal Dam, Minnesota, to Hermann Hagedorn at New York, July 10, 1925. In the Theodore Roosevelt Collection at Houghton Library, Harvard University, Cambridge, Massachusetts.

89. Letter from George Emlen Roosevelt at the Progressive Headquarters at the Manhattan Hotel in New York to Vic Smith at 273 Montgomery Street, Portland, Oregon, July 19, 1912. In the Theodore Roosevelt Collection at the Houghton Library, Harvard University, Cambridge, Massachusetts.

90. Letter from Philip Roosevelt at the Progressive National Committee at the Manhattan Hotel in New York to Vic Smith at Glacier National Park, Columbia Falls, Montana, October 26, 1912. In the Theodore Roosevelt Collection at the Houghton Library, Harvard University, Cambridge, Massachusetts.

91. *Weekly Rogue River Courier*, March 28, 1913.

92. Funeral records for Rae Victor Smith at L. B. Hall Funeral Home in Grants Pass, Oregon. He died March 23, 1913; *Weekly Rogue River Courier*, March 28, 1913.

93. Letter from Vic Smith to Theodore Roosevelt, postmarked Jefferson Hotel in Chicago, April 16, 1913. In the Theodore Roosevelt Collection, Houghton Library, Harvard University, Cambridge, Massachusetts.

94. Letter from Vic Smith to Theodore Roosevelt, postmarked Jefferson Hotel in Chicago, May 12, 1913. In the Theodore Roosevelt Collection, Houghton Library, Harvard University, Cambridge, Massachusetts.

95. Divorce record, April 9, 1917, Eugenia A. Smith and Victor G. Smith, Josephine County, Oregon.

96. Marriage license, April 3, 1918, Alvin Albert Mathes and Eugenia Smith, Josephine County, Oregon.

97. 1920 U.S. Census for Grants Pass, Josephine County, Oregon.

98. Minneapolis City Directories, 1912-1917.

99. Letter from Vic Smith to Theodore Roosevelt, postmarked 613 Sixth Street South, Minneapolis, September 10, 1917.

100. Minneapolis City Directory, 1918.

101. Minneapolis City Directory, 1919.

102. 1920 U.S. Census for Minneapolis, Hennepin County, Minnesota.

103. Letter to Smith from Marquise de Morès, written from the Chateau de la Bocca in Cannes/ Alpes Maritimes, France, postmarked from Switzerland, and dated June 1, 1920. She gave her permanent address as 31, Boulevard Suchest, Passy, Paris. Medora de Morès died in 1921 in France from injuries suffered as a nurse during World War I. See Bruce Nelson, *From the Land of the Dacotahs* (Lincoln: University of Nebraska Press, 1946).

104. *Duluth Herald*, August 10, 1925.

105. Letter from Vic Smith to Hermann Hagedorn at Roosevelt House in New York, New York, written from Federal Dam, Minnesota, July 10, 1925. In the Theodore Roosevelt Collection at the Houghton Library, Harvard University, Cambridge, Massachusetts.

106. The origin of friendship between Smith and Hughes is unknown. The only information known about Hughes is that he was a piano tuner in Duluth in 1928, and that he moved to Maine, Minnesota, in 1929, according to the 1928 Duluth City Directory.

107. A disease of the kidneys.

108. *Duluth Herald*, August 10, 1925.

109. Heart disease and inflammation of the kidneys due to vascular disease. Smith's death certificate was dated August 9, 1925, St. Louis County, Duluth, Minnesota.

110. *Duluth Herald*, August 10, 1925.

111. *Duluth News Tribune*, August 11, 1925.

112. *Duluth Herald*, August 11 and August 12, 1925; *Duluth News Tribune*, August 12, 1925.

113. Personal correspondence from Wallace Finley Dailey, curator, Theodore Roosevelt Collection, Houghton Library, Harvard University, Cambridge, Massachusetts, to Jeanette Prodgers, August 30, 1990.

BOYHOOD

1. Victor Grant Smith was born in New York in 1850, according to the June 14, 1860, U.S. Census, Oshkosh City, Winnebago County, Wisconsin. The 1900 U.S. Census, June 13, 1900, German Township, Silver Bow County, Montana, gives his birth month as January. His marriage license, dated July 27, 1892, lists his birthplace as Buffalo, New York. However, no other official documents could be located showing his exact day of birth. Census records for 1850 for Buffalo, New York, were searched, but researchers did not find his parents listed.

2. This was sometime between 1851 and 1853, because Vic's younger brother Rae was born in Wisconsin in 1853, according to the June 14, 1860, U.S. Census, Oshkosh City, Winnebago County, Wisconsin.

3. This was circa 1863-1865.

4. Smith frequently uses derogatory terms when referring to non-Caucasians, which will offend many readers. During Smith's day, it was not uncommon to see blacks referred to as coons, aunties, etc., in literature and in the press.

5. Some readers may be appalled by Smith's detachment when describing death throughout his narrative. As a survivor of the sometimes ruthless frontier, Smith saw many of his friends and foes die, as well as many thousands of animals. To him, death became a matter of fact, and he didn't expend a lot of emotion discussing it.

6. A coarse, sturdy fabric woven from wool and linen or cotton.

7. Whiskey, especially cheap whiskey.

8. Split logs that have been smoothed.

9. A long, straight-bladed dagger.

10. This was probably *Adventures of Captain Bonneville: Or, Scenes Beyond the Rocky Mountains of the Far West*, a book about Benjamin Louis Eulalie du Bonneville, by Washington Irving, published in 1837 by A. & W. Galignani.

11. This was around 1865 when Vic was about fifteen years old.

12. Rae and Bill are used interchangeably in the manuscript. In most of this chapter, Rae was typed then crossed out and replaced with Bill. Ray and Rae, respectively, are listed in the 1860 U.S. Census for Oshkosh City, Winnebago County, Wisconsin, and the 1870 U.S. Census for Douglas County, Minnesota, but not William or Bill. Bill may be a middle name or nickname for Rae.

13. Rae was about two and a half years younger than Vic, according to the above-cited census records.

14. Originally referred to as a wild horse or a mustang, cayuse became synonymous for any undersized or cow horse.

15. A broken-down horse.

16. Although the Chippewa and Sioux were bitter enemies, it is unknown whether Smith's figures are accurate. In the mid-seventeenth century, the Iroquois drove the Chippewa from their home along the St. Lawrence River. In turn, these displaced Chippewa, equipped with white men's weapons, invaded the Sioux territory in Minnesota, resulting in a half-century of bloody warfare. In the Battle of Crow Wing, the Sioux attacked the Chippewa and captured some women, but they were subsequently defeated and ultimately driven from their lands east of the Mississippi. See William Folwell's *A History of Minnesota* (St. Paul: Minnesota Historical Society, 1921) for more on their embittered rivalry and this particular battle.

17. Throughout his narrative, Smith mentions mistreatment of women by enemy Indian tribes. It is unknown whether such treatment occurred or not.

18. A bundle of floating logs fastened together and placed across a waterway and used as a barrier to retain floating logs.

19. A logging tool similar to a hammer, but with a tapered point and no claw.

20. Frontiersmen often referred to male Indians as bucks, putting them in the same category as animals, and their pursuit of them was akin to hunting.

21. Indian term for the Mississippi River.

22. In August 1862, the Sioux made a final attempt to drive whites from their traditional hunting grounds in Minnesota. The Indians attacked frontier towns, killing hundreds of settlers and destroying their property, until federal troops and Minnesota militiamen quelled their uprisings. Smith's account of the event may be embellished.

23. "St. Vitus's dance" refers to chorea, a nervous disorder marked by incoordination and spasmodic movements of limbs and facial muscles.

24. Smith is relating a tale allegedly told to him and attempting to pass it off as plausible. Disrespect for non-Caucasians was a common attitude among frontiersmen.

25. Jail.

26. Throughout his narrative, Smith tells of numerous white women being raped and tortured by Indians. It is unknown whether any of these events actually happened, or whether Smith is fostering popular frontier myths.

27. It seems incredible that an Indian mother would turn in her own children to the authorities, especially given the animosity between the races at that time.

28. In 1876, eight members of the Jesse James gang tried to rob the First National Bank in Northfield, Minnesota, but the townspeople killed three bandits and captured three. Nineteen-year-old Bill Chadwell was one of the members killed. Only Frank and Jesse James escaped. Chadwell reportedly worked on a farm in Missouri until he joined the James gang in the summer of 1876. If this is true, it is unlikely that this same Bill Chadwell was in Minnesota at the time of these alleged hangings. See Denis McLoughlin, *Wild and Woolly* (New York: Barnes & Noble, 1995) for a detailed discussion. Other sources say William Stiles, a onetime James gang member, was also known as Bill Chadwell. See Dan Thrapp, *Encyclopedia of Frontier Biography* (Spokane, Wash.: Arthur H. Clark Co., 1988-1994).

29. Smith is fond of using the cliché "stoic" when referring to Indians.

30. The editor does not know whether any part of this story actually occurred or not.

INTRODUCTION TO THE FRONTIER

1. Riel led the Métis uprisings against the Canadian government 1869-1870 and again in 1885. The Métis feared that later settlers would take over their land. After the second uprising in 1885, Riel was hanged as a traitor. Since Riel wasn't hanged until 1885, Smith may be blurring his dates here. Preston likely returned after the first uprising.

2. Bob Costello and two other men tried to rob some men who were leaving the Black Hills on their way to Cheyenne, Wyoming, but a young member of the party shot Costello dead. Besides being wanted for various robberies, Costello had been out on bond at this time for shooting his father. See Jesse Brown and A. M. Willard, *The Black Hills Trails: A History of the Struggles of the Pioneers in the Winning of the Black Hills* (Rapid City, S.Dak.: Rapid City Journal Co., 1924).

3. William F. (Doc) Carver traveled with Buffalo Bill Cody in his Wild West show. Although he was an able marksman, his reputation as a champion rifleman has not been documented. See Dan Thrapp's *Encyclopedia of Frontier Biography* (Spokane, Wash.: Arthur H. Clark Co., 1988-1994).

4. Smith was around twenty-one years old when he took the mail carrier position. This route went through some of the most hostile Indian country in the West, and it was considered almost suicidal for an individual to travel alone. In 1868, five mail carriers were killed between Fort Abercrombie and Fort Totten. See Levi Larsen, "Some Chapters in the History of Fort Buford," Master's thesis, Montana State University (Missoula), 1942.

5. The editor does not know the validity of this story.

6. This story is recounted in *The Rockies and N. W. Educator*, March 1892. In that article, it noted that when the dogs became savage with hunger, Smith had to kill the most "turbulent" dog, which he and the other remaining dogs subsisted on until the storm broke. See "Vic Smith, Scout," Vic Smith folder, in the vertical file at the Montana Historical Society, Helena, Montana. Smith was reported to be living in the Centennial Valley when the article was published.

7. Lead dog.

8. As noted in the previous chapter, the Sioux made a final attempt to drive the white men from their traditional hunting grounds in Minnesota in August 1862. After the Sioux had killed hundreds of settlers and destroyed their property, federal troops and Minnesota militiamen finally were successful in subduing the Indians.

9. 1871 to 1873.

10. This is Smith's first reference to his gambling in his manuscript, and throughout the narrative he discusses various types of gambling. In several of her books on North Dakota, author Zena Trinka refers to Smith as an inveterate gambler. See *Medora, The Secret of the Badlands* (Lidgerwood, N.Dak.: First Award Books, 1960) and *"Teddy," The Saga of the Badlands* (Lidgerwood, N.Dak.: International Book Publishers, 1958).

11. James Willert, in *After Little Bighorn: 1876 Campaign Rosters* (La Mirada, Calif.: privately published, 1977), identifies "Jimmy from Cork" as Edward Begley. Smith noted that "Jimmy from Cork" died at Fort Buford on the Big Missouri River while scouting for General Terry.

12. In a side note, Smith wrote that a travois was the Indian mode of carrying the dead or wounded or camp plunder. He said the poles of the tepee or lodge were fastened onto the sides of the horse and to the saddle. A squaw horse (Vic's term for a female horse) was generally used. Crosspieces were fastened on three feet behind the horse, buffalo robes were fastened in, and a very good swing hammock was the result.

13. A practice developed by the military whereby offenses are tried in the field.

14. Luck is a theme that runs consistently throughout Smith's narrative. With a strong belief in luck, it is easy to understand Smith's penchant for gambling.

15. Circa 1873.

16. A cheaply made, flat-bottomed boat with a sharp prow and square stern that is usually propelled by oars and often used just for downstream travel.

17. Sacajawea was actually Snake or Shoshoni, not Nez Perce.

18. Smith shows his disrespect for Indians by concocting this name.

19. Although contemporary accounts noted that Smith was reticent and modest, he does seem to maintain a high opinion of himself throughout his narrative.

20. Circa 1874.

21. In little more than a decade, the buffalo were nearly extinct, and many other wildlife species were dramatically reduced in numbers.

22. Again Smith refers to his luck.

23. Smith notes that a bull boat was made from the skin of a single, large bull buffalo. A frame of willows, in the shape of a bushel basket, only larger, was made. A fresh buffalo skin pulled over the frame and fastened around the rim of the frame completed the boat. Four people could handily ride in one of the boats. A bull boat was propelled by reaching out with the paddle as far as possible in front of the boat and pulling toward the boat instead of paddling beside the boat, which would cause the boat to spin around.

24. Clergyman.

25. Numerous contemporary accounts tell of Smith's reputation with a rifle. See sources in the bibliography by William Hornaday, Joseph Taylor, Theodore Roosevelt, and Philip Rollins. See also the *Anaconda Standard*, *Bad Lands Cow Boy*, *Glendive Times*, and *Dickinson Press*.

26. An article in *The Rockies and N. W. Educator*, March 1892, notes that this is the first Indian Smith killed; Joseph H. Taylor, in *Kaleidoscopic Lives: A Companion Book to Frontier and Indian Life* (Washburn, N.Dak.: Privately published, 1902), also relates this story, but he refers to Smith as "Sunda."

27. [Major] Orlando Moore.

28. Both Indians and frontiersmen scalped and mutilated enemy corpses. According to many Indian tribes' beliefs, corpses would enter the afterlife in the same condition they left their present life. Some frontiersmen adopted similar practices for revenge. See Anthony McGinnis, *Counting Coup and Cutting Horses: Intertribal Warfare on the Northern Plains, 1738-1899* (Evergreen, Colo.: Cordillera Publishers, 1990).

29. This is sometimes spelled Blum.

30. Fort Union was abandoned as a trading post after the army built Fort Buford in 1866. It was the original site of Fort Henry built in 1822, which Indians destroyed. In 1829, Kenneth McKenzie began construction of Fort Floyd, which was later renamed Fort Union. See John Willard, *Adventure Trails in Montana* (Billings, Mont.: Privately published, 1964).

31. Here Smith tells another story of white women being victimized by Indians. Whether this account is fact or fiction is unknown. In his manuscript, Smith also makes the following side note: "A great many cases are on record where whites sacrificed their lives rather than be taken prisoners by their copper-hued enemies. Many white men, both military and civilian, took their own lives to save torture when they saw they would be captured. A half-breed named Louis Labelle, who was condemned to death at Fort Snelling for many murders he committed in the Minnesota Massacre and was pardoned before the fatal day, related to Vic one day how he and several Indians gave chase to a wagon that contained a man and his two daughters who were fleeing to a place of safety. The man fired a muzzle-loading rifle and killed one Indian. Then he pulled out his revolver and shot both of his daughters dead. Placing the revolver to his own head, he blew out his life. He undoubtedly knew the torture awaiting him if captured and the brutal treatment his daughters would have undergone." The editor was also unable to verify this story.

32. This story seems a little farfetched, and Smith may be embellishing an Indian legend. He seems to relate details about O-pah and Wee-no-nah that only the two lovers would know, and it is ironic Smith would be in the camp the same night he not only learned of the story, but also the same night that the lovers eloped.

33. A British term for getting drunk. It can also mean partaking in the various vices offered in town.

34. In 1851, the U.S. government negotiated the Laramie Treaty to establish boundaries for the Sioux nation. However, Americans moving westward violated this agreement, which then began a series of new conflicts between the Sioux and the white invaders. Another treaty was negotiated in 1868, specifying the Black Hills as Sioux territory, but in 1873, Custer led a survey party through the Black Hills. When Custer and others reported the area rich in gold and prime agricultural land, thousands of gold seekers and emigrants flocked to the Black Hills, ignoring the terms of the Laramie Treaty. The government did little to stop the white encroachment, and peace commissions could not persuade the Sioux to relinquish these lands. Deceived by the government once again, many Sioux began to fight for their rights and land; however, Smith's figure of three hundred whites killed may be inflated.

35. Custer was actually only a lieutenant colonel.

36. Custer was fond of hunting with his dogs, which he often brought with him when possible. However, since Custer did not mention Smith in his books, it is unknown whether they actually hunted together.

37. This probably occurred in 1874, because the last of the northern buffalo were slaughtered in 1883.

38. The date should read 1881.

39. Bill Norris ran a saloon, and "germicide" was a euphemism for liquor.

40. Doyle's first name was Patsy.

41. Welch died in the fall of 1881. See the *Glendive Times*, March 2, 1882, in the Appendix for a full account of Welch's death.

42. John Mosby, a noted Confederate ranger during the Civil War, became an independent ranger in 1863. His raids on Union camps were so effective that part of north-central Virginia became known as Mosby's Confederacy.

43. Smith's racist remarks and nonchalant description of killing humans, especially those who were not Caucasian, will offend many readers. His attitude was common in those days among white males.

44. The use of the ball and buckshot in muzzle-loading rifles became popular during the American Revolution. These deadly projectiles, used for maiming and close-range killing, proved effective during the American Revolution and the Civil War. See Joseph Bilby, "A Better Chance Ter Hit: The Story of Buck and Ball," in *American Rifleman* (May 1993).

45. Suspender.

46. Although it is unknown how they met, Joseph Taylor and Vic Smith became friends and trapping partners in western North Dakota in the mid-1870s. They trapped beaver together at a place Taylor called "the spotted otter's playground." Taylor relates some of his experiences with Smith in his book *Kaleidoscopic Lives*. Smith's figures of Taylor's exploits are probably exaggerated.

47. Circa 1875.

48. This means that his door was always open to all.

49. Delmonico, named after Lorenzo Delmonico, was a famous restaurant in New York City in the late 1880s.

50. In 1873, Charley Reynolds was with Custer's expedition to the Black Hills and later helped arrest Rain-in-the-Face for murder. Reynolds was with Major Reno's detachment during the Battle of the Little Bighorn, where he was killed. See Thrapp's *Encyclopedia of Frontier Biography*.

51. To exaggerate when telling stories, a seemingly common phenomenon on the frontier, of which Smith is also guilty.

52. Smith's version of the Mandan legend is similar to other accounts. For example, see G. F. Will and H. J. Spinden, *The Mandans: A Study of Their Culture, Archaeology, and Language* (Cambridge, Mass.: Museum of American Archaeology and Ethnology, 1906).

53. Smith errs in saying the Mandans were the only tribe that ate bear meat. Although many Southwest and Plains tribes would not eat bear meat, because they considered the bear akin to a human, other tribes, especially those who lived in forests, ate bear for survival. However, most tribes universally ascribed special powers to bears, and those tribes that did kill and/or eat bears developed elaborate rituals surrounding the hunt and feast. See David Rockwell, *Giving Voice to Bear* (Toronto: Roberts Rinehart, 1991).

54. This may have been Charles Packeneau.

55. The validity of this story is unknown. Charles Packineau [Packeneau], a French-Canadian who was an interpreter and trader for the American Fur Company at Fort Berthold, died circa 1872.

SCOUTING

1.   At age twenty-five, Smith was already seemingly inured to the vicissitudes of frontier life, where life was cheap and death was common. His willingness to end his friend's life and suffering may seem callous and cold-blooded to some.

2.   As noted earlier, many Plains tribes believed that a corpse would arrive in the afterlife in the same condition that it left. Some tribes delegated the mutilation task to the women and the children. Tribes were more likely to desecrate the remains of their Indian enemies than of their white enemies. See Anthony McGinnis, *Counting Coup and Cutting Horses: Intertribal Warfare on the Northern Plains* (Evergreen, Colo.: Cordillera Publishers, 1990).

3.   This story is recounted in *The Rockies and N. W. Educator* (March 1892), but the men's names in this article were given as Alf. Wickwire and Charlie Johnson instead of Tip Simmons and Charley Sampson.

4.   Loren Fletcher was a representative in the Minnesota Legislature from 1873 to 1883 and served in Congress 1893-1903 and 1905-1907. See *Who Was Who in America* (Chicago: A. N. Marquis Co., 1943) and Warren Upham and Rose Barteau Dunlap's *Collections of the Minnesota Historical Society, Minnesota Biographies 1655-1912*, Vol. 14 (St. Paul: Minnesota Historical Society, 1912), *The Minneapolis Journal*, April 16, 1919.

5.   Colonel Timothy O'Leary was once adjutant general of the Fenians (see note below). He came to Anaconda in 1889, where he started a law practice. See Joaquin Miller, *An Illustrated History of the State of Montana* (Chicago: Lewis Publishing Co., 1894).

6.   In the late 1860s, Irish-American Fenians staged three unsuccessful raids on Canada, which was then part of the British Empire. The Fenians planned to hold Canada hostage until England granted Ireland independence. Irish patriots began the Fenian movement in Ireland in the late 1850s.

7.   A popular western gambling game in which players placed bets on each series of two cards as they were drawn from a box containing the dealer's pack. This is also another reference to Smith's fondness for gambling and squandering money.

8.   Calamity Jane's real name was Martha Jane Canary.

9.   It is unknown whether this particular story is true, but Calamity Jane did have a reputation of shooting things when she was drunk. See Dan Thrapp's *Encyclopedia of Frontier Biography* (Spokane, Wash.: Arthur H. Clark Co., 1988-1994).

10.   Calamity Jane died August 1, 1903. Since Smith remarked that she died "a few years ago," this helps date the manuscript circa 1906-1912. Another source noted that Smith wrote down his experiences before leaving Anaconda in 1909. See *Judith Basin County Press*, 1925, "Death of 'Vic' Smith in Duluth Recalls Many Stories of His Life as a Hunter in Montana," Montana News Association Inserts file, Montana State Historical Society, Helena, Montana.

11.   The editor could not determine who this "villain" may have been. For an informative discussion of Calamity's life, see Roberta Beed Sollid, *Calamity Jane: A Study in Historical Criticism* (Helena, Mont.: The Western Press/Montana Historical Society, 1958, 1995).

12.   Bloody Knife was half-Arikara, half-Sioux.

13. Crook was on his way to join Terry and Custer in Montana. He had a brief skirmish with the Sioux along the Tongue River in Wyoming on the evening of June 9. Eight days later, Sioux and Cheyenne attacked his command along the headwaters of Rosebud Creek. According to John·Finerty in *War-Path and Bivouac, or The Conquest of the Sioux* (Norman: University of Oklahoma Press, 1961), Crook's casualties numbered about fifty. Michael Malone and Richard Roeder in *Montana: A History of Two Centuries* (Seattle: University of Washington Press, 1976) noted that Crook's loss in the Battle of the Rosebud was about twenty-five dead and fifty wounded.

14. Smith noted that Lieutenant DeRudio had been an officer in France and was arrested for complicity in the attempted assassination of Napoleon III. DeRudio and his accomplices were tried and condemned to the guillotine. Although his associates were executed, DeRudio escaped to America and got a commission in the U.S. Army.

15. Smith's figures are exaggerated here. When Terry and Gibbon arrived on the battlefield, they buried just more than 260 men. See Malone and Roeder, *Montana: A History of Two Centuries.*

16. Long, flowing sideburns.

17. For a more accurate account and discussion of the Battle of the Little Bighorn, see Robert Utley, *Custer Battlefield: A History and Guide to the Battle of the Little Bighorn* (Washington, D.C.: National Park Service, 1988).

18. Jerome A. Greene, *Yellowstone Command: Colonel Nelson A. Miles and the Great Sioux War, 1876-1877* (Lincoln: University of Nebraska Press, 1991), uses Wesley as Brockmeyer's first name, while James Willert, *After Little Bighorn: 1876 Campaign Rosters* (La Mirada, Calif.: privately published, 1977), uses William.

19. It is unlikely that Smith witnessed Hickok's death. In an account to the Secretary of War, Major Orlando Moore said he left the mouth of the Rosebud August 1, 1876, on the steamer *Far West* with several companies and scout Vic Smith. These troops were sent to retrieve some forage that had been left behind. Scout Brockmeyer was also killed at this time. Smith's and Moore's accounts of returning for the forage and of Brockmeyer's death are similar, but if Moore's dates are correct, Smith could not have been in Deadwood at the time of Hickok's murder. See Jerome A. Greene, *Battles and Skirmishes of the Great Sioux War, 1876-1877* (Norman: University of Oklahoma Press, 1993).

20. McCall was acquitted after being tried before a miner's jury in Deadwood, under Judge W. L. Kuykendall, who was allegedly bribed. He was rearrested at Laramie, Wyoming, and sent to Yankton, South Dakota, for a new trial. His first trial was declared illegal because Deadwood was not a legally constituted community, and local acts of justice were not recognized by the law. McCall was hanged after the second jury found him guilty. See Joseph Rosa, *They Called Him Wild Bill: The Life and Adventures of James Butler Hickok* (Norman: University of Oklahoma Press, 1974).

21. The bullet in Massie's wrist became a popular barroom topic, and it is unknown whether Smith is telling the truth or drawing upon contemporary myth. See Rosa's *They Called Him Wild Bill.*

22. This was probably Lieutenant Charles Woodruff.

23. This is also sometimes spelled Grouard.

24. Frank Grouard, born in the Society Islands of the South Pacific, was the son of Benjamin Franklin Grouard, a Mormon missionary, and an island native. See Thrapp's *Encyclopedia of Frontier Biography*.

25. Sometimes this is spelled Cushing.

26. To crease an animal, the shooter hit the animal so that the bullet nicked the cords in the animal's neck, close to the spinal column, which temporarily paralyzed a nerve center and knocked the animal down. This was a difficult feat, requiring an excellent marksman and luck.

27. This is sometimes spelled Bloom.

28. Miles's scouts in September 1876 were William Sellew, Albert F. Gaeheder, and James Turner. See Greene, *Yellowstone Command*, and Report of Persons and Articles employed and hired at Cantonment Tongue River, Montana Territory, for October 1876. This story is also recounted by Oskaloosa M. Smith and Alfred C. Sharpe in Greene's *Battles and Skirmishes of the Great Sioux War*.

29. This was Luther S. "Yellowstone" Kelly.

30. See Luther S. Kelly, *"Yellowstone Kelly": The Memoirs of Luther S. Kelly*, edited by Milo. M. Quaife (New Haven: Yale University Press, 1926). Miles named Kelly chief of scouts and sent him to find a camp of hostile Sioux on Frenchman's Creek. Kelly requested to bring Smith, who was then scouting for Colonel Elwell Otis. Kelly noted that he had met Smith before on the Powder River and knew him to be a valuable and experienced scout. Smith also relates this story in a letter to the editor of *Recreation* (July 1897).

31. Veteran Indian fighter Abel Farwell built the trading post for Colonel Campbell K. Peck and Commander E. H. Durfee in 1867. The post became an Indian agency for the Sioux and Assiniboine in 1871. In 1879, the original post was abandoned and was later swept away by the river. See Roberta Carkeek Cheney, *Names on the Face of Montana* (Missoula, Mont.: Mountain Press, 1984) and John Willard, *Adventure Trails in Montana* (Billings, Mont.: Privately published, 1964).

32. Telegraphing by using the sun's rays and their glasses.

33. A frontiersman's derogatory term for an Indian. To siwash means to sleep in the open without shelter.

34. Although Paul McCormick was elected as a delegate to the Montana Legislature from Custer County in 1879, he never served due to a technicality. In 1888, he was a delegate at the National Republican Convention and was listed on the Republican ticket as a candidate for presidential elector in McKinley's second campaign. See *Progressive Men of the State of Montana* (Chicago: A. W. Bowen & Co., 1900).

35. This was Fellows D. Pease, veteran trader and former agent for the Crow Indians. His friends called him "Major" because of his leadership qualities.

36. Locating their post along the route to Yellowstone National Park and near the Crow Reservation, Pease and McCormick thought they could have a profitable business in this game-rich area. In 1873, they and forty-five other men selected a site near the mouth of the Bighorn

River, and in July 1875 they built several log houses and a palisade. See Robert Utley, *The Lance and the Shield* (New York: Henry Holt & Co., 1993) and John S. Gray, *Centennial Campaign: The Sioux War of 1876* (Norman: University of Oklahoma Press, 1988).

37. Clyde McLemore, in an article in *Montana, The Magazine of Western History* (January 1952), identifies this man as James Edwards, who died July 12, 1875.

38. For a more accurate account of Fort Pease's history, see McLemore's article in *Montana, The Magazine of Western History*, or Utley's *The Lance and the Shield*. During the winter of 1875-1876, the Sioux held the post under siege, killing six men and wounding eight. Eventually most of the white men dispersed. Also see "Paul McCormick's Wild Night Ride for His Life," in the *Judith Basin County Press*, 1934, found in the Montana News Association Inserts files, Montana Historical Society, Helena, Montana. The latter also mentions McCormick's hair turning white.

39. Smith sometimes spelled this McMurdy.

40. This was probably Tazewell Woody rather than Frank Woody who was a vigilante and later a judge.

41. McLemore identifies A. S. Hubbell, G. Woody, and A. B. Cocks as the wolfers who were among the men who came to McCormick's assistance when Fort Pease was under attack. Also see "Most Remarkable Indian Battle in State—Three Trappers vs. 1,500 Reds," in the *Judith Basin County Press*, 1936, Montana News Association Inserts file, for a similar account. The wolfers are identified in that article as Tazewell Woody, Lew Hubbell, and Charles Cocke.

42. For another version of this story, see "How Sioux Raiders Slew Pryor Creek Trapper Told by Writer," *Forsyth Independent*, 1941, in Montana News Association Inserts files, Montana Historical Society, Helena, Montana.

43. In *Hunting the Grisly and Other Sketches* (New York: Charles Scribner/G. P. Putnam & Sons, 1893), Theodore Roosevelt mentions Tazewell Woody as a noted bear hunter.

44. Smith writes Sioux here, although he said Cheyenne earlier. Since both tribes had fought against the white men, it is unknown which tribe he really means. He continues to use both interchangeably in this chapter.

45. In his book *Kaleidoscopic Lives: A Companion Book to Frontier and Indian Life* (Washburn, N.Dak.: Privately published, 1902), Joseph Taylor relates a similar story saying his friend, whom he calls Sunda, a.k.a. Smith, killed a hostile Sioux medicine man.

46. This was Private Charles Shrenger.

47. See Greene's *Yellowstone Command* for a more detailed discussion of the incident with Lame Deer.

48. Jack Conley had a long history of law enforcement experience. In 1882, he was deputy sheriff in Miles City, the following year he served as deputy sheriff in Livingston, and in 1884 he was deputy sheriff in Dawson County. From 1885 to 1892, Conley worked at the Anaconda smelter. Then in 1892 he was appointed as a guard at the state penitentiary in Deer Lodge. Conley was deputy sheriff in Deer Lodge County from 1893 to 1896. He was then elected constable in Deer Lodge for two years, and in the fall of 1898 he was elected sheriff of Deer Lodge County and reelected in 1900. See *Progressive Men of the State of Montana*.

49. Other sources give his name as Albert F. Gaeheder. See Greene's *Yellowstone Command*, and Report of Persons and Articles employed and hired at Cantonment Tongue River, Montana Territory, October 1876.

50. One of many references within the manuscript indicating Smith's propensity to gamble and lose money, supporting North Dakota author Zena (also spelled Z'dena) Trinka's assertion that Smith was "an inveterate gambler."

51. Smith probably means rouster, a deckhand.

52. A passenger boat that usually carries cargo or mail.

53. General O. O. Howard mentions meeting "Slippery Dick," whom he identifies as a solitary courier, on October 4, 1877. According to Howard, "Slippery Dick" had just returned from locating Sitting Bull's camp in Canada and was on his way to tell General Miles. Howard and Miles were pursuing Chief Joseph and the Nez Perce who were headed for Sitting Bull's camp. See Howard's account in his book *Nez Perce Joseph* (Boston: Lee & Shephard Publishers, 1881).

54. Scout Milan Tripp is generally credited with killing Chief Looking Glass. See Merrill Beal, *"I Will Fight No More Forever"* (New York: Ballantine Books, 1963) and L. V. McWhorter, *Hear Me, My Chiefs* (Caldwell, Idaho: The Caxton Printers, Ltd., 1952).

55. See Beal, *"I Will Fight No More Forever,"* for a more accurate account of Chief Joseph's surrender. An estimated 150 Nez Perce had escaped to Canada, and 418 surrendered. Of those who surrendered, 87 were men, and some of these were elderly. From his camp in the Bears Paw, Miles listed 23 soldiers as dead and 45 as wounded.

56. In 1887, Jack Johnson was appointed the first marshal of Red Lodge, Montana. See *Crow Killer: The Saga of Liver-Eating Johnson* (Bloomington: Indiana University Press, 1969) by Raymond Thorp and Robert Bunker.

57. This was probably Colonel George Clendennin, Jr.

58. Sarvis berries are also known as Juneberries or service berries.

59. In Eleanor Banks's *Wandersong* (Caldwell, Idaho: The Caxton Printers, Ltd., 1950), Tom Greenwood is identified.

60. In a side note, Smith said a coup stick was a willow eight feet long with three prongs like a three-leaf shamrock; the branches were cut off about five inches long for the scalp to be stretched on.

61. Although no first name is given here, this is probably Frank Smith, the alleged husband of Jennie, rather than Vic Smith.

62. Helen Fitzgerald Sanders and William H. Bertsche, Jr., spell his name as Jimmy Dees rather than Deer in their book *X. Beidler: Vigilante* (Norman: University of Oklahoma Press, 1957).

63. In *Crow Killer*, Thorp and Bunker also relate a similar story. However, they said he earned his nickname of "Liver-Eating" in 1847, many years before this incident. After Crow Indians killed and scalped his pregnant wife, Johnson took revenge by killing and scalping some Crows and eating their livers raw.

64. In Banks's biography of Henry MacDonald, *Wandersong*, Captain Andrews was said to be the only man who mutilated the dead Indians. "He cut off their heads, removed the flesh and brains by boiling, labeled the skulls with awe-inspiring names, and set out on a lecture tour through the States." Similar accounts of this incident appear in numerous books. See Thorp and Bunker's *Crow Killer*, "Teddy Blue" Abbott's *We Pointed Them North* (New York: Farrar & Rinehart, 1939), Joseph Taylor's *Sketches of Frontier and Indian Life on the Upper Missouri and Great Plains* (Bismarck, N.Dak.: Privately published, 1895), and Sanders and Bertsche's *X. Beidler: Vigilante*. In *Wandersong*, the scalping victim is described as a white woman who followed camps. "Her reputation was as ill-favored as her face and figure. Her name was 'Jenny,' but the men had her labeled with a nickname too vile for print. Jenny was tough and impious-tongued. She had to be to survive her grisly lot. But she had a robust sort of loyalty and was as generous-hearted as a child. She even displayed an uncouth vanity." Sanders refers to her as Mrs. Jennie Hawley. Some of the sources identify the trading post as Fort Hawley.

65. This may have been Patrick "Tommy" Tucker, noted cowboy in the Big Hole area.

66. Since her real name is unknown, this date is difficult to verify. However, this date is typescript, which helps date the manuscript.

67. In December 1899, Johnson went to the Old Soldiers' Home in Los Angeles, California, where he died January 21, 1900. He was buried in the San Juan Hill section of the Los Angeles cemetery. See *Crow Killer*.

68. Swatty or Swaddy is slang for soldier.

69. Smith's reputation of modesty does not always apply to his writings.

70. Mazeppa, a famous Cossack chieftain, became a page at the court of King John Casimir of Poland, where he offended a nobleman. As punishment, he was strapped to a wild horse and sent into the wilderness.

BUFFALO DAYS

1. See the Appendix for a similar account that Smith wrote for *Recreation* (May 1899), titled "Roping Buffalo Calves."

2. It was during this time that Smith gained his reputation as "the famous hunter." Many sources cite his expertise with the rifle and his penchant for slaughtering buffalo. Some contemporary sources include Lewis F. Crawford, *The Medora-Deadwood Stage Line* (1925. Reprint. Seattle: Shorey Book Store, 1964); Hermann Hagedorn, *Roosevelt in the Bad Lands* (Boston: Houghton-Mifflin, 1921); William Hornaday, "The Extermination of the American Bison with a Sketch of its Discovery and Life History," *Report of the National Museum* (1887. Reprint. Seattle: Facsimile Reproduction, 1971); A. C. Huidekoper, *My Experience and Investment in the Bad Lands of Dakota and Some of the Men I Met There* (Baltimore: Wirth Bros., 1947); Theodore Roosevelt, *Hunting Trips of a Ranchman* (New York: P. F. Collier & Son, 1885); Joseph Taylor, *Kaleidoscopic Lives: A Companion Book to Frontier and Indian Life* (Washburn, N.Dak.: Privately published, 1902); and articles in the *Bad Lands Cow Boy*, *Dickinson Press*, and *Glendive Times*.

3. Smith reportedly tied a record with noted buffalo hunter Charles Rath, who killed 107 buffalo at one stand in 1873, along the Canadian River. Smith's feat is cited in numerous books on buffalo. It probably first appeared in Hornaday's "The Extermination of the American Bison."

4. As with most figures, Smith tends to overstate. Hornaday attempted to get exact numbers, but found this task impossible. Hide buyer J. N. Davis of Minnesota told Hornaday that he estimated white hunters shipped 50,000 hides and robes in 1881 and 200,000 in 1882 between Miles City, Montana, and Mandan, North Dakota. See Hornaday for a more in-depth discussion of this subject.

5. Smith seems to accept vigilante justice most of the time, except when he discusses "Flopping Bill" later. See pp. 137-139.

6. According to a news article, Rock worked for Smith as a buffalo skinner for nearly three years before going to southeastern Montana, where he discovered a coal mine. In 1886, Rock and Smith again met up near Livingston, Montana. At that time, the two formed a partnership for a big game ranch and guiding outfit, which lasted about five years. See *Anaconda Standard*, April 13, 1902.

7. Conley was deputy sheriff in Miles City in 1882 and deputy sheriff of Dawson County in 1884. See *Progressive Men of the State of Montana* (Chicago: A. W. Bowen & Co., 1900).

8. Spanish monte is a card game similar to faro. Players select any two of four cards turned face up in a layout and bet that one of them will be matched before the other, as cards are dealt one at a time from the deck.

9. A painted tiger often decorates the box of faro cards.

10. The editor was unable to verify this record.

11. In 1876, Anheuser-Busch introduced Budweiser beer, which quickly gained popularity over the heavier, darker beers. See Gary Hoover et al., *Hoover's Handbook of American Business* (Austin, Tex.: The Reference Press, 1994).

12. This was December 1881, on the Sioux Indian Reservation.

13. Again Smith mentions gambling. Although it is difficult to prove, North Dakota author Trinka claimed that Smith was an "inveterate gambler." However, she also said he never drank a drop, which is contradicted in the manuscript.

14. "Flopping Bill" and his band of stranglers was William Quantrill (also spelled Cantrell) and other men hired by Montana and North Dakota cattlemen to round up rustlers. However, according to Smith, "the stranglers" ruthlessly killed innocent people, took their livestock, and rarely went after real rustlers. In *Tales from Buffalo Land* (Baltimore: Wirth Bros., 1940), Usher Burdick also mentions an "Eddie" Bronson being hanged by the vigilantes, under questionable circumstances. See also pp. 137-139 for more on "Flopping Bill" and his band of stranglers.

15. This whiskey smuggling episode was one of the few frontier stories that Smith willingly shared with reporters. He first recounted the tale in a circumlocutory manner for the *Glendive Times*, March 2, 1882. See this account in the Appendix. More details of the story were reported years later in at least two newspapers: the *Anaconda Standard*, December 16, 1900, and the *Fallon County Times*, 1938, "Vic Smith Hid in Graveyard Three Days Eating Rosebuds and Snow Because He Carried Drink of Whisky to Two Friends on Indian Reservation," Montana News Association Inserts file, Montana Historical Society, Helena, Montana.

16. One of Smith's trapping partners, Joseph Taylor, noted in *Beavers, Their Ways, and Other Sketches* (Washburn, N.Dak.: Privately published, 1904) that Smith was one of the best shots in the Upper Missouri country and related how one spring Smith brought down sixty beaver, securing about one in every ten that he killed. Editor A. T. Packard of the *Bad Lands Cow Boy* also reported one of Smith's beaver hunting trips. See the Appendix for this account.

17. Gibbon was actually a colonel.

18. See pp. 137-139 for details on "Flopping Bill."

19. Taylor mentions this tragedy in *Kaleidoscopic Lives*.

20. Although Smith was not married at this time, the 1880 U.S. Census for Dawson County, Montana Territory, lists a Fannie Smith as his wife; notes from Glendive area pioneer Leslie Lovering to local historian Tom Ray also mention a woman living with Smith; and the *Glendive Times*, August 3, 1882, "Notes on Newlon" refers to a Mrs. Smith. For a poignant account of Smith's love affair, see Taylor's *Kaleidoscopic Lives*.

21. In *Tales from Buffalo Land*, Burdick gives her name as Josephine Manuri and says she was part Gros Ventre.

22. Drunk.

23. A long, tapered braided whip made of rawhide or leather.

24. "Freezing onto" was a frontier expression for taking.

25. An article entitled "Death of 'Vic' Smith in Duluth Recalls Many Stories of His Life as a Hunter in Montana," in the *Judith Basin County Press*, 1925, Montana News Association Inserts file, notes that Smith wore a hair-woven watch chain with a gold charm bridle bit given to him by Cole Younger. For a similar account of Grinnell's death, see Bruce Nelson's *From the Land of the Dacotahs* (Lincoln: University of Nebraska Press, 1946). Cole Younger was wounded and captured when he and seven other members of the Jesse James gang tried to rob the Northfield, Minnesota, bank September 7, 1876.

26. *South Dakota Place Names* (Vermillion: University of South Dakota, 1941) gives two versions of the naming of Grover, South Dakota. One is that it was named after a nearby grove of trees, and the other version says it was named after Grover Cleveland.

27. The editor does not know the validity of this story.

28. This may be Arthur Mahoney, who was mentioned earlier.

BIDING TIME IN THE BADLANDS

1. The Marquis de Morès, Antoine-Amédée-Marie-Vincent-Amat Manca de Vallombrosa, came to North Dakota with plans to cash in on the cattle industry by building a packing plant for processing beef to ship East in refrigerated railroad cars.

2. Merrifield was active in local and state affairs for the Republican Party in Montana. See *Progressive Men of Montana* (Chicago: A. W. Bowen & Co., 1900).

3.   Many frontiersmen viewed Indians as animals, something to be hunted, rather than as human beings.

4.   Airtights referred to canned goods such as peaches, tomatoes, or milk.

5.   This account also appeared in the *Anaconda Standard*, December 16, 1900; see the Appendix. There is also an oil painting depicting Smith and Roosevelt hunting buffalo in the badlands in the Theodore Roosevelt Museum in Medora, North Dakota.

6.   Theodore Roosevelt was born October 27, 1858, making him eight years younger than Smith.

7.   For the entire original quote, see Roosevelt's *Hunting Trips of a Ranchman*, Executive Edition (New York: P. F. Collier & Son, 1885). c. 1885 by A.P. Putnam's Sons.

8.   Sitting Bull surrendered to officers at Fort Buford on July 19, 1881. He was then confined as a prisoner of war at Fort Randall until May 10, 1883, when he was allowed to join the Hunkpapa at Standing Rock Reservation. See John Gray's *Centennial Campaign: The Sioux War of 1876* (Norman: University of Oklahoma Press, 1988).

9.   In his "Extermination of the American Bison: With a Sketch of Its Discovery and Life History," *Report of the National Museum*, 1887 (Reprint. Seattle: Facsimile Reproduction, 1971), William Hornaday notes that there were about 10,000 buffalo left between the Black Hills and Bismarck and between the Moreau and Grand Rivers at the beginning of the hunting season in 1883. By October, the herd had been reduced to about 1,200. Smith and numerous other white hunters, along with Sitting Bull and his band, slaughtered the last of these bison within two days. Hornaday quotes Smith: "When we got through the hunt there was not a hoof left." Thereafter, only a stray bull was seen occasionally. Numerous books on buffalo mention the final slaughter of the northern herd, but Hornaday is the primary source. Smith also relates this experience in a letter to the editor of *Recreation* (July 1897), and to the *Anaconda Standard*, December 16, 1900. See the Appendix for these accounts.

10.   In his biography of Sitting Bull, *The Lance and the Shield* (New York: Henry Holt & Co., 1993), noted historian Robert Utley said Sitting Bull's comrades were sometimes known to shout, "Tatanka-Iyotanka!" (Sitting Bull, I am he!) to frighten their enemies. It is unknown whether Smith actually encountered Sitting Bull at this time, or whether he is "drawing the long bow."

11.   In *The Lance and the Shield*, Utley writes that Sitting Bull's father, who was also called Sitting Bull, transferred his name to his son after the youth chased a Crow Indian, smashed him with his tomahawk, and knocked him from his horse.

12.   Sitting Bull actually died December 15, 1890. See Utley's *The Lance and the Shield* or Dorothy Johnson's *A Warrior for a Lost Nation: A Biography of Sitting Bull* (Philadelphia: Westminster Press, 1969).

13.   Dates of Sitting Bull's birth have been given variously between 1831-1838. Dorothy Johnson, in *A Warrior for a Lost Nation*, gives his birth year as 1831. Utley, in *The Lance and the Shield*, also surmises that 1831 is the most likely year.

14.   For a more accurate account of Sitting Bull's death, see Utley's *The Lance and the Shield* or Johnson's *A Warrior for a Lost Nation*.

15. In 1880, Howard Eaton came to the Dakota badlands to hunt and returned the next year as a hunting guide. Howard and his brother Eldon formed a partnership with A. C. Huidekoper called the Custer Trail Cattle Company. Huidekoper furnished the capital, and the Eaton brothers managed the ranch. See D. Jerome Tweton's *The Marquis de Morès* (Fargo: North Dakota Institute for Regional Studies, 1972).

16. Rare; literally, a rare bird.

17. A mild form of bucking.

18. The end of a rope that contains a knotted or spliced eyelet for making a loop.

19. This incident actually occurred in the summer of 1884 and was recounted in the *Bad Lands Cow Boy*, July 31, 1884. Vic had killed a deer about nine miles northeast of Medora before spotting the mountain sheep.

20. Many sources spell his name as Cantrell.

21. The noted Quantrill mentioned, or "Flopping Bill's" uncle, was William Clarke Quantrill, a Confederate guerrilla during the Civil War. William C. Quantrill was accused of stealing cattle and horses and killing people, but he escaped arrest. As a guerrilla leader, he led raids against farmers and others in Kansas and Missouri who favored the Union. In August 1863, his gang burned most of Lawrence, Kansas, killing about 150 people. Some sources say Bill Cantrell rode with Bill Quantrill.

22. Reece Anderson was a partner of prominent cattleman Granville Stuart, who spearheaded vigilantism against alleged rustlers. See *We Pointed Them North* (New York: Farrar & Rinehart, 1939) by "Teddy Blue" Abbott and *Forty Years on the Frontier* (Cleveland: Arthur H. Clark Co., 1925) by Granville Stuart. Stuart refers to Cantrell as his hired stock detective.

23. It is unknown how many people the cowboy vigilantes actually killed, but lynching suspected rustlers was a tacitly accepted practice on the prairie, and more than likely innocent men became victims of the times. In the manuscript, Smith uses the figures eighty-three and eighty-seven, but since he tends to inflate figures when describing the past, either figure is probably too high.

24. Usher Burdick, in *Tales from Buffalo Land* (Baltimore: Wirth Bros., 1940), also mentions "Eddie" Bronson as being hanged by the vigilantes under questionable circumstances.

25. In his autobiography, *We Pointed Them North*, "Teddy Blue" Abbott mentions that Billy Downs, who lived on the Musselshell, was hanged by fourteen "raiders" under orders from Granville Stuart. According to Abbott, Downs's place was a hangout for horse-thieves. However, Downs's wife and friends proclaimed his innocence. Also see Stuart's *Forty Years on the Frontier* and "Mr. Montana Revised" by William Kittredge and Steven M. Krauzer in *Montana, The Magazine of Western History* (Fall 1986): 14-23.

26. What Smith probably means here is that Reece Anderson was Quantrill's (Cantrell's) second boss. Most likely, Anderson's partner Granville Stuart was the leader. In a letter to Hermann Hagedorn, dated July 10, 1925, Smith noted that Granville Stuart hired "Flopping Bill." Joseph Taylor recounts a similar story and gives more details about "Flopping Bill's" background and character in *Kaleidoscopic Lives: A Companion Book to Frontier and Indian Life* (Washburn, N.Dak.: Privately published, 1902).

27. It is unknown how Quantrill/Cantrell died. One source notes that he was run over by a train in the Kansas City, Missouri, yards in 1901. See *Fallon County Times*, 1937, "Prairie Vigilantes Under 'Flopping Bill' Cantrell Outdid Men Who Ousted Mining Camp Outlaws," Montana News Association Inserts files, Montana State Historical Society, Helena, Montana.

28. It is difficult to determine which cold-blooded murder Smith refers to here. It may have been Downs or Bronson. In the same aforementioned letter to Hermann Hagedorn, Smith said Bronson was "a poor weak kid of about seventeen and I do not believe he ever committed a crime as heinous as robbing a hens [sic] nest."

29. For further accounts of "Flopping Bill's" deeds, see the *Anaconda Standard*, August 11, 1901, "When Flopping Bill's Avengers Rode the Range"; the *Fallon County Times*, 1937, "Prairie Vigilantes Under 'Flopping Bill' Cantrell Outdid Men Who Ousted Mining Camp Outlaws," Montana News Association Inserts; the *Great Falls Tribune*, October 3, 1926, "Queer Sobriquets Bestowed on Frontier"; and the *Judith Basin County Press*, 1936, "Horse Rustlers Hanged, 1886," Montana News Association Inserts, Montana State Historical Society, Helena, Montana.

30. Born June 13, 1858, in Paris, France. See n. 1 for this chapter.

31. Louis A. von Hoffman was a Wall Street banker who founded the Knickerbocker Club.

32. On September 27, 1883, Roosevelt bought the Maltese Cross Ranch and hired A. W. Merrifield and Sylvane Ferris as managers. In 1884, he established the Elkhorn Ranch on the Little Missouri River, about thirty-five miles north of Medora. See Chester Brooks and Ray H. Mattison, *Theodore Roosevelt and the Dakota Badlands* (Reprint. Medora, N.Dak.: Theodore Roosevelt Nature and History Association, 1983).

33. A few contemporary sources alleged that de Morès and Roosevelt were enemies, but this was unsubstantiated by either Roosevelt or de Morès. See Brooks and Mattison, *Theodore Roosevelt and the Dakota Badlands*.

34. Armour's packing plant was founded by Philip Danforth Armour, who controlled private railroads and banks.

35. The men were William Riley Luffsey, "Wannegan" a.k.a. John Reuter, and "Cherokee" a.k.a. Frank O'Donald, sometimes spelled O'Donnell.

36. For more on the acquittal and other adventures of de Morès, see Donald Dresden, *The Marquis de Morès, Emperor of the Bad Lands* (Norman: University of Oklahoma Press, 1970); Arnold Goplen, "The Career of Marquis de Morès in the Badlands of North Dakota," *State Historical Society of North Dakota Proceedings* 13 (January-April 1946); or D. Jerome Tweton, *The Marquis de Morès: Dakota Capitalist, French Nationalist* (Fargo, N.Dak.: North Dakota Institute for Regional Studies, 1972).

37. De Morès gave Smith a rifle in the fall of 1884 after a three-day hunting trip. On that trip, the Marquis shot numerous black-tailed deer and several sheep, one of which was described as "the finest specimen of mountain sheep" ever seen around Medora. Smith was impressed by de Morès's hunting abilities and proud of his new acquisition. However, whether this rifle is the one de Morès used to kill Luffsey is questionable. There is a rifle at the Chateau de Morès in Medora identified as the one de Morès used to shoot Luffsey. In a letter to Hermann Hagedorn, dated July 10, 1925, Smith said he still had the stock with the silver plate, but one of his friends had borrowed the rifle, got the barrel full of snow, and shot at an elk before the barrel exploded. See *Bad Lands Cow Boy*, October 23, 1884.

38. As noted earlier, North Dakota author Zena Trinka mentions Smith's gambling in several of her books.

39. When Vic returned from his six-week trip, he said he would not have regretted the trip if it cost him $10,000. See *Bad Lands Cow Boy*, February 19, 1885.

40. A soft stone composed of talc, chlorite, and oftentimes magnetite, which has a soapy feel.

41. The *Dickinson Press*, June 23, 1883, reported that as Vic Smith was about to shoot a deer, his horse stumbled and fell. Smith's gun discharged, killing his horse. It was a close call for Smith, as his head was nearby. Also see the *Glendive Times*, June 30, 1883.

42. The *Bad Lands Cow Boy*, June 18, 1885, reports this suicide, but gives the name as William Higgins.

43. The trip actually occurred in July and August 1885. See accounts in the *Bad Lands Cow Boy*, June 25, 1885, July 16, 1885, August 13, 1885, August 20, 1885, and September 3, 1885, in the Appendix.

44. This date is suspect since the hunting trip occurred in 1885.

45. 1885-1886.

46. The main floor of the theater.

47. A reference to Smith's trick shooting abilities appeared in the *Bad Lands Cow Boy*, January 14, 1886.

48. In his book *The Cowboy* (1922. Reprint. Albuquerque: University of New Mexico Press, 1979), Philip Rollins said Smith was idolized in Montana and Wyoming and had no fear of man or devil. His marvelous accuracy with gun and rifle was known throughout the cattle country. Other accounts of his skilled shooting appear in Zena Trinka's *Medora, The Secret of the Badlands* (Lidgerwood, N.Dak.: First Award Books, 1960) and *"Teddy," The Saga of the Badlands* (Lidgerwood, N.Dak.: International Book Publishers, 1958). Also see the McGill files #945, Mrs. Eda Benson 5-1-39 in the Merrill G. Burlingame Special Collections, Montana State University, Renne Library, Bozeman, Montana.

49. See the *Bad Lands Cow Boy*, May 13, 1886.

ADVENTURES OF AN AGING FRONTIERSMAN

1. This was in the fall of 1886.

2. Although he did put up a good fight, de Morès killed just one assassin. Natives also killed four of de Morès's companions; only one man escaped to tell of the murder. Three natives were later arrested for murder, but one died awaiting trial, and the other two were imprisoned. For a more accurate account of de Morès's African experience and death, see "The African Adventure" in D. Jerome Tweton's *The Marquis de Morès: Dakota Capitalist, French Nationalist* (Fargo: North Dakota Institute for Regional Studies, 1972).

3. An article in the April 13, 1902, *Anaconda Standard* noted that Rock discovered this coal mine, but there is no mention of Smith.

4. A pone is baked or fried bread made of cornmeal.

5. A greaser is usually a piece of pork fat.

6. A dodger is a large slice of bread.

7. Now known as the Ruby River.

8. This was probably a relative of Horace Claflin, noted New York dry goods merchant and millionaire, who died in 1885 at age seventy-three. It is unknown whether this story about Curley Rodgers is true.

9. In frontier slang, coffee-cooling sometimes referred to loafing; Teddy Abbott, in *We Pointed Them North* (New York: Farrar & Rinehart, 1939), says coffee-coolers were Indians who would do anything for a cup of coffee.

10. A piece of cloth containing moist sugar, wrapped to resemble a nipple and used to pacify an infant.

11. They called their ranch Smithrocksian. See the *Anaconda Standard*, April 13, 1902, "Dick Rock, the Trapper, and His Odd Career"; the *Rocky Mountain Husbandman*, February 3, 1938, "Early Day Hunters on Skis Captured Live Elk; Practice Originated by Vic Smith"; and *Fergus County Argus*, 1938, "Hunter on Skis Caught Live Elk," in Montana News Association Inserts file at the Montana Historical Society, Helena, Montana. These three articles are almost identical and mention a lot about Smith, a possible indication that either Smith or a very good friend of Smith's wrote them.

12. Rock used to race "Nellie Bly" against horses and claimed she had never been beaten. He also exhibited her at the World's Fair in Chicago in 1893. See "Killed by Bison He Raised as Pet," *Fergus County Argus*, 1938, in Montana News Association Inserts, Montana Historical Society. Also see "Hunter on Skis Caught Live Elk," *Fergus County Argus*, 1938. Nolie Mumey's *Rocky Mountain Dick: Stories of His Adventures in Capturing Wild Animals* (Denver: Range Press, 1953) has a photograph of this moose.

13. Smith and Rock captured over 300 elk, 40 deer, 25 moose, 10 antelope, three buffalo, 14 bear cubs, and many mountain lions, mountain sheep, and other animals. In addition, they trapped many animals, which they killed for their skins. See *The Youth's Companion*, July 9, 1896, "Trapping Live Game."

14. Using ten-foot skis or Norwegian snowshoes, Smith and Rock ran down the animals in February or March, when the snow was deep and crusted, easy for human movement, but difficult for animals. After securely roping the animals, they would take them on a dog-drawn toboggan to the ranch corral. See *The Youth's Companion*, July 9, 1896, "Trapping Live Game"; the *Rocky Mountain Husbandman*, February 3, 1938, "Early Day Hunters on Skis Captured Live Elk; Practice Originated by Vic Smith"; and *Forest and Stream*, April 8, 1899, "Handling and Breeding Rocky Mountain Game Animals."

15. Austin Corbin was a successful banker and railroad executive who helped develop transportation to New York's beaches. Investing $1,000,000, he created a 26,000-acre game preserve near New Port, New Hampshire. He died June 4, 1896, after he was thrown from his runaway carriage.

16. "Captain John" was John B. Smith, and his Piute wife was Elma Winnemucca. See Gae Canfield, "Sarah Winnemucca of the Northern Paiutes," in *Three American Indian Women* (New York: MJF Books, 1983).

17. The elder Chief Winnemucca was often referred to as "old" to distinguish him from his nephew of the same name. See Canfield, "Sarah Winnemucca of the Northern Paiutes."

18. John Smith died January 19, 1889, near Henrys Lake. See Canfield.

19. Sarah Winnemucca Hopkins wrote *Life Among the Paiutes: Their Wrongs and Claims* (Reprint. Bishop, Calif.: Sierra Medina, 1969) in 1883 and lectured in Boston and other eastern cities. She also served as an interpreter, guide, and scout for the government during the Bannock Indian War in 1878. She died October 17, 1891, while visiting her sister Elma and was buried at Henrys Lake near John Smith. See Canfield's "Sarah Winnemucca of the Northern Piutes" and *Montanian*, November 13, 1891.

20. This sentence was handwritten on the typescript copy, which helps date the manuscript. Based on other accounts in the typescript copy, most of the original manuscript can be dated between 1906 and 1912. However, various handwritten notes indicate that Smith amended the original several times before his death in 1925.

21. Charles Marble was a notorious character around Henrys Lake. In his autobiography, *"Buckskin Charley, Fifty Years in and Around Yellowstone Park"* (typescript at Merrill G. Burlingame Special Collections, Montana State University, Renne Library, Bozeman, Montana, 1932), he claimed Dick Rock and Vic Smith were his partners. Also see Elva R. Howard's interview notes titled "Cowboys," in Park County Biography—WPA files 34-0-1-27 at the Merrill G. Burlingame Special Collections, Montana State University, Renne Library, Bozeman, Montana. Although both sources contain erroneous information about Smith and Rock, Marble probably was one of their hired men.

22. Marcus Daly, an Irish immigrant, made his fortune by investing into the untapped copper market in Butte, Montana, and building a world-class copper reduction works in Anaconda. He and his rival William Clark became known as the Copper Kings, two of the most powerful capitalists in America in the late 1800s.

23. Besides guiding and supplying animals for zoological gardens and menageries, they had a bar and a hotel. Their ranch was the last stopping place on the stage road to Yellowstone Park from Monida. See James Allison and Dean Green, *Idaho's Gateway to Yellowstone—The Island Park Story* (Mack's Inn, Idaho: Island Park-Gateway Publishing Co., 1974). News accounts describe Smith as big-hearted and generous with his money, and Rock as saving and careful. At the end of the five years, Smith had what he started with: a horse, gun, and saddle, while Rock had $5,000 in the bank. Although they dissolved their partnership, "their friendship was like that of Damon and Pythias." See *Anaconda Standard*, April 13, 1902; *Rocky Mountain Husbandman*, February 3, 1938; and *Fergus County Argus*, 1938, "Hunter on Skis Caught Live Elk," Montana News Association Inserts.

24. Dick Rock died March 22, 1902. As he was feeding the buffalo that morning, the bull charged, pinned him to the side of the enclosure, and gored him. When Rock shouted for help, several employees came to his rescue, and his wife summoned the neighbors. He was brought inside for medical treatment but died shortly thereafter. See "Killed By Bison He Raised As Pet," *Fergus County Argus*, 1938, Montana News Association Inserts and Mumey's *Rocky Mountain Dick*.

25. Mumey's account noted that Carrie Rock married John Trout, not Jack Fish.

26. Clergyman.

27. The Salisburys purchased the ranch after Rock's death and renamed it the Salisbury Diamond D Ranch. See Allison and Green, *Idaho's Gateway to Yellowstone—The Island Park Story.*

28. This account is related in a reminiscent obituary in the *Judith Basin County Press*, 1925, Montana News Association Inserts file.

29. Vic was actually forty-two years old, and Eugenia was fifteen. Both lied about their ages on their marriage license. Smith said he was thirty-seven, while Eugenia said she was eighteen. They were married in July 1892 in Silver Bow County.

30. Dengler is also sometimes spelled Dingler or Dingley.

31. Born October 9, 1876, in Cawker City, Kansas, Eugenia was the oldest daughter of Minerva J. Miller Dengler and William J. Dengler. It is unknown when the Denglers moved to Montana.

32. The puppy love may refer to his affair with Fannie Smith in the early 1880s in eastern Montana.

33. A women's tailored blouse with details copied from men's shirts.

34. In addition to the eight goats and the grizzly bear, Turner killed two elk, a marten, a wolf, a badger, and numerous grouse and fish during the four-week trip. The bear reportedly weighed 560 pounds, and Smith claimed that one goat Turner shot weighed 280 pounds, the largest he had ever seen. While guiding Turner, Smith killed a buck antelope and a deer. One day after returning home, Smith was again out in the mountains guiding. See the Appendix, *Anaconda Recorder*, October 13-15, 1896, and *Anaconda Standard*, October 14, 1896, for accounts relating their hunting trip.

35. This trip actually occurred in the summer of 1899. See *Anaconda Standard*, July 27, 1899.

36. Since all of the killings were done outside of the law, it is difficult to know just how many people the vigilantes actually killed in southwestern Montana during this time. However, Smith's figure of sixty is probably high. In *Montana: A History of Two Centuries* (Seattle: University of Washington Press, 1976), Michael Malone and Richard Roeder note that twenty-four were killed between January 4 and February 3, 1864. Thomas Dimsdale suggests at least twenty-nine killed in *The Vigilantes of Montana* (Reprint. Butte, Mont.: McKee Printing Co., 1940) and Hoffman Birney, in *Vigilantes* (Philadelphia: Penn Publishing, 1929), figures thirty-three or thirty-four were killed before March 3, 1866.

37. Beidler was a well-known vigilante but not necessarily the leader. It is interesting to note that Smith seems to approve of vigilantism here, but condemned it when it was done by cattlemen in eastern Montana and western North Dakota in the 1880s.

38. In 1886, Beidler was appointed the collector of customs for Montana and Idaho. See Denis McLoughlin's *Wild and Woolly: An Encyclopedia of the Old West* (New York: Barnes & Noble, 1995).

39. Beidler died January 22, 1890, and was buried in Forestvale Cemetery in Helena.

40. For over twenty-five years, Yankee Jim George made a living from a toll road and hotel that was the only stopping place for travelers through the upper Yellowstone Valley. In 1883, the Northern Pacific Railroad bought the right-of-way. Yankee Jim was unhappy about losing his monopoly, and for twenty years he could be seen cursing at the engineer as the train passed. See Roberta Carkeek Cheney, *Names on the Face of Montana* (Missoula, Mont.: Mountain Press, 1984) and L. W. Randall, *Footprints Along the Yellowstone* (San Antonio, Tex.: Naylor Publishing Co., 1961).

41. A platform scale invented by Thaddeus Fairbanks in 1831 and used to weigh heavy loads.

42. For a more amusing account of their encounter with the bear and additional details of the outing, see the *Anaconda Standard*, July 27, 1899, in the Appendix.

43. Fishtrap Creek is about thirty-five miles south of Anaconda, Montana.

44. This adventure was recounted in greater detail on two different days in the *Anaconda Standard*. The first article appeared September 6, 1902, and the following day the *Standard* devoted nearly a full page to Smith in its Sunday edition, with accompanying photographs and illustrations. See the Appendix for complete accounts.

45. In the Manuscript Collection #945 of the Dr. Caroline McGill Papers, Box 1, Vick Smith Folder, from Montana State University, Renne Library, Special Collections, there is a portion of a typescript article, reportedly taken from the June 1896 *Anaconda Standard*, stating that Smith killed between 700 and 800 bears. However, the figures in Smith's manuscript are probably closer to the truth, although they too may be exaggerated, given Smith's propensity to inflate figures. The typescript article also noted that Smith had never killed any young bears nor had known anyone who did, but this is contradicted by his manuscript. The original news article could not be located.

BIBLIOGRAPHY

Archives and Reference

Anaconda City Directories. Anaconda, Montana: R. L. Polk Co., 1902-1909.

Anaconda School District records for 1906-1907. In Anaconda-Deer Lodge County Courthouse, Anaconda, Montana.

Bradley, John. Letter from Holland House, New York, March 31, 1910, to Vic Smith at 511 Rogue River Avenue, Grants Pass, Oregon. In Theodore Roosevelt Collection at Houghton Library, Harvard University, Cambridge, Massachusetts.

Crawford, Lewis F. Papers. A37 Book #23 p/9. North Dakota State Historical Library, Bismarck, North Dakota.

Dailey, Wallace Finley (curator of the Theodore Roosevelt Collection). Letter from Houghton Library, Harvard University, Cambridge, Massachusetts, August 30, 1990, to Jeanette Prodgers, Butte, Montana.

De Morès, Medora (the Marquise). Letter from the Chateau de la Bocca in Cannes/Alpes Maritimes, France, June 1, 1920, to Vic Smith. In the Theodore Roosevelt Collection at Houghton Library, Harvard University, Cambridge, Massachusetts.

Dillon City Directory. Dillon, Montana: R. L. Polk Co., 1909-1910.

Duluth City Directories. Duluth, Minnesota: R. L. Polk Co., 1913, 1918-1920, 1928.

Great Register of Voters for Anaconda, Montana, April 5, 1909. In collections of the Tri-County Historical Society, Anaconda, Montana.

Grover, Eugene F. (son of Dr. F. C. Grover). Letters to the Theodore Roosevelt National Memorial Park in Medora, North Dakota, July 29, 1958, July 18, 1959, and December 5, 1959. In the collections at the Theodore Roosevelt National Memorial Park in Medora, North Dakota.

Josephine County, Oregon, divorce records, April 9, 1917. Divorce record of Eugenia A. Smith and Victor G. Smith. Circuit Court, State of Oregon, Josephine County Courthouse, Vol. 12, p. 143, Grants Pass, Oregon.

Loeb, William (secretary to President Theodore Roosevelt). Letter to Vic Smith in Anaconda, October 27, 1905. In Theodore Roosevelt Collection at Houghton Library, Harvard University, Cambridge, Massachusetts.

Lovering, Leslie. Undated letter to Tom Ray listing early day settlers in the Lower Yellowstone Valley. In the vertical files at the Mon-Dak Heritage Center, Sidney, Montana.

Marble, Charles "Buckskin Charley." "Fifty Years in and Around Yellowstone Park." Typescript autobiography, 1932. In Merrill G. Burlingame Special Collections, Montana State University, Renne Library, Bozeman, Montana.

———. Interview with Elva R. Howard, Livingston, Montana, November 30, 1940. Park County Biography—WPA files 34-0-1-27. Title: "Cowboys." In Merrill G. Burlingame Special Collections, Montana State University, Renne Library, Bozeman, Montana.

Mathes, Alvin Albert, and Eugenia Dengler Smith. Marriage license, Josephine County, Oregon, April 3, 1918. Josephine County Marriage Records, Josephine County Clerk and Recorder, Vol. 7, p. 77, Grants Pass, Oregon.

Mathes, Eugenia Amelia. Death certificate. Josephine County, Grants Pass, Oregon. April 12, 1945. Oregon Health Division: Center for Health Statistics, Portland, Oregon, #2425.

McGill, Caroline. Typescript article reportedly taken from the June 1896 *Anaconda Standard*. Manuscript Collection #945, Dr. Caroline McGill Papers, Box 1. Vic Smith folder, in Merrill G. Burlingame Special Collections, Montana State University, Renne Library, Bozeman, Montana.

———. Manuscript Collection #945. Mrs. Eda Benson 5-1-39, and 9-8-39, Box 2. Merrill G. Burlingame Special Collections, Montana State University, Renne Library, Bozeman, Montana.

Minneapolis City Directories. Minneapolis, Minnesota: R. L. Polk Co., 1912-1919.

Ray, Tom E. Files at Mon-Dak Heritage Center, Sidney, Montana.

Report of Persons and Articles employed and hired at Cantonment Tongue River, Montana Territory, during the month of October 1876. At Mon-Dak Heritage Center, Sidney, Montana.

Roosevelt, George Emlen. Letter from National Progressive Headquarters at Manhattan Hotel in New York, New York, July 19, 1912, to Vic Smith at 273 Montgomery Street, Portland, Oregon. In Theodore Roosevelt Collection at Houghton Library, Harvard University, Cambridge, Massachusetts.

Roosevelt, Philip. Letter from the National Progressive Committee at Manhattan Hotel in New York, New York, October 26, 1912, to Vic Smith at Glacier National Park, Columbia Falls, Montana. In Theodore Roosevelt Collection at Houghton Library, Harvard University, Cambridge, Massachusetts.

Roosevelt, Theodore. Letter from The Outlook in New York, April 22, 1913, to Vic Smith at 600 West Madison Avenue, Chicago, Illinois. In the Theodore Roosevelt Collection at Houghton Library, Harvard University, Cambridge, Massachusetts.

Smith, Frank, and Mary J. Watson. Marriage certificate #2977, New Lisbon, Juneau, Wisconsin, September 26, 1878. Married September 30, 1878. Wisconsin State Historical Society, Madison, Wisconsin.

Smith, Rae Victor. Entry in funeral records from L. B. Hall Funeral Home in Grants Pass, Oregon, for March 23, 1913.

Smith, Vic. Letter from the Jefferson Hotel, Chicago, Illinois, to Theodore Roosevelt at Oyster Bay, Long Island, New York, April 16, 1913. In the Theodore Roosevelt Collection at Houghton Library, Harvard University, Cambridge, Massachusetts.

————. Letter from the Jefferson Hotel, Chicago, Illinois, to Theodore Roosevelt at Oyster Bay, Long Island, New York, May 12, 1913. In the Theodore Roosevelt Collection at Houghton Library, Harvard University, Cambridge, Massachusetts.

————. Letter from 613 Sixth Street South, Minneapolis, Minnesota, to Theodore Roosevelt, September 10, 1917. In the Theodore Roosevelt Collection at Houghton Library, Harvard University, Cambridge, Massachusetts.

————. Letter from Federal Dam, Minnesota, to Hermann Hagedorn at Roosevelt House in New York, New York, July 10, 1925. In the Theodore Roosevelt Collection at Houghton Library, Harvard University, Cambridge, Massachusetts.

————. Death certificate, St. Louis County, Duluth, Minnesota, August 9, 1925. Minnesota Department of Health, Minneapolis, Minnesota, #26655.

Smith, Vic, and Eugenia Dengler. Marriage license, Silver Bow County, Montana, July 27, 1892. Silver Bow County Courthouse, Butte, Montana, #1378.

————. Marriage certificate, Silver Bow County, Montana, August 1, 1892. (The actual marriage ceremony occurred July 28, 1892.) Silver Bow County Courthouse, Butte, Montana, #1378.

U.S. Department of Commerce, Bureau of the Census. 1850 Census of the United States, Buffalo, Erie County, New York.

————. 1860 Census of the United States, June 14, 1860, Oshkosh City, Winnebago County, Wisconsin.

————. 1870 Census of the United States, Chicago, Dupage County, Illinois.

————. 1870 Census of the United States, Douglas County, Minnesota.

————. 1880 Census of the United States, Chicago, Dupage County, Illinois.

————. 1880 Census of the United States, Dawson County, Montana Territory.

————. June 1900 Census of the United States, Anaconda, Deer Lodge County, Montana.

————. 1900 Census of the United States, June 13, 1900, German Township, Silver Bow County, Montana.

————. 1910 Census of the United States, Grants Pass, Josephine County, Oregon.

————. 1920 Census of the United States, Grants Pass, Josephine County, Oregon.

————. 1920 Census of the United States, Minneapolis, Hennepin County, Minnesota.

Wisconsin Census. 1855 Head of Household Census for Omro, Wisconsin.

Newspapers

Anaconda Recorder
October 13-15, 1896
December 7, 1896
May 26, 1897

Anaconda Standard
October 14, 1896
May 25, 1898
July 27, 1899
November 17, 1900
December 16, 1900
June 2, 1901
June 28, 1901
August 11, 1901
October 21, 1901
April 13, 1902
April 25, 1902
September 6, 1902
September 7, 1902
August 29, 1909
September 5, 1909

Bad Lands Cow Boy
February 28, 1884
March 6, 1884
March 20, 1884
March 27, 1884
April 3, 1884
June 26, 1884
July 31, 1884
September 18, 1884
September 25, 1884
October 2, 1884
October 16, 1884
October 23, 1884
October 30, 1884
November 20, 1884
December 4, 1884
December 25, 1884
January 1, 1885
January 15, 1885
February 5, 1885
February 12, 1885
February 19, 1885
March 5, 1885
March 19, 1885

May 7, 1885
June 25, 1885
July 2, 1885
July 16, 1885
August 13, 1885
August 20, 1885
September 3, 1885
October 22, 1885
January 14, 1886
May 13, 1886

Dickinson Press
June 2-3, 1883
June 23, 1883
July 28, 1883
August 4, 1884

Duluth Herald
August 10-12, 1925

Duluth News Tribune
August 11-12, 1925

Fallon County Times
1937
1938

Fergus County Argus
1938

Forsyth Independent
1941

Glendive Times
March 2, 1882
April 20, 1882
May 18, 1882
July 20, 1882
July 27, 1882
August 3, 1882
March 3, 1883
June 30, 1883

Glendive Times Supplement
June 8, 1882
June 29, 1882

Grants Pass Daily Courier
April 24, 1945

Great Falls Tribune
October 3, 1926

Judith Basin County Press
1925
1934
1936

Minneapolis Journal
April 16, 1919

Montanian
November 13, 1891

New Northwest
April 21, 1894

Rocky Mountain Husbandman
February 3, 1938

Weekly Rogue River Courier
March 28, 1913

Books and Articles

Abbott, E. C. "Teddy Blue," and Helena Huntington Smith. *We Pointed Them North: Recollections of a Cowpuncher.* New York: Farrar & Rinehart, 1939.

Adams, Ramon R. *Western Words: A Dictionary of the Range, Cow Camp and Trail.* Norman: University of Oklahoma Press, 1945.

———. *The Cowboy Dictionary: The Chin Jaw Words and Whing-Ding Ways of the American West.* New York: Perigee Books, 1968.

Allison, James L., and Dean H. Green. *Idaho's Gateway to Yellowstone—The Island Park Story.* Mack's Inn, Idaho: Island Park-Gateway Publishing Co., 1974.

Banks, Eleanor. *Wandersong.* Caldwell, Idaho: The Caxton Printers, Ltd., 1950.

Barsness, Larry. *Heads, Hides, and Horns: The Compleat Buffalo Book.* Fort Worth: Texas Christian University Press, 1985.

Beal, Merrill D. *"I Will Fight No More Forever": Chief Joseph and the Nez Perce War.* New York: Ballantine Books, 1963.

Bilby, Joseph. "A Better Chance Ter Hit: The Story of Buck and Ball," *American Rifleman* (May 1993): 48-49, 78-80.

Birney, Hoffman. *Vigilantes: A Chronicle of the Rise and Fall of the Plummer Gang of Outlaws in and About Virginia City, Montana, in the Early '60s.* Philadelphia: Penn Publishing Co., 1929.

Briggs, Harold E. *Frontiers of the Northwest—A History of the Upper Missouri Valley.* 1940. Reprint. New York: D. Appleton-Century Co., 1950.

Brooks, Chester L., and Ray H. Mattison. *Theodore Roosevelt and the Dakota Badlands.* 1958. Reprint, rev. ed. Medora, N.Dak.: National Park Service and Theodore Roosevelt Nature and History Association, 1983.

Brown, Jesse, and A. M. Willard. *The Black Hills Trails: A History of the Struggles of the Pioneers in the Winning of the Black Hills.* John T. Milek, ed. Rapid City, S.Dak.: Rapid City Journal Co., 1924.

Brown, Mark H., and W. R. Felton. *The Frontier Years: L. A. Huffman, Photographer of the Plains.* New York: Henry Holt & Co., 1955.

Burdick, Usher L. *Tales from Buffalo Land: The Story of Fort Buford.* Baltimore: Wirth Bros., 1940.

Canfield, Gae Whitney. "Sarah Winnemucca of the Northern Paiutes." In *Three American Indian Women*, 1-306 New York: MJF Books, 1983.

Cheney, Roberta Carkeek. *Names on the Face of Montana: The Story of Montana's Place Names.* Rev. ed. Missoula, Mont.: Mountain Press Publishing Co., 1984.

Crawford, Lewis F. *The Medora-Deadwood Stage Line.* 1925. Reprint. Seattle: Shorey Book Store, 1964.

———. "Medora-Black Hills Stage Line." *Collections of the State Historical Society,* Vol. 7, 309-323. Edited by O. G. Libby. Grand Forks, N.Dak.: State Historical Society of North Dakota, 1925.

———. *History of North Dakota.* Vol. 1. Chicago and New York: American Historical Society, 1931.

Dawe, Eva Marie, et al. *Courage Enough: Mon-Dak Family Histories.* Richland County, Mont.: Bicentennial Edition, 1975.

Dimsdale, Thomas J. *The Vigilantes of Montana, or, Popular Justice in the Rocky Mountains.* Reprint. Butte, Mont.: McKee Printing Co., 1940.

Dresden, Donald. *The Marquis de Morès, Emperor of the Bad Lands.* Norman: University of Oklahoma Press, 1970.

Finerty, John E. *War-Path and Bivouac, or The Conquest of the Sioux.* Norman and London: University of Oklahoma Press, 1961.

Folwell, William Watts. *A History of Minnesota.* Vols. 1-4. St. Paul: Minnesota Historical Society, 1921.

Gard, Wayne. *The Great Buffalo Hunt.* New York: Alfred A. Knopf, 1959.

Geil, Marian, comp. *All Things Considered: A History of the Anaconda Methodist Church, Among Other Things (1884-1984).* Anaconda, Mont.: Jean Mills, 1984.

Goplen, Arnold. "The Career of Marquis de Morès in the Badlands of North Dakota." *State Historical Society of North Dakota Proceedings* 13 (January-April 1946).

Gray, John S. *Centennial Campaign: The Sioux War of 1876.* Norman and London: University of Oklahoma Press, 1988.

Greene, Jerome A. *Yellowstone Command: Colonel Nelson A. Miles and the Great Sioux War, 1876-1877.* Lincoln and London: University of Nebraska Press, 1991.

———. *Battles and Skirmishes of the Great Sioux War, 1876-1877: The Military View.* Norman and London: University of Oklahoma Press, 1993.

Hagedorn, Hermann. *Roosevelt in the Bad Lands*. Boston and New York: Houghton-Mifflin, 1921.

Hoover, Gary, Alta Campbell, and Patrick J. Spain, eds. *Hoover's Handbook of American Business 1995*. Austin, Tex.: The Reference Press, Inc., 1994.

Hopkins, Sarah Winnemucca. *Life Among the Piutes: Their Wrongs and Claims*. Mary Mann, ed. 1883. Reprint. Bishop, Calif.: Sierra Medina, Inc., 1969.

Hornaday, William T. "The Extermination of the American Bison with a Sketch of Its Discovery and Life History." *Report of the National Museum*. 1887. Reprint. Seattle: Facsimile Reproduction, 1971.

Howard, Oliver Otis. *Nez Perce Joseph: An Account of His Ancestors, His Lands, His Confederates, His Enemies, His Murders, His War, His Pursuit and Capture*. Boston: Lee & Shephard Publishers, 1881.

Huidekoper, A. C. *My Experience and Investment in the Bad Lands of Dakota and Some of the Men I Met There*. Baltimore: Wirth Bros., 1947.

Irving, Washington. *Adventures of Captain Bonneville: Or, Scenes Beyond the Rocky Mountains of the Far West*. A. & W. Galignani, 1837.

Johnson, Allen, and Dumas Malone, eds. *Dictionary of American Biography*. Vol. 4. New York: Charles Scribner's Sons, 1930.

Johnson, Dorothy. *A Warrior for a Lost Nation: A Biography of Sitting Bull*. Philadelphia: Westminster Press, 1969.

Kelly, Luther S. *"Yellowstone Kelly": The Memoirs of Luther S. Kelly*. Milo M. Quaife, ed. New Haven, Conn.: Yale University Press, 1926.

Kittredge, William, and Steven M. Krauzer. "Mr. Montana Revised." *Montana, The Magazine of Western History* (Fall 1986): 14-23.

Klock, Irma. *All Roads Lead to Deadwood*. Lead, S.Dak.: North Plains Press, 1979.

Lang, Lincoln A. *Ranching with Roosevelt*. Philadelphia and London: J. B. Lippincott Co., 1926.

Larsen, Levi. "Some Chapters in the History of Fort Buford." Master's thesis, Montana State University (Missoula), 1942.

Malone, Michael, and Richard Roeder. *Montana: A History of Two Centuries*. Seattle and London: University of Washington Press, 1976.

McGinnis, Anthony. *Counting Coup and Cutting Horses: Intertribal Warfare on the Northern Plains, 1738-1899*. Evergreen, Colo.: Cordillera Publishers, 1990.

McLemore, Clyde. "Fort Pease: The First Attempted Settlement In Yellowstone Valley." *Montana, The Magazine of Western History* (January, 1952): 16-31.

McLoughlin, Denis. *Wild and Woolly: An Encyclopedia of the Old West*. Rev. ed. New York: Barnes & Noble, 1995.

McWhorter, L. V. *Hear Me, My Chiefs*. Caldwell, Idaho: The Caxton Printers, Ltd., 1952.

Miller, Joaquin. *An Illustrated History of the State of Montana*. Chicago: Lewis Publishing Co., 1894.

Mumey, Nolie. *Rocky Mountain Dick (Richard W. Rock), Stories of His Adventures in Capturing Wild Animals*. Denver: Range Press, 1953.

Nelson, Bruce. *From the Land of the Dacotahs*. Lincoln: University of Nebraska Press, 1946.

Prodgers, Jeanette. "Vic Smith: A Remarkable Frontiersman," *Old West* (Spring 1986): 38-44.

Progressive Men of the State of Montana. Chicago: A. W. Bowen & Co., 1900.

Randall, L. W. (Gay). *Footprints Along the Yellowstone*. San Antonio, Tex.: Naylor Publishing Co., 1961.

Ray, Tom. *Yellowstone Red*. Philadelphia: Dorrance & Co., 1948.

Rock, Dick. "Handling and Breeding Rocky Mountain Game Animals," *Forest and Stream* (April 1899): 263-264.

Rockwell, David. *Giving Voice to Bear: North American Indian Myths, Rituals, and Images of the Bear*. Toronto: Roberts Rinehart, 1991.

Roe, Frank G. *The North American Buffalo: A Critical Study of the Species in Its Wild State*. Toronto: University of Toronto Press, 1951.

Rogers, James. *The Dictionary of Clichés*. New York: Facts on File Publications, 1985.

Rolfsrud, Erling. *The Story of North Dakota*. Alexandria, Minn.: Lantern Books, 1963.

Rollins, Philip Ashton. *The Cowboy: An Unconventional History of Civilization on the Old-Time Cattle Range*. 1922. Reprint. Albuquerque: University of New Mexico Press, 1979.

Roosevelt, Theodore. *Hunting Trips of a Ranchman: Hunting Trips on the Prairie and in the Mountains*. 14 vol. Executive Edition. New York: P. F. Collier & Son, 1893. c.1885 by G.P. Putnam's Sons.

————. *Hunting the Grisly and Other Sketches*. New York: Charles Scribner/G. P. Putnam & Sons, 1904. c. 1893 by G.P. Putnam's Sons

Rosa, Joseph G. *They Called Him Wild Bill: The Life and Adventures of James Butler Hickok*. 1964. Reprint. Norman: University of Oklahoma Press, 1974.

Sanders, Helen Fitzgerald, and William H. Bertsche, Jr., eds. *X. Beidler: Vigilante*. Norman: University of Oklahoma Press, 1957.

Sandoz, Mari. *The Buffalo Hunters*. Lincoln: University of Nebraska Press, 1954.

Smith, Vic. "Where the Buffalo Went," *Recreation* (July 1897): 44.

————. "Roping Buffalo Calves," *Recreation* (May 1899): 365-366.

Sollid, Roberta Beed. *Calamity Jane: A Study in Historical Criticism*. Vivian Paladin, ed. Helena, Mont.: The Western Press/Montana Historical Society, 1958, 1995.

South Dakota Place Names. Federal Writers' Project. Vermillion, S.Dak.: University of South Dakota, 1941.

Stuart, Granville. *Forty Years on the Frontier: As Seen in the Journals and Reminiscences of Granville Stuart, Gold-Miner, Trader, Merchant, Rancher and Politician.* Vols. 1 and 2. Paul C. Phillips, ed., Cleveland, Ohio: Arthur H. Clark Co., 1925.

Taylor, Joseph H. *Sketches of Frontier and Indian Life on the Upper Missouri and Great Plains.* 3rd ed. Bismarck, N.Dak.: Privately published, 1895.

———. *Kaleidoscopic Lives: A Companion Book to Frontier and Indian Life.* 2nd ed. Washburn, N.Dak.: Privately published, 1902.

———. *Beavers, Their Ways, and Other Sketches.* Washburn, N.Dak.: Privately published, 1904.

Thorp, Raymond, and Robert Bunker. *Crow Killer: The Saga of Liver-Eating Johnson.* 1958. Reprint. Bloomington and London: Indiana University Press, 1969.

Thrapp, Dan L. *Encyclopedia of Frontier Biography.* Vols. 1-4. Spokane, Wash.: Arthur H. Clark Co., 1988-1994.

"Trapping Live Game," *The Youth's Companion* (July 9, 1896).

Trinka, Zena [Z'dena] Irma. *Out Where the West Begins—Being the Early and Romantic History of North Dakota.* St. Paul, Minn.: The Pioneer Co., 1920.

———. *"Teddy," The Saga of the Badlands.* Lidgerwood, N.Dak.: International Book Publishers, 1958.

———. *Medora, The Secret of the Badlands.* Lidgerwood, N.Dak.: First Award Books, 1960.

Tweton, D. Jerome. *The Marquis de Morès: Dakota Capitalist, French Nationalist.* Fargo: North Dakota Institute for Regional Studies, 1972.

Upham, Warren, and Rose Barteau Dunlap, comps. *Collections of the Minnesota Historical Society, Minnesota Biographies 1655-1912.* Vol. 14. St. Paul: Minnesota Historical Society, 1912.

Utley, Robert M. *Custer Battlefield: A History and Guide to the Battle of the Little Bighorn.* Washington, D.C.: National Park Service, 1988.

———. *The Lance and the Shield.* New York: Henry Holt & Co., 1993.

"Vic Smith, Scout." *The Rockies and N. W. Educator,* March 1892. Vic Smith folder in vertical file at Montana Historical Society, Helena, Montana.

Watts, Peter. *A Dictionary of the Old West, 1850-1900.* New York: Wing Books, 1977.

Wentworth, Harold, and Stuart Berg Flexner, comps. *Dictionary of American Slang.* 2nd supp. ed. New York: Thomas L. Crowell, 1975.

Who Was Who in America: A Companion Volume to Who's Who in America. Vol. 1. Chicago: A. N. Marquis Co., 1943.

Will, G. F., and H. J. Spinden. *The Mandans: A Study of Their Culture, Archaeology, and Language.* Vols. 3-4. Cambridge, Mass.: Museum of American Archaeology and Ethnology, 1906.

Willard, John. *Adventure Trails in Montana.* Billings, Mont.: Privately published, 1964.

Willert, James. *After Little Bighorn: 1876 Campaign Rosters.* La Mirada, Calif.: Privately published, 1977.

INDEX

A

Adirondack Mountains xxv
Adventures of Captain Bonneville (Irving) 7
African Americans 2–3, 10–11, 106, 110, 140
Aglew, Jim xvi, 111–114
Alberta, Canada 51
alcohol xx, xxvii, 43–44, 48, 57, 58, 99–100, 105, 118, 161, 169–170, 183, 197
  moonshine 6
  smuggling 106–110, 199
Alder Gulch, Montana 169
Alexandria, Minnesota xiv, 1, 7
Alkali Creek 16, 43
American Indians xix, 134, 141–142, 161.
  See also individual tribal names
  burial rituals of 107–108, 125
  conflicts with settlers 10, 11–13, 15–16, 18–19, 26, 27, 29, 32–34, 37, 44, 55–56, 57, 68–71, 76–78, 83, 87, 115
  humiliation rituals of 92–95
  intermarriage 28, 104–105, 116, 120, 157
  intertribal conflict 75
  reservations 71
Anaconda, Montana xxvii–xxviii, 56, 189, 196, 201, 204, 207
Anaconda Company xxvi
Anaconda Recorder 187, 188
Anaconda Standard xvii, xxiv, xxvi–xxvii, xxviii, 188, 190, 194, 195, 196–200, 201, 202, 203, 205, 207
Anderson, Colonel George 29, 150, 202
Anderson, J. W. xvi
Anderson, Reece 137, 139
antelope. *See* pronghorn
Antelope Charlie 81–82
Antelope Creek 27
Armour's Packing Company 139
Assiniboine Indians 176
Ayotte, Aleck 90–92, 109–110

B

badger 52
  methods of cooking 109
badlands 135–136, 186
Bad Lands Cow Boy xvii, xviii, xix, xx, xxi, xxii, 140, 185, 186
Bad Route Creek 68, 83
Bannock Indians 154
Bannock Indian War 157
Baptiste (Chippewa métis) 12–13
Baronette, Jack 154–155
Battle of the Big Hole 112
Battle of the Little Bighorn 52, 60–63, 66–67, 68, 69, 70, 80, 82, 132
Battle of the Rosebud 61
bear xxvi, 4, 7–8, 30, 45, 47, 72, 77, 78, 114–115, 128, 140–141, 154, 156, 163–164, 168, 170–173, 195, 209
  hunting xxi–xxii, xxiv, 44–45, 53, 121, 145–147, 149, 159, 187–188, 189, 190–192, 200, 204, 205, 206–207
Beard, Arthur 98–99
beaver xviii, 14, 52, 76, 120, 182–183
  hunting 110–111
  trapping 25–26, 37
Beaver Creek 110
Beidler, John X. xiv, 169–170
Bell Brothers Mortuary xxxi
Benson, Eda xxi
Benteen, Captain Fred 60
Big Crow (Sioux medicine man) 80
Big Hole Basin xxvi, 162, 167, 187, 189, 190–192, 203
Big Hole River 89
Big Horn Mountains xxi
Big Medicine Hot Springs 164
Big Timber, Montana xxiv, 149, 202
Billings, Montana xx, xxii, 58, 90, 144
Billings Gazette xxii
birth control 6
Bismarck, North Dakota xiv, xv, 26, 44, 56, 91–92, 126, 141
Black Hills 16, 56, 125–126
Black Moon (Sioux chief) 45, 60, 70

Blinkey Jack 12
Bloody Knife (Arikara-Sioux) 61, 63
Blum, Hank 35–36, 68
boars, wild 4–5
boats
    building of 7–8
    bull 31
    Mackinaw 25, 26
    steam 32, 115
    travel by 2–3, 8–10, 25
Bonneville, Benjamin 7
Boots and Saddles (Custer) 62
Botkin, U. S. Marshal 110
Boyd, Jimmie 106, 110
Bozeman, Montana 77, 169
Bozeman Courier 150
Bradley, John xxviii
Brainerd, Minnesota 11–13, 15
Brannigan, Mrs. Peter 127
Brannigan, Pete 127
Bridger Creek 150
Briggs and Ellis Ranch 149
Bright's disease xxxi
Brockmeyer, Yank 63–68, 64, 65–66, 83–84
Brocky 19–24
Bronson, Evan 110, 138
Bronson, Lt. Nelson 110, 138
Brown, Aleck 121–122
Brown, Pussy 6
Bruguier, Johnnie 80
Bruguier, Mitch 60, 61, 63, 80
Buckley, Jenny. *See* Calamity Jane
buffalo xxi, xxvi, 24–25, 29, 43, 44, 45, 51,
    69, 71, 72, 83, 101, 116, 117, 118,
    162, 173, 176, 180, 181, 189–190,
    192–194, 202
    bone gathering industry 132
    calf roping 96–97
    extermination of 98, 128, 130, 132, 143,
        190, 199–200, 208
    hides of 25, 97, 112, 126
    hunting of xv, xvi, xxiii, 24–25, 27, 36,
        97–100, 103–104, 112–113, 125,
        126–127, 129–131, 132–133,
        134–135, 143, 183, 184–185, 208,
        209
    meat 75, 114
    preservation of xvi, 98, 130
    ranching of 28
    skinning of 97, 100–101, 112
    uses of 16, 25
    white 134
Buffalo, New York xiii, 1
buffalo robes 25
Bull Horn (Santee Sioux) 94
Bull Tail (Oglala Sioux chief) 37–41

Bungo (trapper) 10–11
Burns, Johnnie 98–99, 178–179
Burnt Creek 48
Butte, Montana 111

C

Calamity Jane 57–58
Campbell, Dave 65
Campbell, Tom xix
camp food 103, 129, 150–151
Canada 69, 85, 132
Canary, Martha Jane. *See* Calamity Jane
Cannonball River xiv, xxiii, 125, 131
Cantonment at Tongue River 67–68
Cantrell, William 110, 112, 137–139
capital punishment 12–13. *See also* hangings
Carruthers, Tom 137
Carver, Dr. William (Doc) 16
Catfish Joe 121
cattle industry xvii, 29, 116, 128, 129, 139,
    180, 200, 203, 209
    U. S. Government herds 114
Cedar Creek 83
Centennial Valley xxvi, 160
Chadwell, Bill 12
Charbonneau, Mr. 25–26, 28
Charbonneau Creek 25, 33
Charley (Chippewa métis) 12–13
Chase, Frank 142
Cheney, William Harrison xiv–xv
Cherokee Indians xxix
Cheyenne Indians 79–82
Chicago, Illinois xx–xxi, xxviii, xxix, 7,
    28–29, 141, 147, 186
Chicago Northwestern Railway 29
Chief Joseph (Nez Perce) 85–86
Chief Looking Glass (Nez Perce) 85
Chippewa Indians 8, 10–13
Chokecherry Creek 68
chorea 11
Civil War 49
Claflin, Horace 153
Clay Creek 59
Clearwater River 169
Clemming, Captain. *See* Clendennin, Col.
    George Jr.
Clendennin, Col. George Jr. 87
Close, Bill 112, 138
Clough, Reverend H. W. xxxi
coal 128, 150, 202
coal surveys xxviii
Cochran, Johnnie 88–90
Cocks, A. B. 75–78
Cody, William (Buffalo Bill) xiii
Coeur d'Alene, Idaho xvii

Cole Circus xxi, xxv
Columbia Falls, Montana xxviii
Comanche (horse) 84
Conley, Jack 81–82, 102–104
conservation xxiii, 129–130, 173
Cooke City, Montana 155
Corbin, Walter (Austin) xxv, 156
corpse mutilation 56. *See also* scalping
Costello, Bob 15–16
Costello, Mollie 15
Costello, Mr. 15–16
Cowboy, The (Rollins) xxi
Cox (wolfer). *See* Cocks, A. B.
coyote 46, 52, 72, 77, 128, 162–163, 200,
    209
Crawford, Lewis xviii
Crazy Horse (Sioux chief) 60, 80
Crook, General George 61, 64, 67
Cross, Billy 68–69, 189–190
Crow Agency 38
Crow Indians 38–41, 60, 74–75, 77, 79–80
    conflicts with Sioux 39–41
Crow Wing River 8, 9
Culbertson, Jack 176
Cushing, Tom 67, 175
Custer, Lt. Col. George A. 44, 45, 58–63,
    68

D

Daly, Marcus 160
Dawson County, Montana xv
de Morès, Marquis xvii, xxi–xxii, xxiv, xxxi,
    128, 139, 139–140, 141, 144, 148,
    149, 188, 202
de Morès, Marquise Medora xxi–xxii, xxx,
    128, 139, 144–147
Deadwood, South Dakota 43–44, 57, 63
death, attitudes toward 55–56
deer xviii, 7, 29, 30, 35, 128, 154, 156, 159,
    167, 173, 186, 192, 208
Deer, Jimmie 88
Deer Lodge County, Montana 81
Deer Tail, Montana 108
Dees, Jimmie. *See* Deer, Jimmie
Dempsey, C. xxix
Dengler, Eugenia Amelia. *See* Smith,
    Eugenia Dengler
Dengler, Fred xxviii
Dengler, Maud xxviii
Dengler, Minerva J. xxviii
Dengler, Olive (Ollie) xxviii
Dengler, William J. xxviii
Deno, Mr. 201
DeRudio, Lt. Charles 61–62
Devils Lake xiv, 16

Devine, Mr.. *See* Edwards, James
Dickinson, North Dakota xvi, 141, 142
dispatch delivery xiv, 55, 60, 61, 63, 67,
    68–71, 71
dog teams xiv, 17–18, 154
Downs, Billy 138–139
Doyle, Patsy 48, 176–177
Dreaming Eyes (Chippewa) 10
Dubuque, Iowa 2
dude ranching xxiv
dugout canoe 5
dugout shelter 41–43
Duluth, Minnesota xxiii, xxx, xxxi
Dutch Jake 104–106
Dutch Pete 121–122

E

eagles 72
Eaton, Howard 134–135, 137, 143
Edgar, George 184
education 1
Edwards, James 73
elk xxii, xxv, 16, 29, 30, 36, 45, 60, 128,
    143, 146, 154, 156, 159, 164, 167,
    173, 202, 208
Elk Prairie Creek 70
Europeans 90

F

Far West (U. S. Steamer) 61, 64–65
Federal Dam, Minnesota xxx
Figley, Fred 83
Fish Trap Creek 171, 204
Fishbone (Sioux) 11
Fletcher, Loren 56
Fleury, George 67, 80–81, 90–92
Flopping Bill. *See* Cantrell, William
Fort Abercrombie xiv, 16, 56, 198
Fort Benton 26
Fort Berthold 53, 116
Fort Buford xv, 25, 29–32, 60, 61, 68, 82,
    83, 90, 98, 132, 138, 199
Fort Dufferin 56
Fort Galpin xix
Fort Keogh 68, 69, 71, 72, 78, 82
Fort Lincoln 26, 44, 45, 51, 59
Fort Pease trading post 72–74
Fort Peck 48, 69, 70–71, 127
Fort Peck Agency 95, 104
Fort Ransom 14
Fort Rice 37
Fort Snelling 44
Fort Totten xiv, 16, 198

Fort Union 36
Fort Yates 27
fossils xvii, 185
Fountain, Tex 82–83
French George 31
French Gulch 203
frogs 151
funerals 4, 102, 113–114, 119–120
fur trapping and trading xiv, xviii–xix, xxvi,
 9, 11, 14, 52, 76, 77–78, 87, 111, 115,
 182–183, 189, 200

G

Gaeheder, Albert F. 68, 83
Gall (Sioux chief) 60
gambling xx, 19, 57, 83, 103
game laws xxvi, 97–98, 158
game preserves xxv, 156
game ranching xxiv–xxvi, 143, 156, 160,
 162, 193–194, 202
Gardiner, Montana xxi
Geddy, Al. See Gaeheder, Albert F.
geological specimens 185
George, Yankee Jim 170
Gibbon, Colonel John 62, 112
Girard, Fred 60, 61, 66
Glacier National Park xxiii
Glendive, Montana xv, xix, 60, 98, 99, 109
Glendive Times xvi, 175, 178, 180, 181, 183
gold mining 86, 168, 169–170
Goober Bottom, Missouri 5–6
Grand Forks, North Dakota 19
Grand River 57
Grand River, North Dakota 133
Grants Pass, Oregon xxviii, xxix
Greenwood, Bob 88–90
Greybull River 145
Grinnell, Anna Malnuri 116–117, 118–119
Grinnell, George 36, 88–90, 115–120
Gros Ventre Indians 29, 32, 109, 111,
 116–118, 143, 194
Grouard, Frank. See Gruard, Frank
Grover, Bill 125
Grover, Dr. F. C. xxiii–xxiv, xxxi
Grover, Eugene F. xxiv
Grover, South Dakota 125
Gruard, Frank 67
guiding xiii, xvii, xviii, xxi–xxii, xxiv, xxvi,
 78, 89–90, 144–147, 150, 153, 154,
 156, 159–160, 162, 167–168, 186,
 187–188, 197
Gumm, Jeff 4–6
gunfights 28, 48, 85, 142, 176

H

Hagedorn, Hermann xxviii, xxx, xxxi
hangings 12–13, 23–24, 63, 92, 110, 125,
 139
Hardscrabble, Montana xv, 111, 175, 178
Hardscrabble Creek 114
Hargous, Captain Charles 71
Harte, Bret 210
Harvard University xxxi
Healy, Cap 70
Heart River 26, 44, 53
Hederberg, Commissioner 176
Helena, Montana 125, 170
heliography 70–71
Hell Roaring Creek 153
Hemmenway, Deacon 32, 34
Hen Creek 178
Henrys Lake, Idaho xxiv, 156, 162
Heppner, Oregon xxviii
Hickok, William (Wild Bill) 63–64
Hoffman, Louis 139
Hornaday, W. D. 128, 208
horse stealing 39, 45, 47–48, 59, 108, 109,
 137, 141–142
Houghton Library xxix, xxxi
Howard, Elva xxv
Howard, General 157
Hubbell, A. S. 75–78
Huggins, Billy 143–144
Hughes, Cecil R. xxxi
Huidekoper, A. C. xviii
Hults, Jasper 97, 141–142
hunting xiii, xiv, xvii, xviii, xxi–xxii, xxvi,
 4–5, 7, 35–36, 44, 66, 79, 129, 143,
 144–147, 159–160, 162–164, 165,
 167–168, 182, 187–188, 196–197,
 198, 207–208, 209. See also guiding
 for provisions xv, 30–32, 32, 44, 56, 63
 for specimens xviii, 141
Hunting Trips of a Ranchman (Roosevelt)
 xxiv, 131, 208
Huntley, Montana xxi, 76

I

Indians. See American Indians
Indian Wars xv, xvi, xxiii, 58–63, 63–68,
 68–71, 76–78, 79–82, 84, 157,
 189–190
infant mortality 155–156
Ireland 56
Iron Star (Sioux chief) 81
Irving, Washington 7

J

Jackson, Billy xiv, 67
Jackson, Bob xiv, 63, 66, 67, 80, 81
Jackson, William 61
James, Frank xxiii
James, Jesse xxiii, 12, 172
James, Tom 172–173
Jensen, Abe 6
Jensling, Mr. 100
Jesse James Gang xxiii, 12
Jimmy from Cork 20
Johnson, George 67, 78, 80, 86
Johnson, Horace 82–83
Johnson, Jack (Liver-Eating) xiii, xiv, xxiii, 67, 78, 80, 86, 88–90, 145
Jones, Mr. 155–156
Jones, Wood Tick 161–162
Josephine County, Oregon xxix

K

Kaleidoscopic Lives (Taylor) xv, 173
Kalispell, Montana 173
Kansas City, Missouri 139
Keefe, Tom 78–79, 82
Kellogg, Mark 60
Kelly, Luther S. (Yellowstone) xiii, xiv, xxiii, 68–69, 69–71, 189–190
Keogh, Captain Myles 68
Killdeer Mountain 143
Knapp, Dan 106, 110

L

Lake Superior 11
Lambert, Joe 133
Lame Deer (Sioux chief) 80–81
Leader, Jake 89
Leahy, Dan 145
lecture tours xxviii, xxix
Leech Lake 15
Leighton, Joe 119–120
Lewis and Clark Expedition 25
Life Among the Piutes (Winnemucca) 157
Limber Jim 102–104
Little Falls, Minnesota 9
Little Missouri River 135
Livingston, Montana 72, 150, 202
Lodge Pole Creek 45
Loeb, William xxiv
logging 8, 9
Long Prairie River 8
Los Angeles, California 90
Luffsey, Riley 140

Lusierre, Louie 137
Lynch, Jack 160–161

M

MacMurdie, Archie 74–75
Maddox, Mr. and Mrs. 126
Madison River xxv, 171
Madrid, Missouri 3
Mahoney, Arthur 112–114, 126
mail service xiv, 16–19, 82–83, 198
Mandan Indians 53
Mankato, Minnesota 10
Maple River 16
Marble, Charles xxiv–xxv, 160
Marias River 85
marksmanship xiii, xviii, xx, xx–xxi, xxiii, xxiv, 7, 32, 67–68, 94, 147, 186
Marler, Captain Dave 84, 123
marriage 90–92, 165
Marsh, Buck 48–51
Marsh, Grant 64, 66
Marston, C. C. xxxi
Massie, Captain 63–64
Massingale, Ned 127
Mathes, Alvin Albert xxix
McArthur, Don 97, 98–100
McCall, Jack 63–64
McCormick, Paul 71–73
McDougall, Captain Thomas 60
McKenzie, Alec 141
medical care 26–27, 151–152, 157
Medora, North Dakota xvi, xvii, xix, xx, xxi, xxiii, xxiv, xxxi, 128, 135, 137, 139–141, 148, 186, 208
Meeteetse Creek 145
Meeteetse Mountain xxii
Meeteetse River xxi
Merrifield, A. W. 129, 209
Métis Indians 15, 16, 90–92, 120–121
Miles City, Montana xv, 110, 199
Miles, Colonel Nelson A. xiii, xiv, 67, 68–69, 71, 79–82, 85, 189, 198
Milk River xix, 132
Milwaukee, Wisconsin xx
mink 52
Minneapolis, Minnesota xxix–xxx, 7, 9
Minneapolis City Hospital xxix
missionaries 16
Mississippi River xv, xix, 8, 9–10, 10
Missouri River xv, xix, 8, 25, 27–28, 29, 35, 36–37, 38, 48, 51, 69, 115, 120
Mitchell, Major Thomas 127
Mitchell, Mr. 127
Moccasin Foot (grizzly bear) 163
Monida, Montana xxvi
Moore, Major Orlando H. 34, 63–66

Moorhead, Minnesota 16
moose 7, 156, 157
Morley, Bill 6
Mormons 104, 105, 158–159
Mosby, John 49
mountain fever 146
mountain goats 167–168
mountain lions 152, 164, 173
mountain sheep xxi, xxii, 29, 30, 69, 128,
    135, 146, 153, 154, 156, 159, 160,
    208
Mouse River 24, 51
mule trains 115
Mulligan, George 36–37
murder 122, 126, 127
Murphy, Mrs. Frank 179–180
Musselshell River 45, 102, 139
Musselshell trading post 87–90
Muzzy, Frank 96–97, 110–111, 192–194
myocarditis xxxi

N

Native Americans. *See* American Indians
Natooka 87
nephritis xxxi
New Mexico 153
New Orleans Exposition xvii–xviii, xx, 141,
    186
news articles 175–210
Newton, Mr. 114–115
New York Herald 60
Nez Perce Indians 25, 112
    conflicts with settlers 85–86
Nig (horse) xiv–xv
Norris, Bill 49
Northern Pacific Railroad 11, 141
Northfield, Minnesota xxiii, 12
Nye, Jack 149

O

O-pah (adopted Sioux) 37–41
Oakes (V.P. Northern Pacific Railroad) 141
O'Brien, John xxiv
O'Donald, Frank 140
Old Faithful (geyser) 170
O'Leary, Colonel Timothy 56
Olson, Judge 100
Oneota Cemetery xxxi
Ormo, Wisconsin xiii
Osborne, Ben 167, 168, 188
Oshkosh, Wisconsin 1
Otis, Colonel Elwell 68
otter 35, 52, 67–68, 97, 111
Owl River 55, 141

P

Packard, A. T. xix, 137, 140
Packeneau, Charles 53–54
Painted Wood, North Dakota 51
Parsons, Mr. 99–100
Pease, Fellows D. 72–74, 82–83
Peoples, George 127
Piegan Indians 116
Pine City, Minnesota 10
Pinos Creek 152
Pittsburgh University 135
Pittsburgh Zoological Park 135
Piute Indians 157–158
Planters Hotel 141
Plummer, Henry 169
Poplar, Montana xix, 138
Poplar Creek Agency 71, 106, 108,
    122–125, 177, 199
Powder River 63, 64
predator control xxvi, 151, 162–164, 200,
    206
Preston, Billy 14–16, 56–57, 59–60, 145
Procter, Shang 44
pronghorn xviii, xxii, 29, 30, 45, 79, 128,
    156, 159, 173, 182, 186
Pryor Creek 77–78

Q

Quantrill, Bill. *See* Cantrell, Bill

R

Radersburg, Montana 125
Rafello, Rosa 90–92
railroads xvii, 115
Rain-in-the-Face (Sioux chief) 60
Rastus, Mr. 140
Rath, Charles xv
Ream, Richard (Slippery Dick) 84–85
Recreation (magazine) 189, 192
Red Bull (Sioux) 65–66
Red River of the North xiv, 16, 19, 56
Red Rocks Lake xxv
Redwater River 70, 98, 100, 173
Ree Indians 60
religion xxvii
Rembielinski, Count xviii, 186
Reno, Major Marcus A. 61–63
Reuter, John 140
Reynolds, Charley 52–53, 62
Rhode, Captain 138
Riel, Louis 15
robbery 99, 102, 127

Roberts, Bob xvii, xix–xx, 140, 186
Rock, Carrie 162
Rock, Charles W. *See* Rock, Dick
Rock, Dick xxiv–xxvi, 100–101, 150, 153–154, 156, 162, 202–203
rock climbing 166–167
Rocky Mountains 165
Rodgers, Curley 151–153
Rogers, Mr. 107–108
Rollins, Philip Ashton xxi
Roosevelt, George xxviii
Roosevelt, Philip xxviii
Roosevelt, Theodore xxiii–xxiv, xxviii, xxix, xxx, 78, 128–131, 139, 207–210
Roosevelt in the Bad Lands (Hagedorn) xxxi
Rosebud Creek 64, 66
Rounsaville, Fred 99, 110–111
Ruby River 151, 164
Russians xviii

S

Sacajawea 25
St. Anthony, Idaho 105
St. Anthony Falls 10
St. Cloud, Minnesota 9, 29
St. Louis, Missouri 2
St. Paul, Minnesota 2, 7, 44, 141, 148
St. Vitus's Dance (chorea) 11
Salmon River 172
Sampson, Charley 55–56
Savage, Montana xiv
scalping 34, 40, 42, 43, 62, 66, 69, 73, 77, 81, 87
Scott, Charley xxi
Scott, Mrs. Steve 31, 35
Scott, Steve 31, 32, 33–35
scouts, scouting. *See* U. S. Government scouts
Selby Lake Grocery xxix
Seventh Cavalry 60
Seymour Creek 201
Seymour's Ranch xv
Shane, Bat 67, 90–92
sharpshooters xxix
Sheyenne River 14, 16, 18
Shoshoni Indians 25
Shrenger, Charles 81
Shumway, Dan 16
Sidney, Montana xiv
Silver Bow County, Montana xxvi, xxviii
Silvers, Mr. and Mrs. 170–171
Simmons, Tip 55–56
Simpson, J. N. xxi
Sioux Indians xvi, 8, 10, 29, 79–82, 84–85,

116, 131–133, 198, 199
Assiniboine tribe 122–125
battle rituals of 76, 88
burial rituals of 52
conflicts with Crow 39–41
conflicts with settlers xiv, 42–44, 53–54, 58–63, 63, 68–71, 72–74
grieving rituals of 40–41
Hunkpapa tribe 32–34, 46–48
Oglala tribe 37–41, 70, 189–190
Sans Arc tribe 76–78
Santee Tribe 92–95, 104–105
Santee tribe 18–19, 24–25
war dances of 122–123
Sitting Bull (Sioux chief) xvi, 33, 60, 68, 69, 84, 115, 131–133, 190
Skeleton Creek 77
Skinner, Tom xxi
skunk 52
Slue, Jim 68
smallpox 124
Smith, Bill. *See* Smith, Rae
Smith, DeMorny xiii
Smith, Elizabeth Robinson xiii, 28–29
Smith, Eugenia Dengler xiii, xxvi, xxvii–xxix, 165–167, 168, 170–171, 194, 195, 201
Smith, Fannie xv–xvi
Smith, Frank xvii, xix, xxi, xxii, 87, 88, 185
Smith, Glendive 84
Smith, Jennie 87, 89
Smith, John (Captain) 157–158
Smith, Ottram xiii
Smith, Rae xiii, xx, xxvi, xxvii, xxviii–xxix, 7–10, 28–29, 195–196, 196
Smith, Thomas xiii, 29
Smith Creek 98
Smithrocksian Ranch xxiv–xxvi, 156, 160, 162, 202
Smithsonian Institute 128, 208
Smith Valley 98
snakes 5, 151, 153
Snort, Kanudale 180
Spaniards Point 120, 121
Spokane, Washington 44
Spotted Hawk (Gros Ventre chief) 116
Squaw Creek 83
Standing Rock Agency xvi, 27, 38, 132
Stanton, Shang 16
Stillwater Penitentiary xxiii
Stinking Water River. *See* Ruby River
Stone, Dick 44–45
Stranger (murder victim) 19–24
strychnine 151–152
Sunday Creek 82–83

T

Taylor, Joseph xv, xvi, xviii–xix, 51–53, 173
Terry, General Alfred xiii, xiv, 58–59, 60,
    62, 63, 64, 66, 198
Theodore Roosevelt and His Hunting Guide,
    Vic G. Smith (painting)
    xxiii–xxiv
Theodore Roosevelt Association xxxi
Theodore Roosevelt Museum xxiii, xxiv
tobacco, as wound dressing 4
Tom Miner Creek 153
Tongue River 60
Toole, Jim 154–155
Trail Creek 150, 153
Trapley, Mr. 126
trick shooting 92, 147–148, 186
Trinka, Zena xx
Tripp, Bartlett 121
Tripp, Milan 67, 85
trout xxii, 145, 152, 154, 158
Trout, John 162
Tubbs, Jimmie 3–4
Tucker, Patrick (Tommy) 89
Turner, Captain W. S. 167–168, 187–188
Turner, James (a.k.a. Bill) 68
Twenty Years on the Trap Line (Taylor) 52

U

U. S. Government scouts xiv, 57, 59–63,
    63–68, 67, 68, 69–71, 80, 82, 85, 112,
    157, 189–190, 198–199
    Indian scouts 60, 61
Utter, Charley 63

V

Van Driesche, William xxi
vigilante justice 12–13, 20–24, 100,
    137–139, 169
Virginia City, Montana 168

W

Wapiti Creek 22
Wee-no-nah (Oglala Sioux) 37–41
Welch, Mike (Red) 45–48, 176
White, J. L. xviii
White Earth Reservation, Minnesota
    10–11, 52
White Tail (Sioux) 10
Wild Rice Creek 16
wild west shows 44

Williams, Morgan 80
Williamson, Jack 112, 138
Winnemucca, Elma 157–158
Winnemucca, Sarah 157–158
Winnemucca (Piute chief) 157
Wisdom, Montana 89
Wise River 167
Wolf Point, Montana xix, 109, 110, 177
Wolftown (wolfing camp) 19
wolves 18, 46, 70, 77–78, 111, 128,
    162–163, 165, 209
    hides 43–44, 97
    hunting 19, 41–43, 72–73, 78–79
    poisoning 37, 97
    wolfers 72–73, 75–78, 87–90
Woodard, Lieutenant. *See* Woodruff,
    Lieutenant Charles
Wood Hawk John 35
Woodruff, Lieutenant Charles 66
Woody, Tazewell (a.k.a. Frank) 75–78
woodyards 31, 32–36, 115, 121, 122
World War I xxix

Y

Yancy Ranch 78
Yankton, Dakota 121
Yellowstone National Park xxiv, 78, 153,
    154, 156, 168, 170–171, 194–195
Yellowstone River xv, 25, 29, 38, 60, 66, 72,
    98, 149, 170
Younger, Cole xxiii, 120

ABOUT THE EDITOR

Jeanette Prodgers spent over a decade gathering information on Victor Grant Smith, or "Yellowstone Vic," as he was once known. Her interest in Vic Smith was piqued in 1984 when she was collecting stories for a book of western bear tales. While perusing frontier newspapers, she frequently found articles about or by Smith. Over the years, Prodgers acquired numerous anecdotes, documents, photographs, and news clippings about him. In 1990, she discovered his unpublished manuscript at Harvard and began editing it for publication.

Jeanette Prodgers has enjoyed western history since she was a child growing up in Helena, Montana, where she spent many hours at the Montana Historical Society Library and Museum. When not requesting arcana from the local librarians, Prodgers works as a Regional Program Officer in the Senior and Long Term Care Division for the State of Montana. She lives in Butte with her husband Rich and their black lab Kate. Prodgers has a bachelor's degree in journalism and a master's degree in counseling from The University of Montana. Her other published books include: *Butte-Anaconda Almanac*, a day-by-day history of Butte and Anaconda, Montana (recently reprinted), and *The Only Good Bear Is a Dead Bear— A Collection of the West's Best Bear Stories*, now in its fourth printing.

HOW THE WEST WAS WON